Bed, Breakfast & Bike
Western Great Lakes

by

Michele Gast & Byron Glick

Bed, Breakfast & Bike Western Great Lakes
Copyright 2000 by Michele Gast and Byron Glick

Cover: *photos by the authors; design by Jean Sullivan*

Maps: *Richard Widhu*

ISBN: 0-933855-20-6
Library of Congress Control Number: 00-132769

Also available:
Bed, Breakfast & Bike Mid-Atlantic
Bed, Breakfast & Bike Northeast
Bed, Breakfast & Bike Pacific Northwest
RIDE GUIDE: Covered Bridges of Ohio
RIDE GUIDE: North Jersey 2nd Edition
RIDE GUIDE: Central Jersey 2nd Edition
RIDE GUIDE: South Jersey 2nd Edition
RIDE GUIDE: New Jersey Mountain Biking
RIDE GUIDE: Mountain Biking in the New York Metro Area
RIDE GUIDE: Hudson Valley New Paltz to Staten Island 2nd Edition
and
Happy Endings by Margaret Logan

Send for our catalog or visit us at www.anacus.com

Published by

PRESS INC.

P.O. Box 156, Liberty Corner, New Jersey 07938

"Ride Guide" and "Bed, Breakfast and Bike" are trademarks of Anacus Press, Inc.

Printed in the United States of America

Acknowledgments

When so many people contribute so much to a book it sometimes seems as if the authors are the last people whose names should appear on the cover. Patricia Gast deserves special attention for her excellent suggestion of a dictaphone for recording directions and mileage while riding. Especially out on the trails, recording accurate directions would have been almost impossible otherwise. Chuck Lennon at the Minnesota Department of Tourism was tireless in helping us identify both inns and rides across Minnesota. We want to thank our families on both sides for their patience with us missing all kinds of family events because we were "out on the bikes." We also want to thank Shirley Mand of Abacus Pet Sitting on behalf of Leo, Sasha, and Flex. Christian Glazar, our editor, deserves a special thanks for getting the whole project started and providing invaluable guidance and support along the way.

The good folks at the Budget Bicycle Center in Madison, Wisconsin, provided all kinds of insight, support, and—oh yes—help with Big Green, the Cannondale tandem that carried us through many happy miles of riding. If you're in the area drop by and say hello. Any bike-loving soul will enjoy the visit to their many buildings scattered along Regent Street. Roger Charly and his staff know everything about anything cycle-related in Dane County and the surrounding areas.

Throughout the book we mention the many helpful public servants, forest rangers, and other kind folks who gave us excellent on-the-spot information about trails, rides, and bike-related events, but we'd also like to tip our hats to them here. Though we didn't see many of them, we'd also like to thank all the folks who work so hard maintaining the trails, paths, and parks we've included in this book.

We must thank the many friends and family who provided leads on interesting rides or their favorite inns. Last, but surely not least, we want to express our gratitude to the innkeepers and hosts who not only served us all those delicious calories needed to keep the pedals turning, but spent time discussing their inns and local events and history, gathering copious amounts of local biking information, and just generally helping out wherever they could.

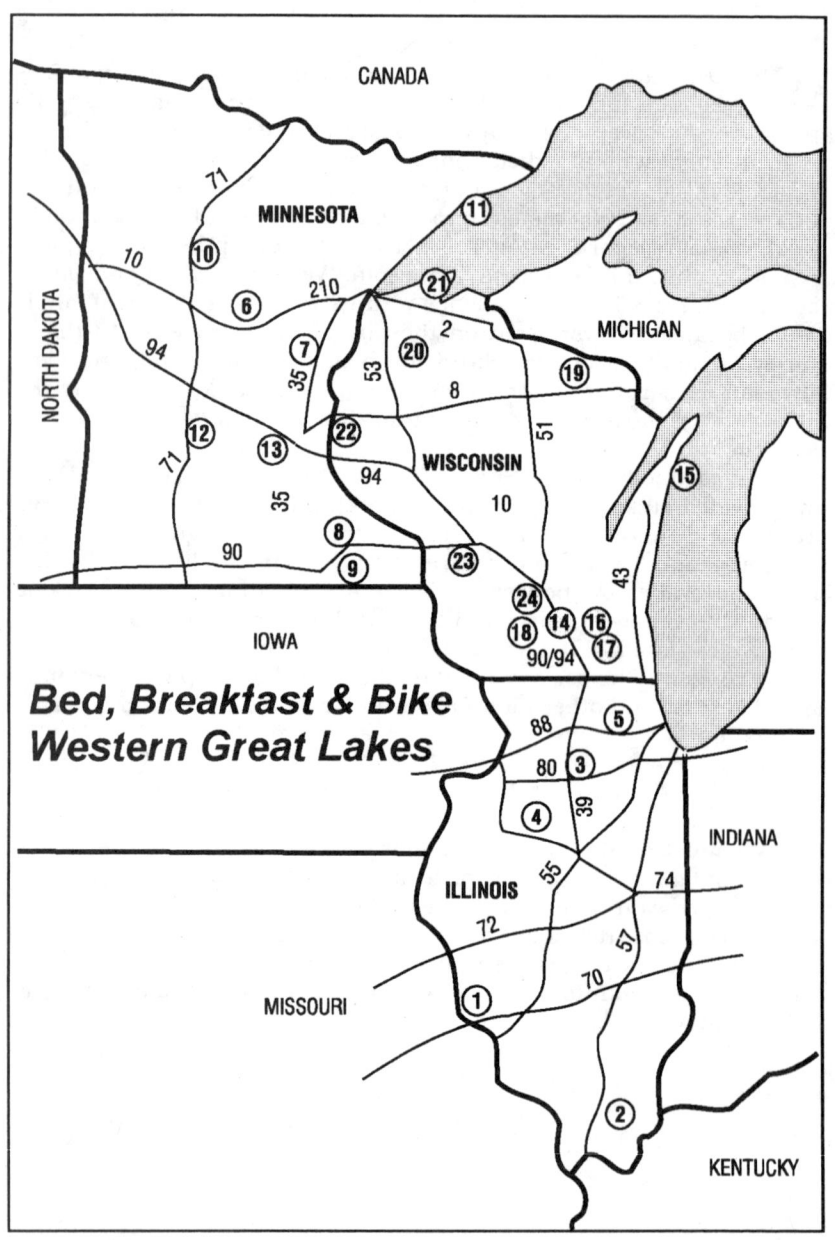

Numbers on map correspond to numbers in the Table of Contents

Contents

INTRODUCTION
Acknowledgements.. 3
Inn Locator Map... 4
How To Use This Book.. 7
Before You Go... 9

ILLINOIS INNS AND RIDES.. 11
1—The Green Tree Inn.. 13
2—House of Nahum.. 21
3—Landers House Country Lodging... 29
4—Rockwell's Victorian Bed & Breakfast.................................... 35
5—Villa Batavia Bed & Breakfast.. 45

MINNESOTA INNS AND RIDES... 53
6—Birch Hill Inne... 55
7—Dakota Lodge.. 61
8—Inn at Rocky Creek.. 69
9—JailHouse Inn... 79
10—The Park Street Inn.. 87
11—Pincushion Mountain Bed & Breakfast.................................... 95
12—The Spicer Castle.. 101
13—Wander Inn Bed & Breakfast... 107

WISCONSIN INNS AND RIDES... 113
14—Arbor House, An Environmental Inn...................................... 115
15—The Blacksmith Inn... 127
16—Fargo Mansion Inn.. 135
17—Hamilton House Bed & Breakfast... 143
18—The Hill Street Bed & Breakfast.. 149
19—Inn at Pinewood.. 157
20—Lumberman's Mansion Inn.. 163
21—The Old Rittenhouse Inn.. 171
22—St. Croix River Inn.. 179
23—The Strawberry Lace Inn.. 185
24—Victorian Treasure... 193

SELECTED RECIPES... 201

How to Use This Book

Information About the B&Bs

When it comes to B&Bs, no two establishments are alike—not even remotely alike. They all reflect the individual styles and tastes of their owners. Nevertheless, virtually everyone will find something that tickles their fancy in the selected cyclist-friendly accommodations in this book, from farms and lakefront mansions adapted for use as B&Bs to a tastefully converted county jail. Some are popular because of their setting, some because of their rich history or distinct architecture. The entry for each inn contains descriptions of ambiance, amenities, and locale to guide your selection.

From a management and hospitality perspective, the lodgings fall, in general, into two different categories: B&Bs, which tend to be smaller, family-run businesses where the innkeeper will greet you at the door and even serve you breakfast, and inns, which are somewhat larger establishments with larger staffs and slightly less personal—albeit hospitable and professional—service. If you're the kind of person who can't live without a TV, phone, and mini-bar in your room and who must have porters, fax machines, and room service on-demand, you probably won't enjoy a stay at a small, intimate, relaxed B&B or inn. That said, many B&Bs and small inns are adding amenities, such as in-room phones with voicemail, and some may even offer a television or a mini-bar in your room. In any event, if there is an amenity that you can't live without it's best to check with the innkeeper before booking a room. Many establishments also have non-smoking policies, so if you're a smoker ask about the smoking policy when you make a reservation.

The heading for each listing includes all contact information, including Web addresses and e-mail where available, plus rate information. The rate description is based on the rates when we visited the inns in 1999, and is subject to change. Rather than give a specific rate, which can quickly become dated, we have instead placed the rates in a range as follows:

Budget: $90 or less
Moderate: $91-140
Deluxe: $141-199
Luxury: $200 and up

Cycling

At least two recommended road rides with maps are included for each inn; however, in many cases innkeepers or local bike shops can make additional recommendations.

Descriptions of each ride cover terrain, road and traffic conditions, as well as interesting sites and landmarks along the way. The authors rode a tandem bike with regular road tires on most routes, and mountain bikes on off-road rides. Where road conditions are better suited to either a mountain or hybrid bike, it's noted.

The ride cues are well documented and mapped; however, it is a good idea to carry a detailed local map when riding the routes. Sometimes innkeepers will have them on hand; otherwise, they usually can be found at a local gas station, convenience store, bike shop, outdoor recreation or book store, or through a tourist bureau or chamber of commerce. In some areas, maps especially designed for cyclists are available. In a few instances, free maps are available from local real estate offices.

Cue Sheets

The cue sheets are presented in a standard format, providing information about mileage, landmarks, and turning points. The abbreviations represent:

Pt.-Pt.	Point-to-point, distance between turns or points of interest
Cum.	Cumulative, total miles from start point
Street/	
Landmark:	Description of street names or distinguishing landmarks
Turn	Direction in which to turn
L	Left
R	Right
S	Straight
BL	Bear left
BR	Bear right
TA	Turn around
R,L or **L,R**	Turn in one direction followed by another quick turn in another direction
-	Cross street or landmark where a stop or turn is not required

Before You Go

Preparing for the Trip

Everyone has his or her own idea about what makes a good bike ride. There are those who enjoy leisurely, low-impact tours along rail trails, and roadies who prefer wide, fast shoulders and the occasional strenuous climb. All will discover destinations to their liking in this collection of cue sheets, maps, and descriptions.

The write-up for each inn and related rides includes descriptions of the locale, bike routes, and noteworthy sites along the way. Most of the routes in this book are designed for recreational cyclists and can be handled by riders in moderately good physical condition. Stronger riders will find that there are a number of longer routes and some with challenging hills. In all cases, the ride descriptions will indicate for which kind of cyclist the route is suited.

In any event, if you haven't been on a bike for a while, you'll find your trip more enjoyable—and more endurable—if you do some training in advance.

Your Cycling Gear

Since the most critical item for a bicycle tour is your bicycle, you'll want to make sure that it's in good repair. If it hasn't been serviced for a while, head down to the local bike shop and have it fine-tuned to make sure everything is in excellent working order. When riding, it's a good idea to carry a tool kit and know how to use it. Likewise, since one of the most common on-the-road equipment problems is a flat tire, carry a pump and a spare inner tube—and know how to replace it.

Most touring cyclists like to mount a bag on their handlebar or rear rack for carrying items such as a camera, snack food, picnic lunch, sun block, and foul weather gear. How much and what you carry in your bag is a matter of personal style and preference.

In any event, carry plenty of water and drink it frequently to avoid dehydration.

What to Wear

What you wear is going to depend on the time of year and where you're riding. Summers in this part of the country tend to be warm, with slightly cooler temperatures as you move north, so a t-shirt and shorts are usually adequate. However, it's always best to be prepared for a change of weather by taking along a windbreaker or lightweight rain jacket. Spring and fall temperatures vary from pleasantly warm to chilly. During these seasons, particularly near Lake Michigan and Lake Superior, the weather can change quickly. Take along a warm sweater or pullover and consider wearing long tights over your bike shorts so that you can peel off or add layers as the day warms up or cools down. What starts out as a chilly morning can turn into a glorious afternoon, and you don't want to be excessively dressed for the warmer part of the day.

Wearing bright colors makes you more visible to oncoming motorists.

Finally, no matter how experienced you are, wear an ANSI- or SNELL-approved helmet.

Safety Tips

- Obey traffic laws and posted trail regulations
- Ride with traffic, as close to the shoulder as safely possible
- Avoid riding double except on extremely remote roads
- Use extra caution when crossing busy routes or intersections
- Use hand signals to indicate turns
- Cross railroad tracks at right angles
- Watch for sewer grates, pot holes, rocks, wet leaves, and other obstacles

---

—Important Disclaimer—

While this book provides as accurate a description of these rides as possible, road conditions and other critical information provided in these pages can change overnight. It is your own responsibility to have a thorough understanding of the routes you ride, the mechanical condition of your bike, and your riding ability. By purchasing this book or borrowing it from a friend, you have released Anacus Press, the authors, and the artists from any liability for injuries you may sustain while using this book as a guide.

Illinois

We've only included five inns from Illinois, but they represent five very different riding experiences. Though known as the Land of Lincoln, Illinois could also be called the Transition State as it seems one moves between the urban and rural, the agricultural and aquatic, the civilized and the wild as one traverses the state. Just outside of Chicago, the riding around the Villa Batavia has a park-like feel with many paved paths, benches and other accommodations. At the other end of that scale is the riding in the Shawnee National Forest just outside of the House of Nahum. The definition of "road" was definitely stretched to include some of the forest roads we covered there. Mountain bikes only need apply.

Not quite so far away either geographically or in feeling are the Illinois and Michigan Canal rides near the Landers House in Utica. The man-made features of the Canal are evident even as nature begins to reclaim lost ground, almost filling in the canal in places or throwing trees up through the supports of an abandoned bridge. One further step in that direction is the Rock Island Line ride out of Rockwell's Victorian B&B in Toulon. Though we've plowed the prairies, even agriculture can't hide nature's amazing reach across these flat expanses crisscrossed with the ravines of creeks, streams, and rivers. The Mississippi River is the dominant shaping force all along its reach and the town of Elsah, home of the Green Tree Inn, falls under that spell. Nestled in the cleft of a river bluff, this town came into being because of the river and owes much of its character and history to the river's proximity.

Taking proper advantage of all this diversity may require a bit of planning. We found a wealth of information on the Internet, primarily at the following two sites:

http://www.state.il.us/tourism/
http://dnr.state.il.us/parks/bike/bikegde.htm

Different states handle biking differently. Most of the Illinois paths are under the auspices of the Department of Natural Resources, but we found Department of Transportation bicycling maps quite helpful. They can be obtained at:

Map Sales - Room 121
Illinois Department of Transportation
2300 South Dirksen Parkway
Springfield, Illinois 62764
Telephone: (217) 782-0834

The Green Tree Inn, Elsah, Illinois

Green Tree Inn

Mike & Pauline Pitchford
15 Mill Street, PO Box 96,
Elsah, IL 62028
Rates: Moderate

Phone: (800) 701-8003
Web: www.greentreeinn.com

When you book rooms at the Green Tree Inn, it's almost as if you make a reservation for the whole town. The town of Elsah, not more than about four blocks wide, is nestled in a cleft of the high bluffs along the Mississippi River. It seems like the newer houses were built in the 1920s and '30s and many of the locals trace their homesteads here back three or four generations. As a result, Elsah has the authentic look and feel of a cozy turn-of-the-century river town.

Elsah got its start in the 1840s feeding wood to the boilers of Mississippi steamboats. James Semple bought land, laid out plots, and by the 1850s it became a commercial hub for the surrounding farms up on the bluffs. During the railroad boom in the late 1800s, track was laid down through town to avoid local St. Louis bridge-building politics, and Elsah boomed too. Over time, however, the politics got resolved, the bridge was built, and Elsah's railroad began to wither. By the end of the century, Elsah's boom was over. What must have seemed like a disaster then is the modern traveler's boon, as the town has been effectively preserved in its early 1900s state. The day-to-day work of this preservation is carried on by the Historic Elsah Foundation.

The geography around Elsah essentially comes in two gigantic stories. The first floor is at river level and the second is at the top of the high bluffs. Between Alton and Grafton, there are a handful of steep valleys (including Elsah's) that cut into the face of the bluffs. While the roads along the river and across the plains behind the bluffs are relatively flat, the lanes winding up these valleys are as steep as they are picturesque, reminiscent of New England.

That impression carries over to The Green Tree Inn, which could have been transplanted from the roadside of a colonial village. Though only built a dozen or so years ago, the two-story building with porches and balconies still carries the flavor of a New England saltbox. Most of the first floor is given over to a large dining room with a beautifully painted and stenciled wide-plank floor. When not in use as a dining hall, this room, decorated in a nautical theme, also serves as a common area for conversation or games. There's a small souvenir shop across the porch from the dining room. Two of the inn's nine rooms are also on this floor.

The Green Tree was purpose-built as an inn so you won't find some of the eccentric little nooks and corners in the rooms that you might in an old Victorian home. What you will find are spacious rooms with antique furniture, Victorian-inspired wallpaper and stenciling, and private bathrooms. Almost anywhere you look in Elsah, you'll find beautiful old houses and village scenes. This is true for all the rooms as well. Look out any window and you'll see something that makes you wonder if you stepped through a time warp.

Breakfast in that beautiful green-floored dining room is a satisfying affair. Our breakfast started with coffee, juice, and a cup of fresh fruit. That was followed by a crustless quiche that was so rich and fluffy it must have drained the cream and egg reserves for the county. Accompanied by a sausage patty side, this breakfast filled us up for a day of riding.

Elsah and surroundings provide ample opportunity for cyclists, but if you can't spin the pedals one more time around, there are many other diversions available. The area has over 75 antique and specialty shops. A floating casino, the Alton Belle, is just a few minutes away in Alton. If you prefer more outdoorsy pursuits, the Riverlands Sanctuary offers bird watching, including the occasional over-wintering eagle, and the Père Marquette State Park has hiking in and around the bluffs.

Rides from Green Tree Inn
The position of the Green Tree Inn presents you with a dilemma. In one direction you find two really interesting rides along the great river. But in addition to the two Great River Trail rides documented below, there are miles of rolling country roads atop the bluffs over the river to explore. In fall, you can take the Brussels ferry over to a slip of land between the converging Missouri and Mississippi rivers and wander the roads among orchards heavy with fruit.

Terrain: Flat—very flat. The Great River Trail runs on bike lanes on the road, which is right on the edge of the river. If you go all the way up to Père Marquette State Park, there are a few places where the trail climbs away from the river and the road, but mostly this is flat riding.

Road Conditions: The bike lanes are very well marked and generous. In those sections where there's actually a separate path, it's paved and well maintained.

Traffic: Though we were riding in bike lanes on the street for most of these rides, we were not conscious of the traffic. The bike lanes provide a very comfortable space for cycling along this well-traveled road.

Best Time to Ride: We really enjoyed our stay here in the spring though the high river changed our course a bit. This is far enough south that high summer can be quite hot. In general, the locals seem proudest of their fall weather and color.

Nearest Bike Shop
Bike Gear
2603 State Street
Alton, IL 62002
(618) 467-2453

Père Marquette State Park Picnic Ride (20.9 miles)
This ride runs right along the Mississippi River, so close that part of the trail was flooded out while we were there. Locals assure us that this is unusual and definitely only a problem in April or May. If you choose to come for the fall colors, which are supposed to be spectacular, the river will be more accommodating. On an early spring ride, we were able to take town streets past the flooded section. There was a small sidewalk and a marginal shoulder on the relatively lightly-traveled road.

Pt.-Pt.	Cume	Turn	Street/Landmark
			From the Green Tree Inn
0.0	0.0	R	**Mill St.**—head out towards Highway 100
0.0	0.0	-	Alpa St.
0.0	0.0	-	Elm St.
0.1	0.1	R	**Mississippi St.**
0.0	0.1	R	Just past parking lot **turn onto trail**
1.5	1.6	-	Chatauqua Rd.
1.2	2.8	-	Palisades Parkway
1.1	3.9	L	**Grafton Hills**
0.1	4.0	R	**Water St.**
0.1	4.1	-	Oak St.
0.2	4.3	R	**Market St.**; trail goes straight but was flooded
0.0	4.3	L	**Main St.**; trail parallels Main to the left
0.1	4.4	-	Sycamore
0.2	4.6	-	Mulberry St.
0.2	4.8	-	End of road shoulder
0.1	4.9	-	Edward St.
0.1	5.0	-	Canal St.

Pt.-Pt.	Cume	Turn	Street/Landmark
0.1	5.1	-	Mason Hollow
0.4	5.5	-	Daggett Hollow
0.3	5.8	**BR**	**Onto trail** as it crosses Main St.
0.2	6.0	-	Unmarked road
0.3	6.3	-	Parking lot for path
0.6	6.9	-	Graham Hollow
1.3	8.2	-	**Père Marquette Riding Stables** & **Mark Twain Wildlife Refuge**
1.6	9.8	-	Entrance to east **parking lot for park** (picnic area, bathrooms, water)
0.6	10.4	**TA**	**Main entrance**—lodge, picnic table, restaurant
0.5	10.9	-	East parking lot entrance
1.6	12.5	-	**Mark Twain Wildlife Refuge**
1.3	13.8	-	Graham Hollow
0.6	14.4	-	Parking lot for path
0.3	14.7	-	Unmarked road
0.2	14.9	**L**	Turn left off trail onto **Main**
0.3	15.2	-	Daggett Hollow
0.4	15.6	-	Mason Hollow
0.1	15.7	-	Canal St.
0.1	15.8	-	Edward St.
0.3	16.1	-	Mulberry St.
0.1	16.2	-	Sycamore St.
0.2	16.4	-	Market and Route 3 (going back through town)
0.2	16.6	-	Oak St.
0.2	16.8	-	Grafton Hills (pick up **bike path** on right)
3.8	20.6	**L**	**Mississippi Street** into town of **Elsah** (*use caution* crossing Rt. 100
0.0	20.6	**L**	**Mill St.**
0.2	20.8	-	Elm St.
0.0	20.8	-	Alpa St.
0.1	20.9	-	End of ride at **Green Tree Inn**

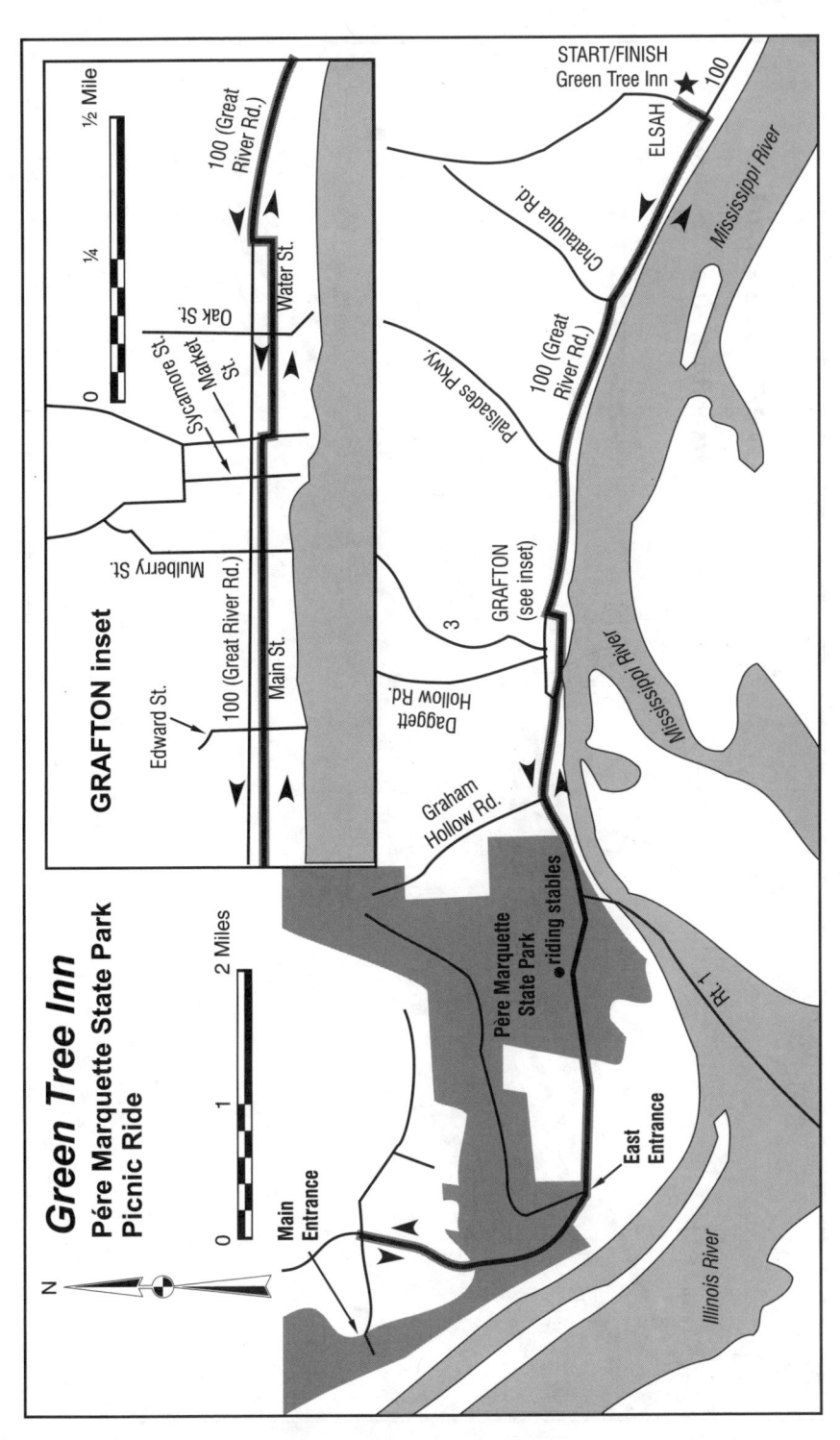

Green Tree Inn
Pére Marquette State Park
Picnic Ride

N

0   1   2 Miles

Main Entrance

Pére Marquette State Park

riding stables

East Entrance

Rt. 1

Illinois River

Mississippi River

GRAFTON inset

0   ¼   ½ Mile

Edward St.

100 (Great River Rd.)

Main St.

Mulberry St.

Sycamore St.

Market St.

Oak St.

Water St.

100 (Great River Rd.)

START/FINISH
Green Tree Inn

100

ELSAH

Chatauqua Rd.

100 (Great River Rd.)

Palisades Pkwy.

GRAFTON
(see inset)

3

Daggett Hollow Rd.

Graham Hollow Rd.

Mississippi River

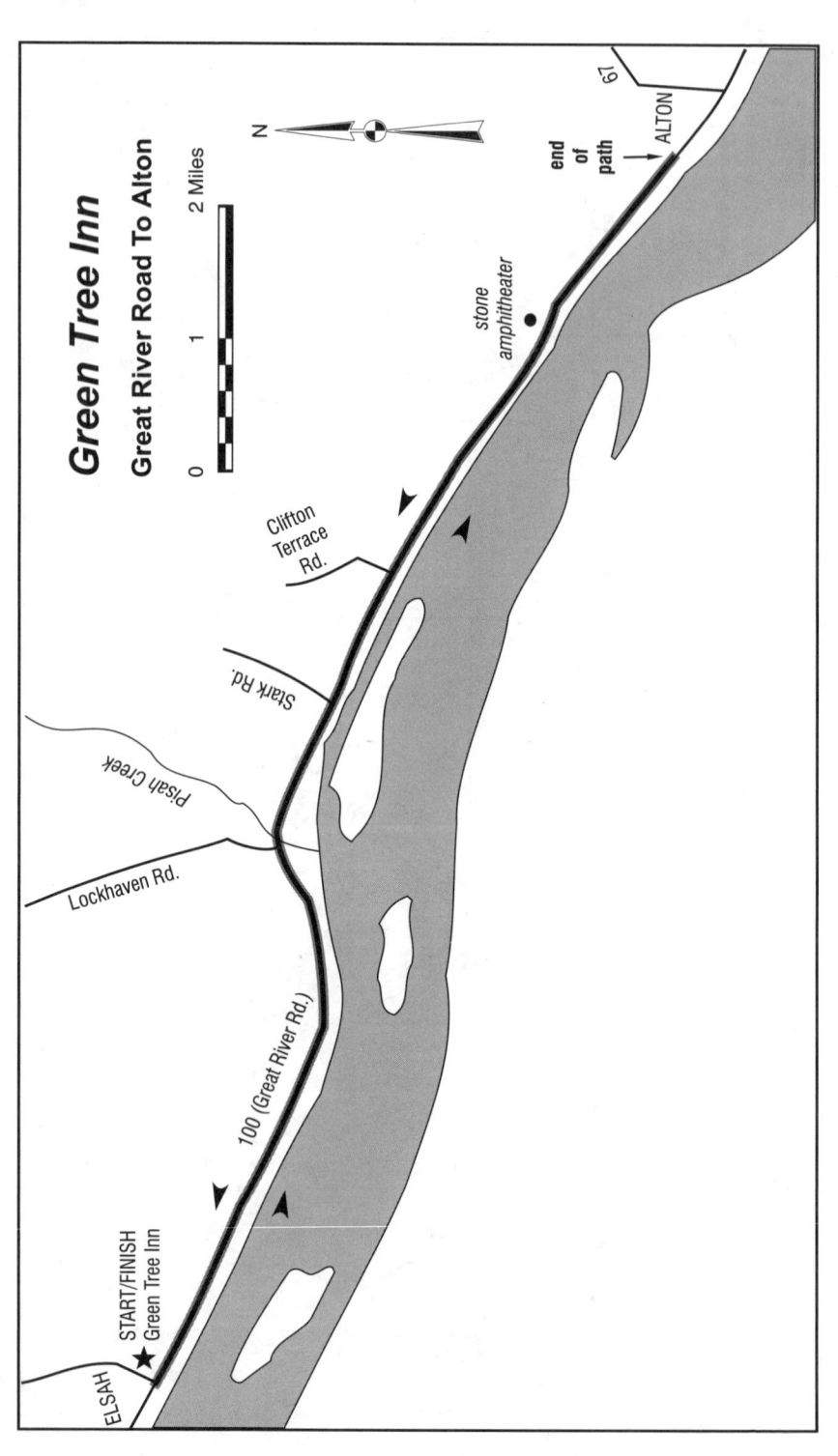

Green Tree Inn
Great River Road To Alton

N

0   1   2 Miles

ELSAH

★ START/FINISH
Green Tree Inn

100 (Great River Rd.)

Lockhaven Rd.

Pisah Creek

Stark Rd.

Clifton
Terrace
Rd.

stone
amphitheater

end
of
path → ALTON

67

Great River Road Ride to Alton (20.3 miles)

On the day we chose this ride over the bluffs, we were curious about all those antique shops in Alton. Though we didn't bring back any treasures, we did have a relaxing, fun ride on this easy trip down to Alton.

Pt.-Pt.	Cume	Turn	Street/Landmark
			From the Green Tree Inn
0.0	0.0	R	**Mill St.** towards Highway 100
0.0	0.0	-	Alpa St.
0.0	0.0	-	Elm St.
0.1	0.1	R	**Mississippi St.**
0.1	0.2	L	Trail along **Great River Rd. (Rt. 100)**, *be careful* crossing
4.3	4.5	-	Lockhaven Rd.
0.1	4.6	-	Piasa Creek
0.2	4.8	S	**On path** as it crosses Great River Rd. and continues east
0.7	5.5	-	Stark Rd.
1.1	6.6	-	Clifton Terrace Rd.
0.2	6.8	-	Unmarked Rd.
0.2	7.0	-	Iroquois Rd.
1.4	8.4	-	Large stone amphitheater
1.9	10.3	TA	**End of separate path**, though bike lane continues on other side into Alton which is less than a mile away
1.9	12.2	-	Large stone amphitheater
1.4	13.6	-	Iroquois Rd.
0.2	13.8	-	Unmarked Rd.
0.2	14.0	-	Clifton Terrace Rd.
1.1	15.1	-	Stark Rd.
0.3	15.4	S	**On path** as it crosses Great River Rd. and continues west
0.2	15.6	-	Piasa Creek
0.1	15.7	-	Lockhaven Rd.
4.3	20.0	R	**Mississippi St.**; town of **Elsah**
0.1	20.1	L	**Mill St.**
0.1	20.2	-	Elm St.
0.0	20.2	-	Alpa St.
0.1	20.3	-	End of ride at **Green Tree Inn**

House of Nahum, Harrisburg, Illinois

House of Nahum

Sona Thomas   **Phone:** (618) 252-1414
90 Sally Holler Lane   **Web: compuserve.bbchannel.com:**
Harrisburg, IL 62946   **8010/bbc/p210771.asp**
Rates: Budget to Moderate

The most compelling memory of the House of Nahum is not the building itself, comfortable as it is, or even the surrounding woods, green,
deep, and still. Sona Thomas, the House of Nahum's innkeeper, is at
the heart of our warm memories of this inn. From the cool drink and
cookies she offers when you arrive, through a chat about what to make
for breakfast, to a discussion of how to spend the day, Sona was not
only available and helpful, but downright accommodating and a pleasure to be around. Her personable hospitality made this feel more like a
visit with a favorite aunt than a stay at a place of business.

The House of Nahum is down a country gravel lane with a driveway
that winds down a slope between the trees. The driveway ends in a
slight rise, which meets the bricked driveway and wide front porch of
the inn. On sunny days Caleb the Cat will call a greeting—if he's not
snoozing on the warm bricks. Though this inn was built in 1992, it
could be from another era. When you walk in the front door, you step
into a Victorian parlor with every nook and cranny given over to some
small decoration or object. Sona's sense of style and taste bring all the
pieces together into a harmonious whole that provides endless detail for
the eye to settle on and savor.

The guestrooms are all on the second floor up an open wooden staircase that fills the entryway. The landing has antique blocks and other
children's toys. Each room has a theme, with matching quilts and comfortable chairs. The house is set down at the end of a country lane in the
Shawnee National Forest, so every window looks out into the trees; you
might catch a glimpse of a red-headed woodpecker or a ruby-throated
hummingbird. There is one suite—the Serenity Suite—which has a large
comfortable bed, a wicker couch, and whirlpool bath. As with the rest of
the house, Sona has skillfully and tastefully filled the rooms with Victorian antiques and reproductions. Picture books, dried flower arrange-
ments, and even the ornate wallpapers combine to provide a taste of
Victorian sensibilities. Every room has a private bath.

If you're lucky to have nice enough weather, you may get to eat breakfast on the patio at the back of the house. Nestled between two sides of
the house and bordered by an arbor, this cozy little nest seems like a
storybook house in the woods. Though Sona will tell you cooking isn't
her thing, the waffles we had one day and French toast the other tell a

different story. Breakfast started with juice and coffee and cup of fresh local fruit. The entrée came with maple syrup and homemade strawberry jam. It was all served on antique china. We can't guarantee the company of hummingbirds, but they floated over our breakfast both mornings, adding to the sense of enchantment.

The Shawnee National Forest is just beyond the back patio's arbor, but to appreciate its over 270,000 acres, you'll probably have to travel back down the country lane and out into the reaches of the forest. There are any number of natural attractions, including the Garden of the Gods, a collection of intricate and mysterious sandstone formations shaped by exposure to over 300 million years of wind and water. Numerous swimming, hiking, and other recreation areas are also scattered throughout the forest. To get the complete scoop on forest activities, visit the Shawnee National Forest Headquarters (800/699-6637) just outside of Harrisburg. Jean Glore, Barbara Casey, and the other rangers are a treasure trove of information.

You can choose to just sit on the inn's porch sipping lemonade, watching Caleb sleep. Pushing a mountain bike up through the bush on a forest road is another option, but nothing except comfort and relaxation is mandatory. Between the natural expanse of the forest and the serenity of the House of Nahum you will find an easy retreat from whatever stress and strain you might have.

Rides from House of Nahum
In the Shawnee National Forest there are over 1,250 miles of roads with surfaces ranging from pavement all the way to grass (we did see a forest road marker in the middle of what appeared to be an untouched meadow). All of these "roads" are open to cyclists, though road bikes will not get very far on some of them.

Terrain: The terrain for the Shawnee National Forest ride was everything from hilly to grassy to streambeds—a real mountain bike experience. The Tunnel Hill State Trail ride seems to be a steady incline from Vienna to the Tunnel Hill turnaround and is relatively secluded from roads or other signs of civilization for most of its length.

Road Conditions: The national forest ride covers a wide variety of surfaces and conditions will vary greatly depending on the recent weather. Parts of this path are only maintained by the apparently infrequent passage of trail users—in other words, it's a perfect, remote mountain bike ride. The Tunnel Hill Trail was a nice ride with a well-groomed trail surface and smooth entrances and exits to the bridges.

Traffic: We did not see a soul on either of these rides. Sweet.

Best Time to Ride: The House of Nahum is in the southern tip of Illinois and consequently has a more southern climate. Riding early in the spring or in the fall is characterized by balmy weather. July and August are quite hot.

Nearest Bike Shop: Jeff Jones, local biking enthusiast that we met at the Shawnee National Forest headquarters, tells us there is "no nearest bike shop." He goes across the border into Paducah, Kentucky, when serious bike attention is required.

Shawnee National Forest (7.3 miles)

The Shawnee National Forest ride has a little bit of everything. After an uphill start through the woods, the back section is a gravel forest road. The trail dives back into the woods and a downhill traverse follows which includes washouts and two short rides in a stream bed (dry when we visited in late May). You've got a bit of a drive from the inn to get here, but once you arrive, it's real mountain biking time. To reach the trailhead, follow these cues with your car:

Pt.-Pt.	Cume	Turn	Street/Landmark
0.0	0.0	**R**	Turn right onto **Rt. 35** headed towards Herod
5.0	5.0	**R**	Turn right onto **gravel road** at sign for Williams Hill
0.3	5.3	**BR**	Follows main road
0.3	5.6	-	unmarked road to right
1.2	6.8	-	dirt road to left, continue on main road
1.6	8.4	-	Pope Country Road from right
0.4	8.8	-	Trail meets road from left
0.4	9.2	-	unmarked road to right
0.6	9.8	**L**	Drive up **dirt road** to left; **park here**.

Shawnee National Forest Ride Cue Sheet

0.0	0.0	**S**	Straight up **dirt track** passing path up into cemetery
0.1	0.1	-	Trail to left continue straight
1.5	1.6	**L**	Left onto a **gravel road**

Pt.-Pt.	Cume	Turn	Street/Landmark
0.4	2.0	-	Trail to left, continue straight
0.1	2.1	-	Trail to left, continue straight
0.2	2.3	**BL**	Trail to right, continue on **gravel road**
0.1	2.4	-	Trail to left, continue straight
0.2	2.6	-	Trail to left, continue straight
0.3	2.9	-	Trail to left, continue straight
0.4	3.3	-	Foot path to right, continue straight
0.6	3.9	-	Path to right
0.3	4.2	**L**	Turn left onto **grass trail**
0.1	4.3	**BL**	Trail joins from right **continue to left**
0.1	4.4	-	Trail to right
0.3	4.7	-	Trail to right, continue straight down hill
0.5	5.2	-	Downhill through dry (hopefully) streambed
0.2	5.4	-	Foot trail comes in from right
0.1	5.5	-	Trail joins from left
0.4	5.9	**L**	**Turn left** as another trail joins from right
0.3	6.2	-	Cross creek and come out to gravel road at outfitters shop
0.0	6.2	**L**	Left onto the **gravel road** you drove in on
0.4	6.6	**BL**	Road joins from right; *loose gravel in intersection*
0.6	7.2	**L**	Turn left on **dirt road** at cemetery
0.1	7.3	-	Back at beginning of ride

Tunnel Hill State Trail (19.6 miles)

While you'll have to drive a bit to get to this recreational trail, it's worth the trip. There's a fascinating rail museum at the Vienna trailhead that made the ride a kind of journey into the recent railroad past as well as a delightful ride in the woods. This trail has the railroad's gentle grades and there are some beautiful views into gorges along the way from the old railroad bridges that have been remodeled for biking convenience. To reach the trailhead, follow these cues:

Pt.-Pt.	Cume	Turn	Street/Landmark
0.0	0.0	**L**	Turn left on **Rt. 34** (head back towards Harrisburg)
0.0	0.0	**L**	Turn left on to **Rt. 145**

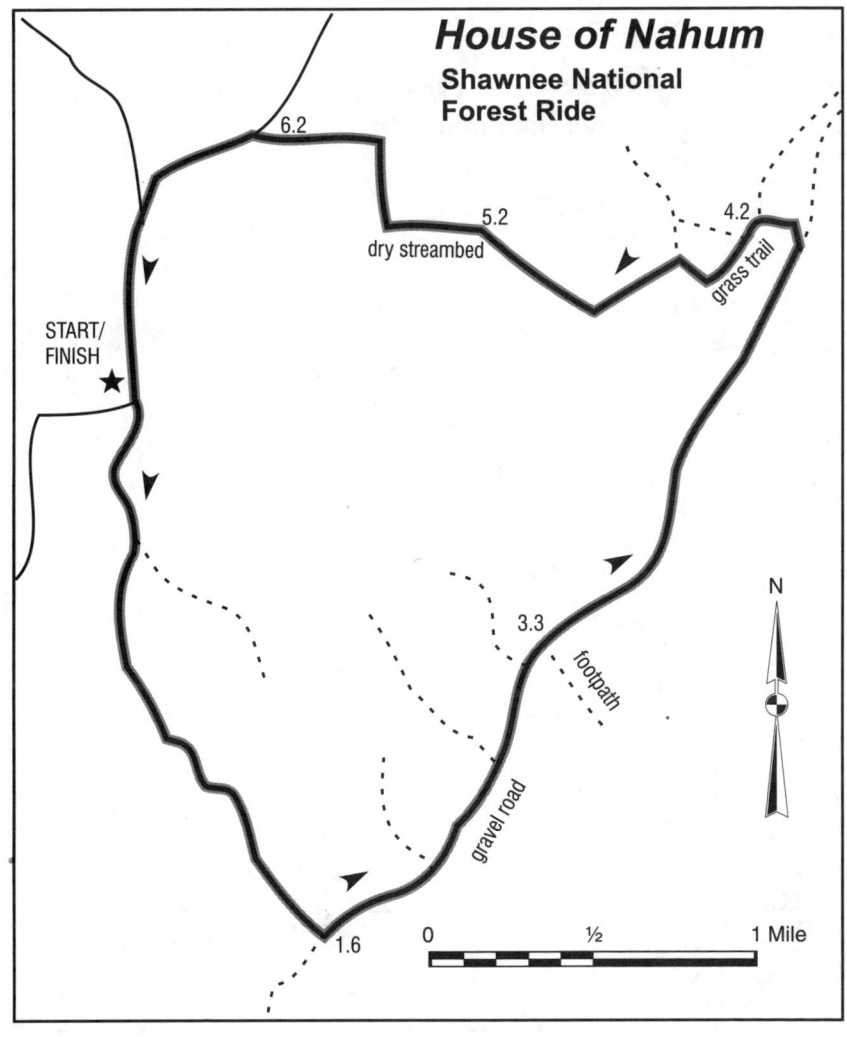

House of Nahum

Shawnee National Forest Ride

6.2

5.2

dry streambed

4.2

grass trail

START/
FINISH

3.3

footpath

gravel road

1.6

N

0   ½   1 Mile

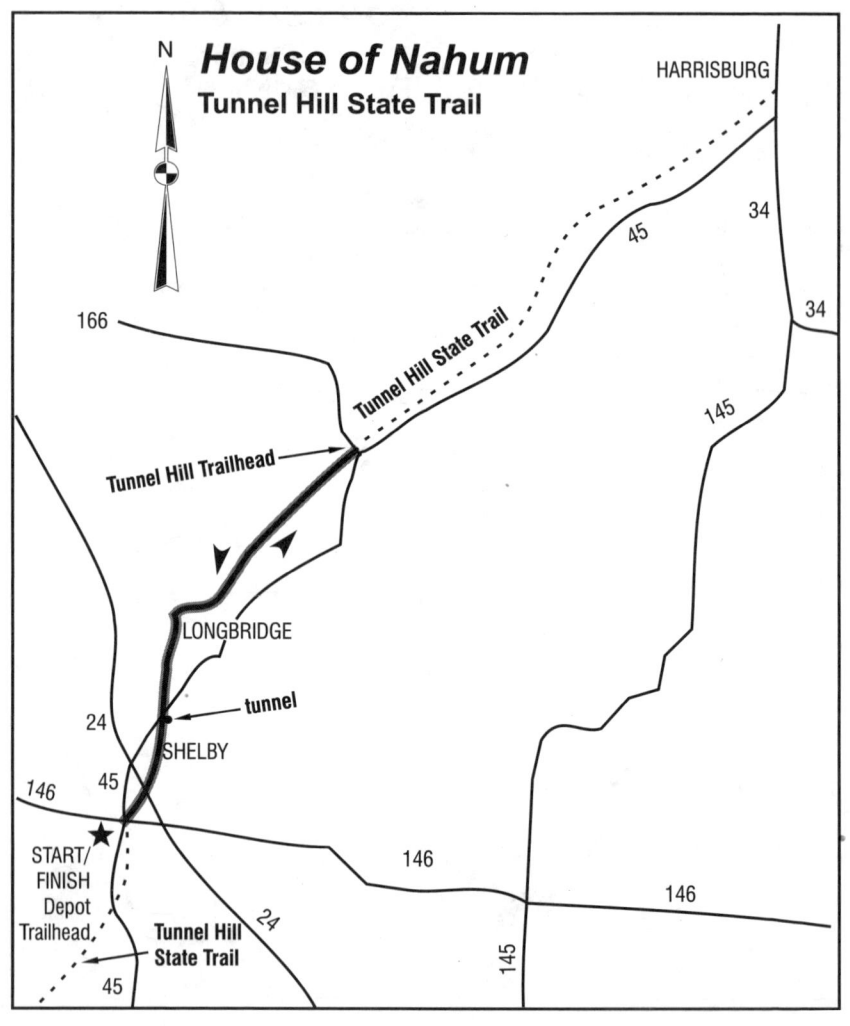

Pt.-Pt.	Cume	Turn	Street/Landmark
22.0	22.0	**L**	Exit Rt. 145 to **Rt. 146** turning left at bottom of ramp towards Vienna
13.0	35.0	**R**	Coming into Vienna, the **Depot Trailhead** is on the right

Tunnel Hill State Trail Cue Sheet

0.0	0.0	**L**	Starting **from flag pole** in front of depot
0.0	0.0	-	**Rail bridge**
0.8	0.8	-	Farm road
0.1	0.9	-	Farm road followed by **underpass**
0.1	1.0	-	Farm road
0.5	1.5	-	Farm road
1.3	2.8	-	**Shelby**
0.1	2.9	-	**Tunnel** under highway
0.2	3.1	-	Farm road
2.8	5.9	-	River to River **horse trail** crosses path
1.1	7.0	-	**Long Bridge**
1.7	8.7	-	Unmarked road
0.7	9.4	-	**Tunnel** of Tunnel Hill fame
0.4	9.8	**TR**	**Tunnel Hill Trailhead**
0.3	10.1	-	**Tunnel**
0.7	10.8	-	Unmarked road
1.7	12.5	-	**Long Bridge**
1.2	13.7	-	River to River **horse trail** crosses path
2.7	16.4	-	Farm road
0.2	16.6	-	**Tunnel** under highway
0.1	16.7	-	**Shelby**
1.3	18.0	-	Farm road
0.6	18.6	-	Double **underpass**
0.2	18.8	-	Farm road
0.8	19.6	-	**Vienna Trailhead**

Landers House, Utica, Illinois

Landers House Country Lodging

Dorelle Denman
115 East Church Street
Utica, IL 61373
Rates: Budget to Luxury

Phone: (815) 667-5170
Fax: (815) 667-5170
Web: www.inn-dex.net/landers

A drive through the cornfields southwest of Chicago to Landers House in Utica, Illinois, finds you in an African safari camp—or, for that matter, in a north woods fishing lodge, or a log cabin off the Appalachian Trail. Innkeeper Dorelle Denman's skill in creating various faux finishes and interior atmospheres has created an inn unlike any other we've seen. You simply must see this place.

From the exterior you'd never know that the two neighboring houses that make up Landers House contain a world of exploration and comfort. The two houses have seven guestrooms of varying sizes, but of unvarying creativity and uniqueness. A suite in the second house is an ideal setting for a small family vacation. A large deck overlooks a shared yard and gazebo, which provide an outdoor shelter from sun and wind. Down a short walk to the back of the property is a barn, which has been converted into two ample cottage suites.

We stayed in one of the cottages decorated with rustic Americana in a fishing camp theme. Most of the first floor is taken up with a comfortable sitting room that has a fireplace on one wall and a large two-person Jacuzzi in the far corner. A roomy bathroom with shower is off to one side, and in the crook of the stairs up to the bedroom loft is a guest kitchen with wet bar, coffee maker, and microwave. Whether by accident or design, all the windows in the cottage are situated high up on the walls, creating light that saturates the sitting area without any visual distraction. The loft bedroom has balcony rails and bed furniture made out of rough limbs and twigs, which only accentuates the decadent comfort of bed itself.

The African Safari room in the main house centers around a large bed tented in thick creamy fabric. African art and artifacts collected by Dorelle while visiting Africa carry out the theme. The log cabin room has been painstakingly painted to resemble the inside of a log cabin. Even after running your fingers across the smooth surfaces you'll find yourself believing the walls are made out of stacked-up tree trunks. It almost comes as a shock that the snowshoes crossed on the wall are real. Each of the seven rooms has a distinct theme and all have private baths.

The food at the Landers House continues the high production values evidenced in the interior decorating. On suitable summer days, breakfast is served on the patio and in the gazebo. It starts with a sideboard full of juices, signature coffee and teas, as well as pastries to keep you distracted as you anticipate your entrée. This becomes a more difficult task on your second or third day, as experience with these delightful breakfasts makes waiting for them less easy with each repetition. In between the juice and the main course there's a fresh fruit smoothie with an unexpected but wonderful secret ingredient from a childhood favorite sandwich. Finally, the entrées arrive: Lobster quesadillas or blueberry blintz soufflés or maybe marmalade-stuffed French toast. It doesn't really matter what's on the menu any given day, because it's all wonderful. As if breakfast weren't enough, you can arrange for box lunches to take on the trail or to the State Park, or have lunch or supper served in your room as part of the Cottage Packages.

Though you may be tempted to spend your entire stay without stepping out the front door, there are a number of reasons to venture out in addition to cycling. Starved Rock State Park has 15 miles of hiking trails as well as canoe rentals. There are a number of golf courses in the area as well as canoeing, pedal boats, and motor boating on waterways such as the Fox and Illinois Rivers.

The town of Utica is sweet little town ready to shake your hand and show you around. One day we got to meet Joe Carey, His Honor the Mayor, just walking across the street. Missy Herman, the proprietor of Canal Port, a Main Street watering hole and restaurant, has a welcoming smile and winning menu for all who come through the front door. We ended up going back to the Canal Port a second night despite both Mexican and Cajun temptations elsewhere.

Our stay at Landers House came at the end of long trip. It took us one night and one breakfast to change from wanting to be home to wanting to stay just a little longer. You don't need a long trip to appreciate this place, though. It's a destination worthy of a trip all by itself.

Rides from Landers House Country Lodging
In addition to the biking along the Illinois and Michigan Canal Tow Path Trail documented below, there are a number of other bike routes and trails within a short drive, including the Old Plank Road Trail and the Tiskilwa Bike Route. The Buffalo Range Shooting Club has mountain and dirt bike trails on the bluffs above the canal.

Terrain: The bike trail runs along the old towpath of the canal, so it is very level.

Road Conditions: The path is crushed limestone for most of its length, with a paved section at the LaSalle/Peru end of the trail. The trail is easily wide enough for bicyclists, joggers, etc. to pass in opposite directions.

Traffic: The trail is a popular site for not only riding and walking, but also for folks fishing down towards LaSalle. Heading towards Ottawa, we ran into fewer people, but still did not have the trail to ourselves.

Best Time to Ride: Because the summer temperatures tend towards the hot side, fall or spring tend to be better times for a visit to Landers House.

Nearest Bike Shop: Mix's Trading Post rents bikes locally, but the nearest full-service bike shops are in LaSalle.

Lunch in LaSalle (11.4 miles)

This is a casual ride along the I&M Canal to LaSalle. The ride has a kind of park atmosphere to it, with historical markers and benches periodically positioned along the path. We were serenaded by a giant bullfrog at one such stop. Once in LaSalle you can cross the canal on a footbridge. Dorelle can give you recommendations on where to eat.

Pt.-Pt.	Cume	Turn	Street/Landmark
0.0	0.0	R	Facing Landers House head **towards downtown Utica**
0.0	0.0	L	**Mill St.**
0.1	0.1	R	**Canal St.**
0.1	0.2	L	**Cross bridge to trail**
0.5	0.7	-	Turnout on trail
1.4	2.1	-	Doubletrack to left
0.1	2.2	-	**Old lock**
0.4	2.6	-	**Picnic place**
0.1	2.7	-	**Split Rock Historical Marker**
0.1	2.8	-	Dirt road heading down to Illinois river underneath I-39
1.4	4.2	-	**Aqueduct** and **historical marker**
0.6	4.8	-	**Lock 14:** toilets, parking lot, bridge to downtown **LaSalle** (lunch here!)
0.9	5.7	TR	**Lock 15**
0.9	6.6	-	**Lock 14**
0.5	7.1	-	**Aqueduct** and **historical marker**
1.6	8.7	-	**Split Rock Historical Marker**
2.3	11.0	-	**Stay left** under bridge

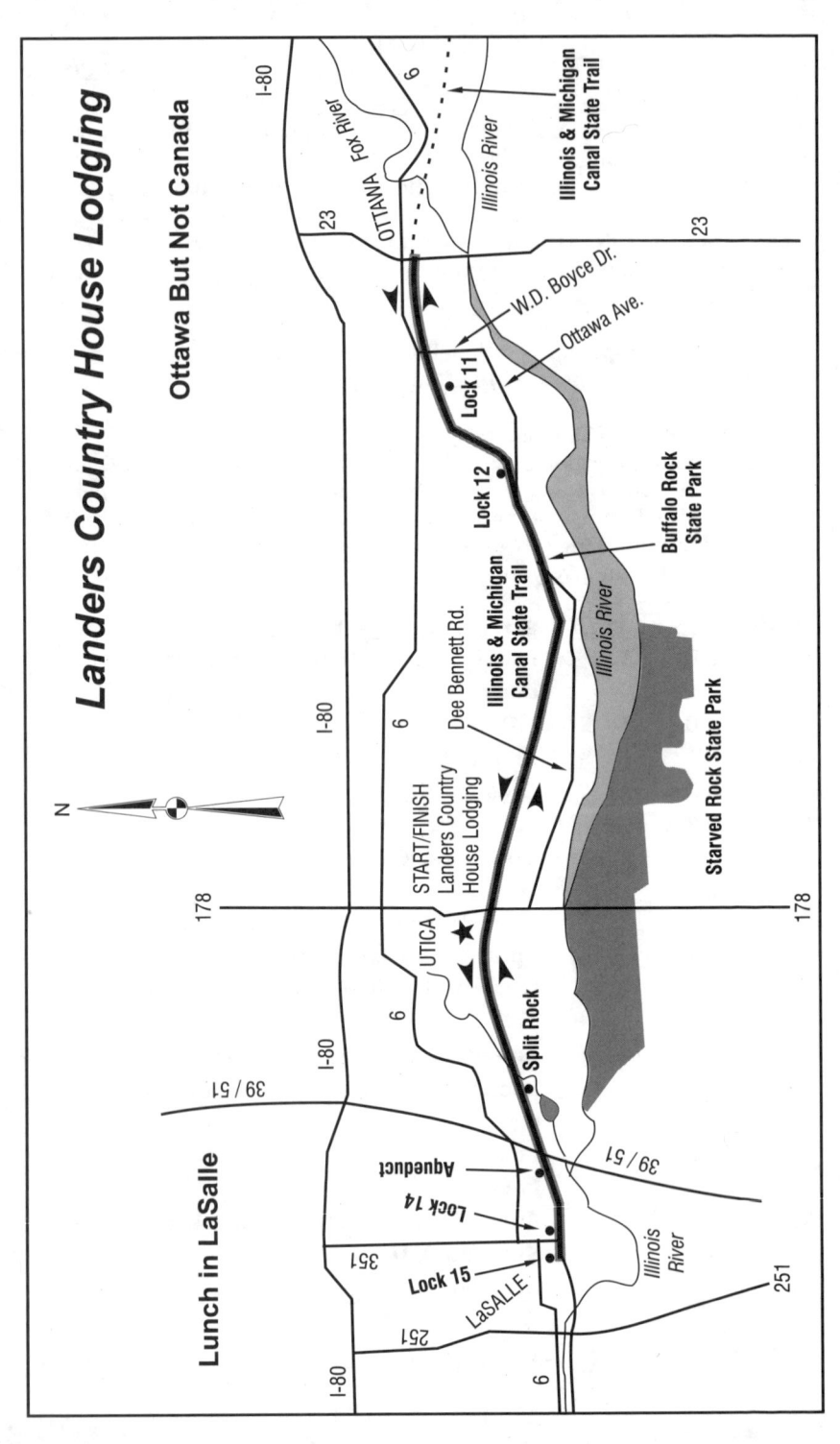

Landers Country House Lodging

Ottawa But Not Canada

Lunch in LaSalle

N

I-80

Fox River

OTTAWA

23

Illinois River

9

Illinois & Michigan
Canal State Trail

23

W.D. Boyce Dr.

Ottawa Ave.

Lock 11

Lock 12

Buffalo Rock
State Park

Illinois River

I-80

6

Dee Bennett Rd.

Illinois & Michigan
Canal State Trail

START/FINISH
Landers Country
House Lodging

Starved Rock State Park

178

178

UTICA

6

Split Rock

I-80

39 / 51

39 / 51

Aqueduct

Lock 14

Lock 15

LaSALLE

Illinois River

351

251

I-80

6

251

PtPt.	Cume	Turn	Street/Landmark
0.1	11.1	L	**Cross bridge**
0.1	11.2	R	**Canal St.**
0.1	11.3	L	**Mill St.**
0.1	11.4	R	**Church St.**
0.0	11.4	-	**Landers House** on **right**

Ottawa but not Canada (16.8 miles)

Headed east from Utica, this ride is a bit more scenic than the ride to LaSalle, with more woods and water. There is also access to Buffalo Rock State Park in the middle of the ride.

0.0	0.0	L	Facing Landers House, **away from downtown Utica**
0.0	0.0	R	**Vine**
0.1	0.1	BL	Cross Canal and jog left to **cross bridge to trail**
0.0	0.1	L	Left on **trail**
0.6	0.7	-	Driveway
0.6	1.3	-	Driveway (watch for gate across trail, which you'll ride around)
1.6	2.9	-	High bluffs on left
0.2	3.1	-	**Shelter** to right
1.4	4.5	-	**Camping**
0.2	4.7	-	**Camping**
0.6	5.3	-	Parking lot and **Buffalo Rock State Park** access
0.5	5.8	-	Pillars for abandoned bridge
0.4	6.2	-	underpass
0.2	6.4	-	**Lock**
1.5	7.9	-	**Lock**
0.1	8.0	-	Train tracks
0.4	8.4	TR	**West Ottawa Trailhead** (trail continues into town) with bathroom
0.4	8.8	-	Train tracks
0.1	8.9	-	**Lock**
1.5	10.4	-	**Lock with foot bridge**

Pt.-Pt.	Cume	Turn	Street/Landmark
0.6	11.0	-	abandoned bridge
0.5	11.5	-	Parking lot and **Buffalo Rock State Park** access
0.6	12.1	-	**Camping**
0.2	12.3	-	**Camping**
1.4	13.7	-	**Rest area**
1.7	15.4	-	**Rest area**
0.1	15.5		Gate
1.2	16.7	**R**	Turn **onto bridge across canal**
0.0	16.7	**BL**	Jog left to get on **Vine.**
0.1	16.8	**L**	**Church St.**
0.0	16.8	-	**Landers House**

Rockwell's Victorian Bed & Breakfast, Toulon, Illinois

Rockwell's Victorian Bed and Breakfast

Fred & Elizabeth Rockwell   **Phone: (309) 286-5201**
404 N. Washington
Toulon, IL 61483   **Rates: Budget**

Victorian mansions are often known for their woodwork. Rockwell's Victorian Bed and Breakfast carries this detail to the next level. Built in 1889 for local lumber baron Levi Silliman, this inn showcases some of the finest hardwoods and millworks available in the last half of the 1800s. As if that weren't enough, the building has had only three owners since it was built. Carefully maintained throughout its more than 100 years on the corner of Washington and Commercial streets, the house has had little need for restoration.

From the outside, there is little to advertise the museum-quality finish inside. The first hint is across the diminutive porch when one encounters the substantial front door. Just beyond, the entryway is done in oak with intricate inlays edging the floor and complex spindlework throughout the banister of the staircase, which curves up to the second floor. Everywhere, the eye catches some other fascinating detail in wood.

Just beyond the entryway is the library/living room done in a cherry that has aged to a deep warm maroon color. Built-in bookshelves rise up to the 12-foot ceilings and are topped with delicate carvings of single branches across the top. The faces of the huge pocket doors are covered with cherry on the sides facing into the living room as well. If you walk into the front parlor, the other side of the pocket door is covered in walnut, the predominant wood in that room. The parlor also has a fireplace with a tile face and walnut mantel. The tile came from Italy and features a boy's profile in one corner and a girl's profile in the other, a common motif at the turn of the century. One could spend the entire stay examining just the walnut mantel in the parlor. One can only imagine the long hours and many days required to craft the many nooks and detailed three-dimensional carvings.

If you don't inspect every room from the fine wood flooring to the details of the plaster work on the ceiling, you'll miss some intriguing and pleasing detail. For example, both the parlor and the entryway have elaborate leaded glass transom windows filled with cut glass and prisms which fill the rooms with a rainbow of light when the afternoon sun shines through them.

Upstairs, the inn has three rooms, which, while not quite as spectacular as the first floor rooms, are still a feast for the eyes. The smallest room is still quite roomy with two twin beds. Its high windows share the carved wood finish found throughout the downstairs. Down the hall and around a slight bend is the Walnut room. It is slightly larger with a queen bed and fills up with light in the late afternoon. The third room is a suite with a sitting room and generous sleeping area separated by a large pocket door. The sitting room also has another of the Italian-tiled fireplaces, and is filled with antiques including a loveseat, rocker, and oak checker table. There's a single bathroom on the second floor with a huge old tub, suitable for soaking after a long ride.

Elizabeth Rockwell serves a delicious breakfast with a light touch. Breakfast starts out with a cup of mixed fresh fruit. We enjoyed a combination of fresh strawberries, particularly succulent watermelon, and bananas. Though it was too early for blueberries, we could almost taste them anyway as Mrs. Rockwell regaled us with stories of blueberry picking during her girlhood. One day the main course for breakfast was a well-turned mushroom, scallion, and cheese omelet with a spray of perfect hash browns, crispy on the outside, soft on the inside. For another breakfast we were lucky enough to have "Mom's French Toast" served with a spicy sausage. All in all, they were ideal breakfasts before hopping on the bikes.

If you were to pull a small prairie town from the collective American consciousness and make it a county seat, something much like Toulon would emerge. The county courthouse is the main fixture on Main Street. It's flanked by a high stone monument to Toulon's civil war veterans to the left and a solid obelisk dedicated to the pioneer founders on the right. No small town would be complete without a bit of conversational history: Toulon had a dentist shop, whose most famous customer was Abraham Lincoln. He left behind a couple of teeth, which have since disappeared in the mists of time; rumor has it that they were stolen.

All in all, our visit to the Rockwell Victorian bed and breakfast seemed more like a visit to grandma's than a stay at an inn. The amazing woodwork details of the house, the charming county seat, and even Elizabeth Rockwell herself all harmonized into a comfortable and familiar Americana.

Rides from Rockwell's Victorian Bed and Breakfast

We came to Toulon to ride the Rock Island Line Trail. It's a good ride, but the area has much more to offer. It is very rural and has miles of roads suitable for riding. The prairie views are spectacular and if you happen to find the right tailwind you might not have to pedal for miles. The Illinois Department of Transportation (217/782-0834) publishes bicycle route maps, and Map #4—the Spoon River Valley Map that covers this region—shows literally hundreds of miles of rideable roads.

Terrain: You're on the prairie now! The Rock Island Line Trail is a true rails to trails conversion and you won't find any significant hills. You might want to check the wind direction before you leave, though. On the day we rode this trail we had a none-too-light and always-present head wind, which made it feel like a 15-mile uphill. On the Wyoming Loop the ride starts out flat, but the further into the ride you get the more hills you encounter, with more steeply-pitched grades.

Road Conditions: The Rock Island Line is a delightful trail on crushed limestone. It is not heavily used and is in excellent shape. The roads in the Wyoming Loop ride are in good condition though without significant shoulders for riding. The one exception is the short stretch on Route 91 south of Wyoming where there are shoulders.

Traffic: On the Rock Island Line Trail we saw next to nobody. On the Wyoming Loop we saw ... nobody. We were riding in the middle of the week in late May, before summer really got started, but it didn't seem to us that this was an unusual occurrence.

Best Time to Ride: The upside of riding early in the season is milder temperatures, as it can get hot later in the summer. The downside is that this time of year brings ample and seemingly unrelenting breezes. Later in the summer will be hotter, but calmer as well.

Nearest Bike Shop: Come prepared for all minor maintenance tasks because there is no full service bike shop close at hand.

The Rock Island Line Trail (32.5 miles)
This is a beautiful secluded trail, especially up towards the Toulon end. The number of beautiful small birds we saw along this path—including orioles, indigo buntings, and a bluebird—astounded us. There's also a spectacular old railroad bridge on the trail that reminds you this was once the Rock Island Line of train song and story.

Pt.-Pt.	Cume	Turn	Street/Landmark
0.0	0.0	**L**	Starting from the corner of Commercial St. and Washington, turn left onto **Franklin**
0.1	0.1	-	Greenwood St.
0.1	0.2	**R**	**Clinton St.**
0.1	0.3	-	Miller St.
0.0	0.3	-	Olive St.
0.1	0.4	**S**	Cross Union St.
0.5	0.9	**R**	**Downend St.**

Pt.-Pt.	Cume	Turn	Street/Landmark
0.2	1.1	-	Surface changes to gravel
0.3	1.4	L	**Rock Island Line Trail**
0.2	1.6	S	Cross N. Grainbin Rd.
0.4	2.0	-	Rock Island Trail parking lot
0.5	2.5	S	Cross 800N and gate
0.4	2.9	S	Cross 750N
0.7	3.6	S	Cross 900 E; careful of blind hill on road near crossing, gates on both sides
0.5	4.1	-	**Old railroad bridge** over Spoon River
1.7	5.8	S	Cross road at gate
0.0	5.8	R	**Sixth St.**
0.1	5.9	L	**Thomas St.**
0.1	6.0	R	**Seventh St.**
0.0	6.0	L	**Alleyway behind Williams**
0.1	6.1	L	At intersection of Galena and Williams, **cross diagonally** and follow **Williams** east towards water tower
0.1	6.2	-	Main St.
0.1	6.3	R	**Wyoming Trailhead** and **Train Depot**; trail resumes
1.1	7.4	S	Gate, Cross 500N, Gate
1.0	8.4	S	Cross 1200E
0.2	8.6	S	Cross 400N
1.2	9.8	S	Cross 300N
1.5	11.3	S	Cross 150N
0.8	12.1	S	Cross 75N
0.8	12.9	S	Cross 00N; **Rock Island Trail Nature Preserve**
1.1	14.0	S	Cross Streitmatter Rd.
1.0	15.0	S	Cross Mendell Rd.
0.3	15.3	L	Trail ends at **unmarked road**, take it left
0.1	15.4	R	**Town Ave.**
0.3	15.7	-	Woertz Rd.
0.0	15.7	-	Craig Rd.
0.3	16.0	R	**North Rd.**
0.1	16.1	L	**Walnut St.**

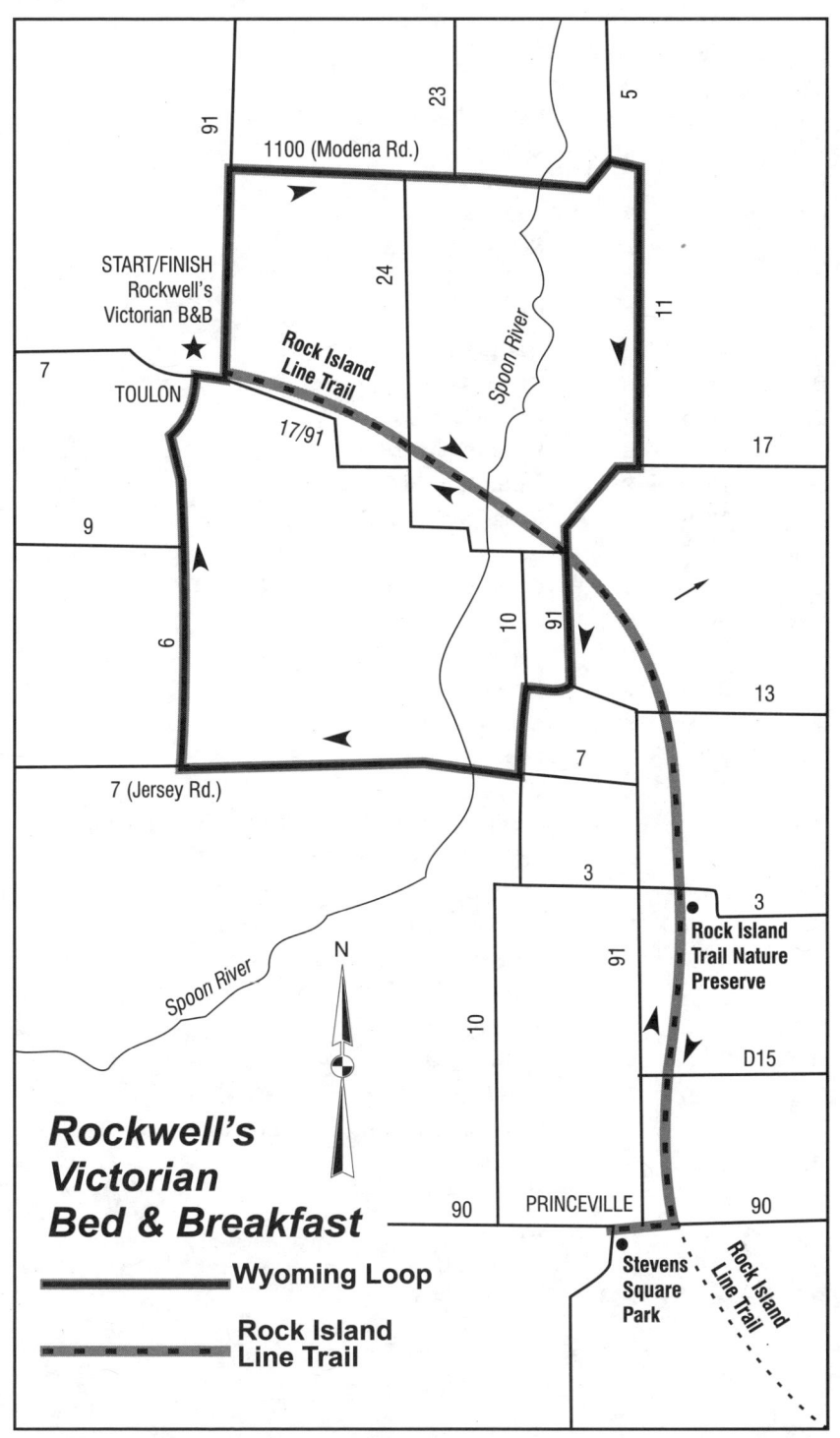

91

23

5

1100 (Modena Rd.)

START/FINISH
Rockwell's
Victorian B&B

24

Spoon River

11

Rock Island
Line Trail

7

TOULON

17/91

17

9

10

91

6

91

13

7

7 (Jersey Rd.)

Spoon River

N

3

Rock Island
Trail Nature
Preserve

3

91

10

D15

Rockwell's
Victorian
Bed & Breakfast

90

PRINCEVILLE

90

Stevens
Square
Park

Rock Island
Line Trail

Wyoming Loop

**Rock Island
Line Trail**

Pt.-Pt.	Cume	Turn	Street/Landmark
0.0	16.1	-	High St.
0.1	16.2	-	Evans St.
0.0	16.2	**R**	**Main St.**
0.1	16.3	**TR**	**Stevens Square Park**
0.1	16.4	**L**	**Walnut St.**
0.0	16.4	-	Evans St.
0.1	16.5	-	High St.
0.0	16.5	**R**	**North St.**
0.1	16.6	**L**	**Town Ave.**
0.5	17.1	**L**	**Unmarked road**
0.1	17.2	**R**	**Rock Island Trail**
0.3	17.5	**S**	Cross Mendell Rd.
1.1	18.6	**S**	Cross Streitmatter Rd.
1.1	19.7	**S**	Cross 00N; **Rock Island Trail Nature Preserve**
0.8	20.5	**S**	Cross 75N
0.7	21.2	**S**	Cross 150N
1.6	22.8	**S**	Cross 300 N
1.1	23.9	**S**	Cross 400N
0.2	24.1	**S**	Cross 1200E
1.0	25.1	**S**	Cross 500N
1.1	26.2	**L**	Onto **Williams St.** at Wyoming Trailhead and Train Depot; bathrooms
0.1	26.3	-	Main St.
0.1	26.4	**R**	At Intersection of Galena and Williams, **cross diagonally** and **follow alley** towards Seventh St.
0.1	26.5	**R**	**Seventh St.**
0.0	26.5	**L**	**Thomas St.**
0.1	26.6	**R**	**Sixth St.**
0.0	26.6	**L**	**Rock Island Line Trail** resumes to left
2.3	28.9	**S**	Cross 900 E
0.7	29.6	**S**	Cross 750N
0.4	30.0	**S**	Cross 800E
0.5	30.5	-	Trailhead
0.4	30.9	**S**	Cross N. Grainbin Rd.

Pt.-Pt.	Cume	Turn	Street/Landmark
0.2	31.1	R	**Downend St.**
0.3	31.4	-	Surface changes to asphalt
0.2	31.6	L	**Clinton St.**
0.5	32.1	S	Cross Union St.
0.1	32.2	-	Miller St.
0.1	32.3	-	Olive St.
0.0	32.3	L	**Franklin St.**
0.1	32.4	-	Greenwood St.
0.1	32.5	R	**Commercial St.**
0.0	32.5	-	Corner of Commercial St. and Washington—head east on Commercial

The Wyoming Loop (28.1 miles)

Fear not, you don't have to get out your ten-gallon hat and cowboy boots to enjoy this ride. Wyoming is the next town over and this ride heads out north and east before looping back through Wyoming and then back south and west. On the flat parts northeast of Toulon we saw a number of pheasants along the road but had to settle for contented-looking cows to amuse us for the rest of the ride.

0.0	0.0	-	Corner of Commercial and Washington
0.0	0.0	L	**Franklin St.**
0.1	0.1	-	Greenwood St.
0.1	0.2	R	**Clinton St**
0.1	0.3	-	Miller St.
0.0	0.3	-	Olive St.
0.2	0.5	L	**Union St. (Highway 91)**
0.4	0.9	-	900N
1.1	2.0	-	1000N
1.0	3.0	R	**1100N** (Also **Modena Rd.**)
1.5	4.5	-	800E
1.0	5.5	-	900E
0.5	6.0	-	950N
1.5	7.5	-	1100E
0.7	8.2	-	1175E
0.5	8.7	-	1215E

Pt.-Pt.	Cume	Turn	Street/Landmark
1.0	9.7	-	1000N
0.5	10.2	-	950E
2.5	12.7	**R**	**Rt. 17**
0.8	13.5	-	Entering **Wyoming**, Rt. 17 becomes **Diagonal St.**
0.3	13.8	-	Madison
0.2	14.0	-	Main St.
0.1	14.1	-	Galena St.
0.1	14.2	-	**Diagonal St. merges with Seventh St.**
0.1	14.3	-	Butler St.
0.1	14.4	-	Thomas/Park St.
0.0	14.4	**S**	Cross Williams St. (**Seventh** is also known as **Rt. 91** here)
0.1	14.5	-	Elm St.
0.1	14.6	-	Smith St.
0.1	14.7	-	Agard St.
0.0	14.7	-	South St.
0.7	15.4	-	500N
0.9	16.3	**R**	**Route 10**
0.5	16.8	**BL**	Road forks; take the left branch which is still **Route 10**
1.1	17.9	**R**	**Route 7** (also known as **Jersey Rd.**)
0.5	18.4	-	1120E
0.6	19.0	-	950E
1.4	20.4	-	815E
0.1	20.5	-	800E
1.5	22.0	-	650E
0.5	22.5	**R**	**Route 6 (600E)**
1.5	24.0	-	450N
0.5	24.5	-	500N
1.0	25.5	-	600N
0.2	25.7	-	620N
1.8	27.5	-	Prairie St.
0.1	27.6	**R**	**Turner St.**
0.1	27.7	**L**	**Henderson**

Pt.-Pt.	Cume	Turn	Street/Landmark
0.1	27.8	**S**	Cross Main St.
0.1	27.9	-	Vine St.
0.1	28.0	-	Thomas St.
0.0	28.0	**R**	**Commercial St.**
0.1	28.1	-	Back at the **Rockwell's Victorian**

Villa Batavia Bed & Breakfast, Batavia, Illinois

Villa Batavia Bed and Breakfast

Dick Palmer & Fran Steiner   **Phone: (630) 406-8182**
1430 S. Batavia Ave   **Fax: Same (call first)**
Batavia, IL 60510
Web: http://compuserve.bbchannel.com: 8010/bbc/p210515.asp
Rates: Budget – Deluxe

Riding the bicycle paths from the Villa Batavia, you'll probably never forget that you're in and about the outer suburbs of Chicago. On the other hand, riding through the miles of well-groomed trails and parks along the Fox River, you might come to believe you're lost in a really large country estate. The Villa Batavia itself is more than ready to play the role of country manor.

The Villa was built in 1844 as a farmhouse, and the enormous dining room could have accommodated the family, the farmhands, and all the neighbors that came to help bring in the harvest. The visitors probably would have been on their best behavior in this formal space, which includes several heirloom murals. The 1833 paintings, collectively titled "Scenic America," are duplicates of panels hanging in the Oval Reception Room of the White House in Washington, D.C. Once you manage to pull your eyes away from the fantastic details of the murals you'll notice the generous dining room table, the large crystal chandelier, and formal fireplace at one end of the dining room. The only other public room is the adjoining living room. Though not quite on the grand scale of the dining room, it is a very comfortable space with several couches, games, and local information in an antique desk.

Upstairs, the Villa has two generous guestrooms. The centerpiece of the Caroline Room is an antique fourposter bed and antique spread. Across the room is a small comfortable loveseat next to an antique desk. A toasty gas fireplace, warm hardwood floors, and a large throw rug set the room's comfortable ambiance. Connected to the main room is a spacious bathroom with a large bath surrounded in marble taken from the old Kane County Courthouse.

The other upstairs room is the Selbourne Suite, which consists of a bedroom full of Victorian furniture, a sleeping porch with television and telephone, and a bath and dressing room. Just across from the bed is a fireplace with a hand-carved wooden frontispiece from the 1700s. Earlier in this century, the suite served as the apartment of a University of Chicago professor who used the larger bedroom as her library, leaving the porch to serve as her bedroom.

The only other room in the Villa is the Garden Room, which is downstairs just off the dining room. Far simpler than the other two rooms, this room has a twin bed and a television. Its private bathroom is just down the hall. Though the room is much smaller than the other two, it has a great view of the Villa's gazebo and gardens.

The ample grounds of the Villa include several flower gardens, a meadow, and a small Christmas tree farm. Last but not least, a wooded path leads down to the Fox River Trail. The grounds of the Villa are adjacent to the trail with the Fox River itself just on the other side.

Before you head off down the trail, be sure to stoke up on one of Dick's breakfast creations. We had a fresh fruit cup to start, with a very attractive set of pastries including an apple cinnamon combination on phyllo and several bear claw donuts. The main course, Eggs Benedict Arnold, was a unique and delicious interpretation of the traditional eggs benedict with homemade bread, eggs poached with sweet vidalia onions, and a very light and tasty cilantro hollandaise sauce.

If you somehow manage to exhaust the 100+ miles of bike trails out the back door of the Villa, there are plenty of other activities in the surrounding area. Without leaving the Fox Valley, you'll find boating, horseback riding, and cross-country skiing in season. The first Sunday of the month, St. Charles (just a short drive north) has an antiques fair, and there are many antiques stores and over 30 museums in the area as well. The scientifically-inclined might want to visit the nearby Fermi Labs, featuring the most powerful particle accelerator on the planet. The Villa Batavia will provide a relaxing home base whether you want to spend all your time on the bike, exploring local attractions, or just reading a good book in the gazebo.

Rides from Villa Batavia
The bike trail and path system out the back door of the inn provides several hundred miles of trails ranging from the very rural to the noticeably urban. You can do any number of loops and out-and-back rides depending on your whim.

Terrain: Though the largely developed environment hides it, this really is the edge of the prairie; consequently, most of the riding is pretty level.

Road Conditions: The Aurora Ride is all on nicely paved trail. The Wheaton Triangle ride combines all kinds of surfaces including compacted gravel, paved trails, sidewalks, and paved roads.

Traffic: There are places in the Wheaton Triangle ride where you'll be sharing the roads without the benefit of bike lanes or paths. While we did not feel the conditions were dangerous at any point, some vigilance is required as some of the road portions are fairly heavily traveled by those large four-wheeled distractions.

Best Time to Ride: As one moves further south in this region, there is a marked difference in climate. Batavia is in northern Illinois, but the high summer months can still be quite hot. Riding earlier in the spring or early in the fall will probably provide the most comfortable rides.

Nearest Bike Shop
Pedal and Spoke
1575 Lincoln Way
North Aurora
(630) 892-1010

Wheaton Triangle Ride (33.5 miles)
This ride includes samples of every possible riding environment. It starts out along the Fox River against a park-like backdrop. There are flat country sections once you leave the river valley, followed by some fairly urban riding through the outskirts of Wheaton. The ride heads back into a more rural setting before returning to the river valley on the way home.

Pt.-Pt.	Cume	Turn	Street/Landmark
0.0	0.0	L	At path from Villa Batavia. Head **left towards Geneva on Fox River Trail**
0.9	0.9	-	*Caution:* Gate foundation in middle of trail
0.3	1.2	-	Trail merges with road at water treatment plant
0.1	1.3	-	Trail diverges to right
0.0	1.3	-	Trail joins **Flinn Drive**
0.1	1.4	L	**Schumway**
0.2	1.6	S	Cross Wilson St. Shumway becomes **Island Ave.**
0.1	1.7	L	**Houston St.** Get onto sidewalk to pick up trail in one block
0.1	1.8	R	**Trail resumes** to right
1.2	3.0	-	**Park** and parking lot
0.3	3.3	R	**Cross bridge to small park** in middle of river
0.3	3.6	L	After crossing another bridge **trail resumes** to left

PtPt.	Cume	Turn	Street/Landmark
0.1	3.7	-	**Dutch Windmill**
0.8	4.5	**S**	Intersection with another trail, continue straight
0.4	4.9	-	Rt. 38 underpass, trail curves a bit right and then left, continue along the river
0.1	5.0	**BR**	**Trail merges with sidewalk on Bennett St.**
0.1	5.1	**BL**	**Trail diverges from sidewalk**
0.5	5.6	**R**	**Illinois Prairie Path** goes up to right. It's easy to miss this turn. It's just after a curvy section through some trees.
0.0	5.6	**S**	Cross Riverside Dr. and walk up wood walkway to **Illinois Prairie Path**
0.4	6.0	-	**Trail joins Locust Drive**, go one block to Eastside Rd.
0.0	6.0	**R**	**Eastside Rd.**
0.3	6.3	**S**	Cross Geneva Dr.
0.2	6.5	-	Woodward Dr. to left
0.0	6.5	**SL**	**Sharp left** off sidewalk **onto trail**
0.5	7.0	**S**	Cross unmarked highway; _busy, be careful_
1.2	8.2	**S**	Cross unmarked road
0.2	8.4	-	Golf course crossing
1.0	9.4	**S**	Cross unmarked road
0.3	9.7	-	Railroad crossing
0.2	9.9	-	Unmarked road followed immediately by gate
1.0	10.9	-	Bridge over railroad yard
0.2	11.1	-	Trail merges with **Yale St**. for short distance and then curves right away from street
0.4	11.5	-	Unmarked road at entrance to **West Chicago** (follow markers through town)
0.6	12.1	-	**West Chicago Community Center** (old depot)
0.1	12.2	-	Trail goes along **Chicago Ave.**
0.1	12.3	**R**	Steep uphill and right turn **onto sidewalk**
0.3	12.6	**S**	Cross Rt. 59
0.1	12.7	**S**	Cross Easton
0.5	13.2	**S**	Cross Prince Crossing Rd. Trail picks up on other side

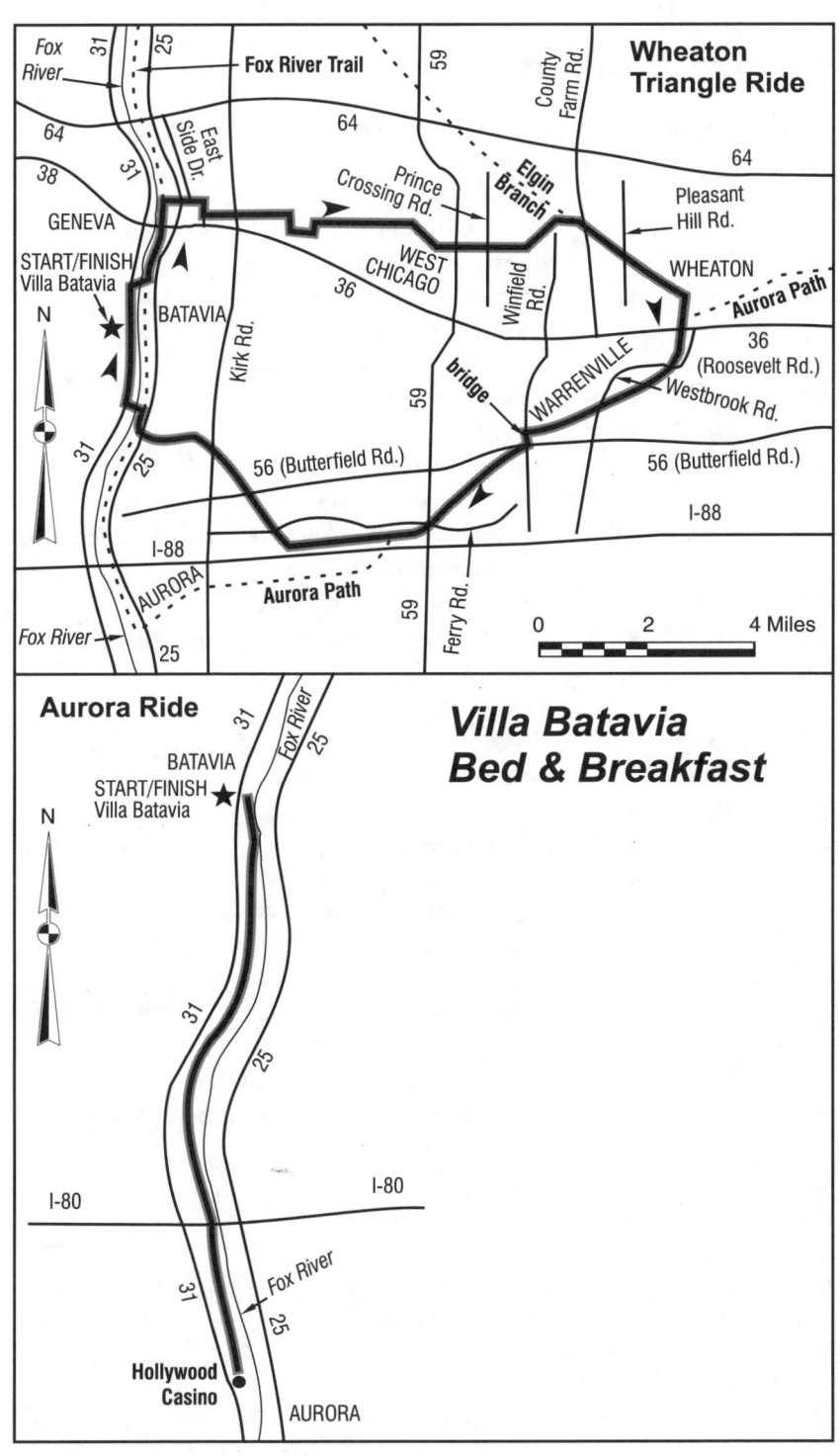

Pt.-Pt.	Cume	Turn	Street/Landmark
0.1	13.3	**S**	Cross Sunset
0.1	13.4	**S**	Cross Lake
1.4	14.8	**S,R**	Cross **Winfield Rd.** and turn right; **trail continues along road**
0.4	15.2	**S**	Across Geneva Rd. and Country Farm Rd., ending up diagonally across the intersection where **trail picks up again.**
1.0	16.2	**S**	Cross Pleasant Hill Rd.
0.3	16.5	**S**	Cross unmarked road
0.5	17.0	-	**Lincoln Marsh National Wildlife Area**
0.4	17.4	**S**	Cross Lincoln Street
0.5	17.9	**S**	Intersection of Aurora and Illinois Prairie Path, continue straight
0.1	18.0	-	Trail runs on **Chilton St.**
0.2	18.2	**S**	Cross Roosevelt Street, pick up trail on other side
0.1	18.3	-	**Prairie Path Park** on left
0.1	18.4	**S**	Cross Arbor Rd.
1.0	19.4	**S**	Cross unmarked road
1.0	20.4	**S**	Cross Westbrook Rd.
0.5	20.9	**S**	Cross unmarked road
0.2	21.1	**S**	Cross unmarked road
0.6	21.7	**L, SR**	**Trail turns left under a bridge** and then makes a **sharp right**
0.4	22.1	**L**	Intersection of Butterfield and Winfield. Cross **Winfield** and **turn left, trail continues along road**
0.6	22.7	**R**	**Trail leaves road** to the right
0.7	23.4	**S**	Following a river crossing, stop at unmarked road
0.1	23.5	-	Warrenville
0.2	23.7	**S**	Cross Rockwell St.
0.4	24.1	**S**	Cross Williams Rd.
0.8	24.9	-	One-lane underpass; walk bike
0.3	25.2	**S**	Cross Ferry Rd.

Pt.-Pt.	Cume	Turn	Street/Landmark
0.7	25.9	**BR**	Fork in the path; **right goes to Batavia**, left to Aurora
0.7	26.6	-	Railroad crossing
0.6	27.2	**BL**	Fork in path; **stay left, go under underpass**
0.6	27.8	-	Trail angles away from I-88
0.5	28.3	**S**	Cross unmarked road
0.7	29.0	**S**	Cross unmarked road
0.5	29.5	-	Trail from left
0.7	30.2	-	Bridge over Rt. 56
0.4	30.6	**S**	Cross Kirk Rd.
0.3	30.9	**S**	Cross Wagner Rd.
0.5	31.4	**S**	Cross Raddant Rd.
0.6	32.0	-	Trail merges from right
0.9	32.9	**L**	Cross **bridge over Fox River** to island
0.1	33.0	-	Continue through park to walking bridge across to far side
0.1	33.1	**S**	Cross Shumway and take **Flinn** up hill
0.0	33.1	**L**	½ block from river, **trail resumes** to left
0.1	33.2	-	**Trail merges with Pamarco rd**
0.1	33.3	-	Trail diverges to left
0.2	33.5	-	**Path to Villa Batavia**

Aurora Ride (10.4 miles)

This is an out-and-out pleasure ride. The paved trail sticks pretty close to Fox River. It doesn't present much in the way of riding challenge, which means you can sit back, relax, and really enjoy the passing scenery. While we might not ride that way every day, it was a delightful change for us on the morning we did this ride.

Pt.-Pt.	Cume	Turn	Street/Landmark
0.0	0.0		Starting where the path from Villa Batavia joins the trail, **head south on the Fox River Trail**
0.0	0.0	**S**	Feeder trail goes off to right to park, continue straight
0.4	0.4	**S**	Cross trail, continue straight
0.3	0.7	**S**	Cross trail, continue straight

Pt.-Pt.	Cume	Turn	Street/Landmark
0.6	1.3	-	Driveway
0.4	1.7	**BL**	Feeder Path goes up to road, stay left and **go through underpass**
0.7	2.4	-	Underpass
1.2	3.6	-	Underpass
0.8	4.4	**S**	Cross Illinois Ave.
0.8	5.2	**TR**	Park on the river, at the **Hollywood Casino**
0.8	6.0	**S**	Cross Illinois Ave.
0.8	6.8	-	Underpass
1.1	7.9	-	Underpass
0.7	8.6	**BR**	feeder path goes left to a parking lot, stay right and **go through underpass**
0.4	9.0	-	Driveway
0.7	9.7	**S**	Cross trail, continue straight
0.3	10.0	**S**	Cross trail, continue straight
0.4	10.4	-	Feeder trail from Park
0.0	10.4	-	Look for the stone to the left of the trail, it marks the **Villa Batavia Path**

Minnesota

Minnesota is well known for its winters and its lakes. There's also a wealth of biking opportunities for every taste. As we traveled across Minnesota and Wisconsin we joked that in Minnesota they have gravel country roads and paved bike paths while in Wisconsin they have gravel bike paths and paved country roads. Some of the best and most beautiful recreational rides we've ever done fall within Minnesota's borders. Minnesota also has some of the most exciting and challenging mountain biking in the Midwest.

One of the best recreational trails we've ever ridden is the Root River Trail just down the street from the JailHouse Inn in Preston. Other riding in this general area includes the excellent city trails of Rochester near the Inn at Rocky Creek and the relaxing Luce Line Trail that runs just beyond the side porches of the Wander Inn in Watertown.

If you want to sample some of Minnesota's lake country, the rides from the Birch Hill Inne in Cross Lake are a good bet. The Heartland Trail and the Paul Bunyan State Forest rides from The Park Street Inn in Nevis will also put you among the woods and waters of northern Minnesota. The Glacial Lakes Trail and roads around Spicer Castle on Green Lake provide a wonderful ride among the lakes as well.

The riding around the Dakota Lodge is not so easily categorized. The Willard Munger trail is one of the straightest—but most enchanting—trails we've experienced, while St. Croix State Park offers a complete smorgasbord of riding opportunities. For pure mountain biking enjoyment, nothing beats the private trails of the Pincushion Mountain Bed and Breakfast in Grand Marais. The drive along Lake Superior's north shore is spectacular, the trails are wonderful, and so is the hospitality.

For general information on Minnesota tourism, the Office of Tourism can be reached at:

Minnesota Office of Tourism
100 Metro Square
121 7th Place East
Saint Paul, Minnesota 55101-2146
(651) 296-5029
(800) 657-3700
E-mail: explore@state.mn.us
Web: www.exploreminnesota.com

Birch Hill Inne, Crosslake, Minnesota

Birch Hill Inne

Steve & Heidi Engen   Phone: (218) 692-4857
Brian & Julie Engen   (800) 769-8619
P.O. Box 468   E-mail: stay@birchhillinne.com
Crosslake, MN 56442   Web: www.birchhillinne.com
Rates: Budget

The Birch Hill Inne feels like the prototype for that wonderful old summer resort that we all have rumbling around in our collective consciousness. That could be because The Birch Hill Inne is a wonderful old summer resort. The Oscawana Resort was established in 1926 between Ox Lake and Loon Lake. The original layout included several log cabins and a carriage house. Though the rest of the resort has been divided up into private lake homes, the carriage house carries on the resort lineage as The Birch Hill Inne today.

Just after World War II, Ted and Betty Ball purchased the carriage house and remodeled it into an eating establishment. They had originally intended to open a kind of summer snack bar, but quickly began serving full meals and established a reputation for hearty meals with "hamburgers, more burger than bun," turkey or ham dinners, and tempting desserts, all for 95¢. In 1947, living quarters were added and the whole enterprise was named The Birch Hill Inne. The name and the knack for welcoming visitors and making them feel at home are still part of the inn today.

The inn has five rooms all decorated in the up-north lodge idiom with rustic wood furnishings and quilts. All have private baths and cable TV. A telephone is available in the common area. The Norway Pine and Birch Rooms are on the first floor, well removed from the common areas. The Norway Pine is one of the larger rooms, with a double Jacuzzi, private deck, and queen-sized bed. The Birch Room is slightly smaller with a double brass bed and views of Loon Lake peeking between the trees from across the road.

The upstairs has the Lake View Room, the Up North Room, and the Garden Room. Up North is another large room with a queen bed, Jacuzzi, and a view of the trees surrounding the inn. Lake View has a pine double bed and looks west over Loon Lake for special sunset viewing. The Garden Room has an iron double bed. It also features a charming one-person sun porch looking east across the inn's gardens to Ox Lake.

Melissa, our host, served up a more-than-continental continental breakfast. Served buffet style, we had juice, coffee, warm muffins, and fruit to start. A good selection of cereals was laid out, as well as some cinnamon swirl bread that, when toasted and buttered, caused at least one guest to eat entirely too much. Part of the breakfast experience is the dining room itself, which has been preserved from the original restaurant. The etched and deeply lacquered old pine tables are set out across the dining area. A solid stone fireplace seems to occupy one whole wall with some comfy chairs and a couch in attendance. One can imagine a blustery winter day, eating breakfast, looking out a window, smiling, and settling onto the couch with a book in front of that fire. In warmer seasons, a screened-in porch or even the garden can be a breakfast setting as well.

The Birch Hill Inne has several nature trails and lake access as well; Ox Lake is just a short trail away. Canoes are available, as well as a cheery old metal-frame-and-drum pedal boat. Either mode of water transport will take you across Ox Lake to private hiking trails along the shoreline. If you're lucky, you might catch sight of the eagle that sometimes nests here. In addition to the Ox Lake trails, the inn has private wildflower gardens with hiking and ski trails. These "gardens" are more like meadows in size; we saw an amazing expanse of lupines on our visit.

Between the lakes, the wildflowers, and the hiking trails—and the fact that most major logging ended early in the century—means that the Cross Lake area has some wonderful wooded scenery. One has the feeling of being out in the woods even when driving through town—which is not to suggest that there aren't ample services, activities, and events to divert the vacationer if desired. The area has a good number of golf courses, parks, antique shops, and local museums. Fairs, parades, flea markets, and sporting events dot the calendar year-round, as well. While you might find a few fast food chain outlets, the local restaurants are well worth a visit. We had a sunset drenched supper at The Manhattan Beach Lodge that satisfied every sense. Whether seated in the dining room or out on the patio overlooking the adjacent lake, you'll enjoy great views and superbly prepared dishes of a varied menu.

The Birch Hill Inne and the Cross Lake area are perfectly tuned for your relaxation and enjoyment. There's plenty to do, but none of it's urgent. Almost from the moment you turn on to State Route 66 you can feel yourself beginning to slow down, take deeper breaths, and maybe even grin a little bit.

Rides from Birch Hill Inne
In addition to the road rides documented below, the Birch Hill Inne is about half an hour from the Paul Bunyan State Trail. The trail stretches 100 miles from Brainerd to Bemidji, and the southern half is paved. The nearest access to the trail is either the town of Jenkins or Pine River, depending on which direction you want to head.

Terrain: There are some gentle hills, but most of this riding is around or near lakes so the changes in elevation are modest.

Road Conditions: The roads for these rides are in good shape. In the middle third of the ride around Lower Whitefish Lake, you'll find interesting reddish-pink road surfaces, but we found no unpleasant surprises anywhere on these rides.

Traffic: Traffic speeds and volumes are not high on any of the roads included in these rides. Route 66 has the highest volume but it has broad shoulders and felt very safe. Route 16 and County 1 do not have shoulders, but generally the traffic was not an issue on these roads.

Best Time to Ride: All summer long you'll find decent weather for riding in this region. There are a variety of festivals and bike races on the regional calendar. Fall comes a little earlier as one gets further north in the state, but September should provide some beautiful riding days.

Nearest Bike Shop: There are a number of hardware stores that can provide basic supplies (tubes, etc.). The nearest full-service shops are in Brainerd.

The Whitefish Chain Ride (28 miles)

This ride circles Lower Whitefish Lake as well as a few other nearby lakes. The first portion of the ride is through fairly populated territory, and none of the ride is completely out in the wilderness. However, on the backside of the ride deer stood by the side of the road and watched curiously as we glided by. This is a pleasant road ride with good road surfaces, pleasing vistas, and accommodating grades.

Pt.-Pt.	Cume	Turn	Street/Landmark
0.0	0.0		Across the street from the Birch Hill Inne, heading into Cross Lake
0.4	0.4	-	Anchor Point Rd. to right
0.2	0.6	-	Eagle St.
0.4	1.0	**R**	**Rt. 16**
0.1	1.1	-	Hidden Valley Rd.
0.2	1.3	-	First St.
0.3	1.6	-	Island View St.
0.6	2.2	-	Gladick Ln.
0.4	2.6	-	Rushmore Blvd.

Pt.-Pt.	Cume	Turn	Street/Landmark
0.2	2.8	-	Johnie St.
0.0	2.8	-	West Shore Dr.
0.3	3.1	-	ABC Dr.
0.2	3.3	-	Harbor Ln.
0.0	3.3	-	Gail Ln.
0.9	4.2	-	Pine Tr.
0.2	4.4	-	Silver Peak Rd.
0.6	5.0	-	Fox Hunter Rd.
0.3	5.3	-	Star Lake Dr.
0.7	6.0	-	North View Harbor Dr.
0.1	6.1	-	Little Whitefish Dr.
0.2	6.3	-	Butternut Point Rd.
0.3	6.6	-	County Rt. 69
0.6	7.2	-	Schaller Rd.
0.4	7.6	-	Rutger Rd.
0.4	8.0	-	Timber Ln.
0.1	8.1	-	Timber Ln.
0.1	8.2	-	South Clamshell Dr.
0.6	8.8	-	Birchdale Blvd.
0.4	9.2	-	Forest Knoll Rd.
0.2	9.4	-	Blueberry Bay Rd.
0.7	10.1	-	Peoria Rd.
0.5	10.6	**R**	**Rt. 145**
0.4	11.0	**BL**	**Rt. 145** takes a 90-degree turn to left; unmarked road goes straight
0.7	11.7	**R**	**Silver Sands Rd.**
0.5	12.2	-	Hidden Acres Rd.
1.5	13.7	**R**	**Rt. 15**
0.2	13.9	-	Red Rambler Dr.
0.3	14.2	-	Driftwood Ln.
0.5	14.7	-	Old Farm Ln.
0.5	15.2	**BR**	**Rt. 15** goes right, follow it
0.6	15.8	-	Wildamere Ln.
0.3	16.1	-	Long Farm Rd.
1.2	17.3	**R**	**County Rt. 1**
0.8	18.1	-	Long Farm Rd.

Pt.-Pt.	Cume	Turn	Street/Landmark
3.5	21.6	-	West Arrowhead Dr.
1.2	22.8	-	Rt. 134
3.1	25.9	**R**	**Rt. 66**
1.7	27.6	-	Manhattan Point Blvd.
0.4	28.0	-	**Birch Hill Inne**

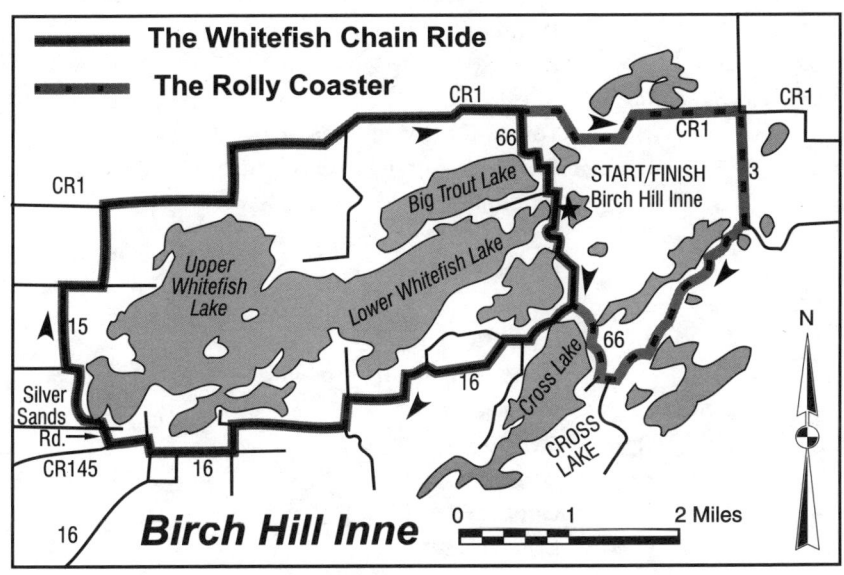

The Rolly Coaster (16 miles)

This ride is named for the middle stretch on Route 3. The whole section seemed to be a series of short, not-too-steep hills. On this early morning before breakfast, we found a rhythm on the road that made us feel like we could have cycled all day. A good portion of this ride is away from the populated areas and we mostly had only swallows for company.

Pt.-Pt.	Cume	Turn	Street/Landmark
0.0	0.0		In front inn, **head north on Rt. 66**
0.2	0.2	-	Manhattan Point Blvd.
1.8	2.0	**R**	**Rt. 1**
0.2	2.2	-	Fifty Lakes town line
2.5	4.7	-	Peninsula Rd.
1.0	5.7	-	Kego Rd.
0.8	6.5	**R**	**Rt. 3**
1.5	8.0	-	Township line of Cross Lake
0.5	8.5	-	Entrance to boy scout camp
0.1	8.6	-	Pinemiller Dr.
0.3	8.9	-	Bayshore Rd.
1.1	10.0	-	Birch Narrows Rd.
0.5	10.5	-	Wolf Trail
1.3	11.8	-	Pine Bay Rd.
0.3	12.1	-	*Caution:* golf cart crossing
0.4	12.5	-	County 37
0.3	12.8	**R**	**Rt. 66**
0.9	13.7	-	Edgewater Ln.
0.4	14.1	-	Dagget Bay Rd.
0.9	15.0	-	County 16
0.4	15.4	-	Eagle St.
0.2	15.6	-	Anchor Point Rd.
0.4	16.0	-	**Birch Hill Inne**

Dakota Lodge

Tad Hilborn
Route 3, PO Box 178
Hinckley, MN 55307
Rates: Budget to moderate

Phone: (320) 384-6052
Fax: (320) 384-0336

The Dakota Lodge is an unassuming collection of buildings along a quiet country road running from rural central Minnesota to rural northern Wisconsin. There are chickens clucking and scratching in the flowerbeds and lawn or taking an occasional peck at a wandering cat. One of the first things you'll see inside is an entire wall of books, followed by a number of antiques, decorative rugs, and comfortable chairs. Everything about the Dakota Lodge promotes relaxation.

Built in 1971 as a roadhouse along State Route 48, Tad bought the property in the early '90s and renovated and redecorated it into the lodge. The main building is a long, low ranch structure with log exterior. The front door is across a small porch with several rockers. Sitting in one seems to be an open invitation to the cats that frequent the yard. We spent a pleasant evening on the porch with a big yellow tabby rumbling away in our lap.

Once inside you'll find a sitting room, with the aforementioned wall of books and chairs. There is a small smoking/television room off the sitting room and the dining room is just a little further back in the house. Tad used to run a renovation and decorating business and says he was never able to throw anything away. Judging by the high quality antiques throughout the house, it's easy to see why.

Did we mention that the Dakota Lodge is chock full of books? There's a small library's worth, and it's almost impossible not to pick one up and begin browsing. Don't worry if you don't have time to finish your selection; Tad will let you "check out" what you're reading and mail it back when you're done.

The Dakota's five guestrooms all exhibit Tad's skill as a decorator. The Pinkham is the largest room, with a king bed and double whirlpool. An antique sofa sits on burnished oak floors across from a wood-burning fireplace. The Pinkham is on the east side of the house, and its three windows light up with the morning sunrise. It also has a private full bath just off the sleeping area. The Bentley is another large room with a queen bed, a dressing area with table and chairs, and a sitting area with a comfortable couch across from a fireplace. It's decorated in blue with pink and gray accents, and looks west into a grove of birch trees. It also has a roomy three-quarter bath with double whirlpool off the sitting area.

The Kathryn has a more romantic feel to it, though it's still quite roomy, featuring a canopied queen-sized bed and double whirlpool in the sleeping area. A table for two and fireplace all contribute to the intimate feeling of this room. It has a private half-bathroom in addition to the whirlpool. The Medora has a more open and light feel with windows on the south and east. It also features a queen-sized bed, private half-bath and a fireplace with a love seat strategically positioned for gazing into the fire. The Eastedge leans towards the nostalgic with lace curtains and an antique dresser. It has a queen-sized bed and, just outside the room, a private full bath.

Tad advertises the morning meal as a "full country breakfast," and you won't be disappointed. We had wonderfully light eggs scrambled with scallions and basil. He also provided sides of sausage, country-style potatoes, and pancakes. There was plenty of coffee and juice as well as a heaping plate of strawberries, cantaloupe, honeydew melons, and grapes. We'd gone for a ride in the St. Croix State Park before breakfast and had second helpings of everything, twice.

Hinckley and surrounding areas have beautiful natural scenery and make the most of it with the Willard Munger Trail and two state parks. In addition to the riding at St. Croix State Park, there is the fascinating Civilian Conservation Corps historical site, built to house the workers who created the park. You can rent canoes and paddle down the St. Croix River or just hike on the park's many trails. If you're more drawn to the pursuits of civilization, there's a golf course and a casino in the opposite direction of the park from the lodge. Whichever direction you choose, the lodge will be waiting when you return at end of the day, ready with a cup of coffee, a good book, and a soft couch.

Rides from Dakota Lodge

Both of the rides we've included are just samples of what you'll find in these respective areas. The Willard Munger Trail runs over 80 miles north, with most of that length paved. St. Croix State Park has miles of forest roads and several additional miles of trails open to mountain bikes as well. For more information and maps of the park contact:

St. Croix State Park
Rt. 3, Box 450
Hinckley, MN 55037
(320) 384-6591

For more information on the Willard Munger Trail:

The Munger Trail Towns Association
P.O. Box 276
Moose Lake, MN 55767

Terrain: The southernmost paved section of the Willard Munger Trail is flat. While there are some minor changes in elevation, you'll probably not notice much. The St. Croix-St. Park ride has a little more geographical variety but you still won't be challenged by the terrain unless you venture out on some of the park's forest roads.

Road Conditions: The Willard Munger Trail is paved and well maintained. You'll find good signage all along the trail, though some point out snowmobile trails that in late summer are completely overgrown. The main trail has wide grassy shoulders on either side of the paved portion. The St. Croix Sampler has a little bit of everything. It starts out on packed dirt, which becomes interspersed with not-so-packed sand once you cross the access road. The trail and road portions of this ride all have impeccable surfaces.

Traffic: Traffic is not an issue on either of these rides. We were visiting on a summer weekend during high tourist season and down by the St. Croix campground saw a few people. For the most part, however, we were alone on the trails.

Best Time to Ride: In this part of Minnesota, there isn't a bad time to visit during the summer months. We were here in mid-August and still had balmy temperatures and clear blue skies, with the exception of one out-of-the-blue rain shower on the Willard Munger Trail which was actually refreshing, coming late in the ride as it did.

Nearest Bike Shop: There really isn't a bike shop close at hand. The Twin Cities are about 45 minutes south and provide a large number of possibilities for bike assistance.

Willard Munger State Trail Ride (26 miles)

There's a fairy tale quality to this trail. At the second or third road crossing you can look down this perfectly straight trail for miles between the
high green banks created by the trees. The trail shimmers in the distance as if it might ride up into the wedge of blue sky on the horizon.
The possibilities seem endless. We saw deer all along this trail and a
variety of bird life both in the wooded portions and the wet lands. The
trail truly seemed enchanted. To reach the trailhead by car, follow these
cues:

Pt.-Pt.	Cume	Turn	Street/Landmark
0.0	0.0	**R**	Out of Lodge driveway onty Highway 48
10.0	10.0	-	Interstate 35
0.6	10.6	**R**	**Old Highway 61**
0.5	11.1	**L**	**Rt. 65**
0.1	11.2	**R**	**Willard Munger State Trail trailhead**

Willard Munger State Trail Cue Sheet

Pt.-Pt.	Cume	Turn	Street/Landmark
0.0	0.0	-	Trailhead at Hinckley
0.5	0.5	**S**	Cross unnamed road
3.3	3.8	**S**	Cross unnamed dirt road
1.0	4.8	**S**	Cross unnamed road
1.0	5.8	**S**	Cross unnamed road
0.2	6.0	-	**Skunk Lake**
1.0	7.0	**S**	Cross unnamed road, spur to Sandstone, **toilets**
1.1	8.1	**S**	Cross unnamed road
1.3	9.4	**S**	Cross unnamed road
1.9	11.3	**S**	Cross unnamed road
0.7	12.0	**S**	Cross unnamed road
1.0	13.0	**TR**	**Finlayson Train Depot**
1.0	14.0	**S**	Cross unnamed road
0.7	14.7	**S**	Cross unnamed road
1.9	16.6	**S**	Cross unnamed road
1.3	17.9	**S**	Cross unnamed road
1.1	19.0	**S**	Cross unnamed road, spur to Sandstone, **toilets**

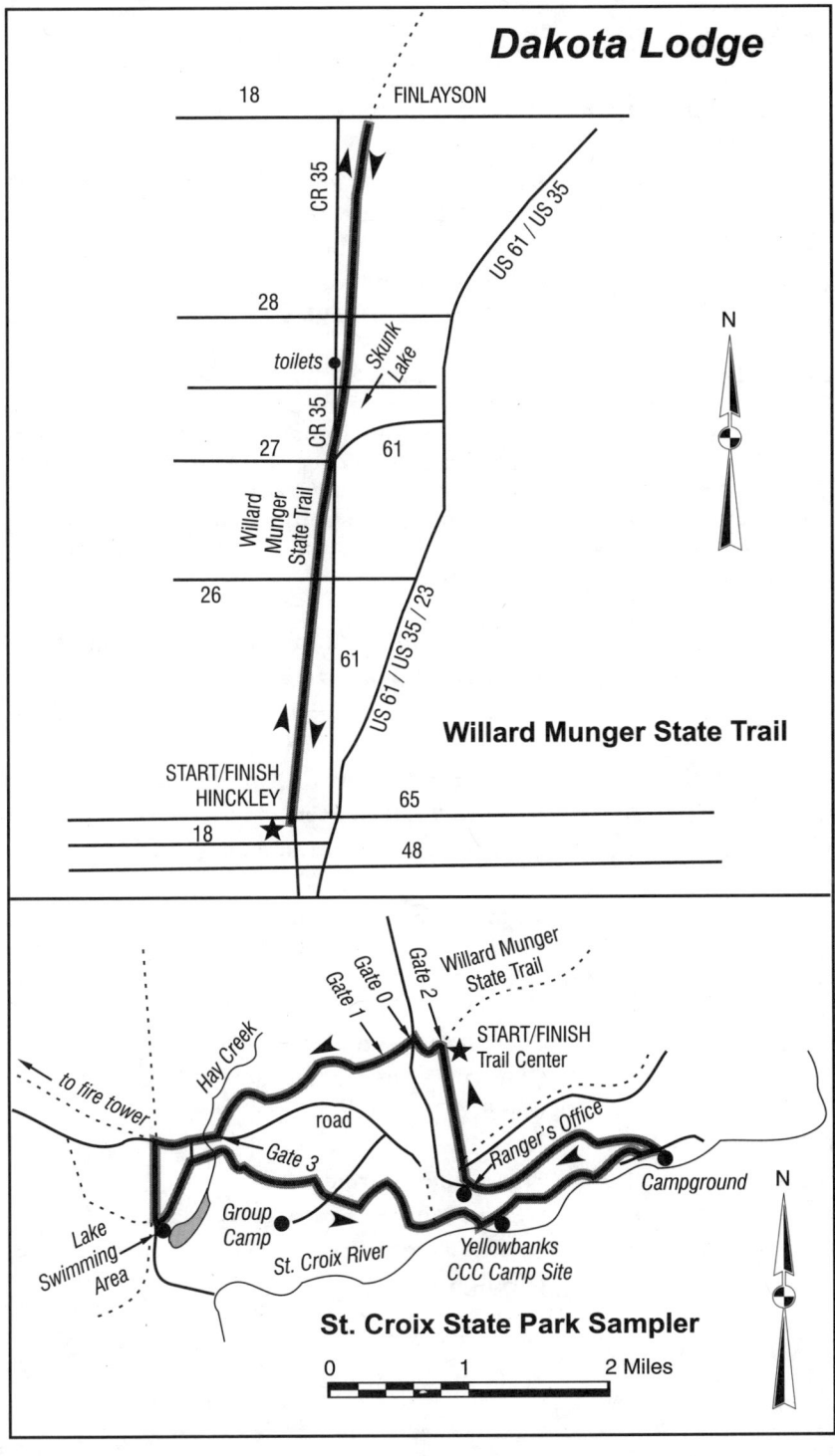

Dakota Lodge

FINLAYSON

18

CR 35

US 61 / US 35

28

toilets •

Skunk Lake

CR 35

27   61

Willard Munger State Trail

26

61

US 61 / US 35 / 23

Willard Munger State Trail

START/FINISH
HINCKLEY

65

18   ★

48

N

Willard Munger State Trail

Gate 0
Gate 1
Gate 2

START/FINISH
Trail Center

to fire tower

Hay Creek

road

Gate 3

Ranger's Office

Lake
Swimming
Area

Group
Camp

St. Croix River

Yellowbanks
CCC Camp Site

Campground

N

St. Croix State Park Sampler

0   1   2 Miles

PtPt.	Cume	Turn	Street/Landmark
1.0	20.0	-	**Skunk Lake**
0.2	20.2	S	Cross unnamed road
1.0	21.2	S	Cross unnamed road
1.0	22.2	S	Cross unnamed dirt road
3.3	25.5	S	Cross unnamed road
0.5	26.0	-	**Trailhead at Hinckley**

St. Croix Sampler Ride (10.9 miles)

This ride gives you a little bit of everything the park has to offer. Though most of it is on paved trails or roads, you'll want to take your mountain bike for that first two miles of trail. If you really prefer the pavement, you can do basically the same ride by riding out the way you drove in and just going straight past the ranger station. You'll pick up the path just a few miles down at the signs to the swimming beach. To drive to the starting point, follow these cues:

0.0	0.0	L	Turn left onto **Highway 48** from Dakota Lodge
5.2	5.2	R	**St. Croix State Park access road**
3.7	8.9	-	Maurie Krier Trail. We'll be back on bike!
1.1	10.0	-	Park Office; stop to get $4 parking sticker
0.0	10.0	L	**Road to Trail Center**
0.1	10.1	L	**Road to Trail Center**
0.6	10.7	S	First entrance to parking lot
0.1	10.8	R	Look left as you're turning right into parking lot to see the first trail sign

St. Croix State Park Cue Sheet

0.0	0.0	S	Just off the road **at the Yellow Trail marker**. Gate Two is visible ahead at the edge of the woods
0.0	0.0	-	**Gate Two**
0.1	0.1	BR	Trail comes in from left
0.1	0.2	L	**Willard Munger State Trail**
0.1	0.3	S	At **Gate Zero**, cross park access road, **continue through Gate One**

Pt.-Pt.	Cume	Turn	Street/Landmark
1.8	2.1	-	**Gate Three** (following lots of sand)
0.0	2.1	**R**	Stop and turn right **onto the paved park road**
0.3	2.4	**L**	**Road to picnic and swimming area**; straight leads to fire tower on gravel roads
0.3	2.7	**L**	**Across parking lot to gate labeled "Service Road."** Go around it
0.0	2.7	**L**	A few steps down a gravel path you'll find the **paved bike path**
0.3	3.0	-	Bridge over Hay Creek
1.6	4.6	**S**	Cross Group Camp Road
0.0	4.6	-	Hiking trail to right
1.0	5.6	**BR**	Spur to left to Ranger's Office
0.4	6.0	-	**Civilian Conservation Corps Yellow Banks Camp Historical Site**
0.8	6.8	-	Hiking trail to right
0.1	6.9	-	Hiking trail to right
0.3	7.2	**L**	Straight goes to campground
0.6	7.8	**L**	Parking, bike rentals, etc. Follow paved path through all this.
0.1	7.9	**L**	**Camping access road**
0.1	8.0	**L**	**Road to park entrance**
2.1	10.1	**R**	**Road to Trails Centers**
0.0	10.1	**L**	**Road to Trails Centers**
0.7	10.8	-	First entrance to parking lot
0.1	10.9	-	Back at **trailhead**

Inn at Rocky Creek, Rochester, Minnesota

Inn at Rocky Creek

Jane & Robert Hanson
2115 Rocky Creek Drive N.E.
Rochester, MN 55906
Rates: Budget — moderate

Phone: (507) 288-1019
Web: www.bbhost.com/
innatrockycreek

As part of our travels we've stayed in many wonderful old Victorian houses, summer retreats built many years ago, and lodges with venerable histories. It's easy to wonder which structures being built today people will want standing forty or a hundred years from now. The Inn at Rocky Creek provides a sure answer to that question. This recently constructed Inn in a new neighborhood on a high bluff outside of Rochester will be a welcome traveler's stop for years to come.

The spacious dining room, airy great room, and the three guestrooms all seemed arranged for the ease and comfort of the guest. This happy situation is the result of Jane and Robert's decision to build a home in 1997 with the specific goal of opening a bed and breakfast. Though the inn is newly built, Jane and Robert have borrowed the style of the house from the past, including a roomy entryway with a high window above it, a wide oak stairway leading to the second floor, and fine woodworking in the crown moldings, fireplace mantel, and pocket doors. Exquisite antique furniture and heavy oriental rugs over hardwood floors lend an air of permanence and serenity to every room. Even from the outside, the porch with rocking chairs and the beautiful perennial gardens contribute to a unified look that will age very gracefully.

We stayed in the Morning Primrose Room. With its high arched window under a vaulted ceiling, Morning Primrose is filled with light. Decorated in a gentle, warm yellow with green, blue, and pink flower accents, this room is the perfect place to while away a summer afternoon with a book or a nap. The room has a fourposter queen bed, comfortable chair, and ample closet space for an extended stay. This room, like all the others, has a private bath with tub and shower.

The Woods View Room looks out the back of the house to—what else—a wooded view. A steep, tree-filled ravine crosses the back of the property and gives this room its name. A wrought iron queen bed, private bath, and an overstuffed chair complete the décor of this cozy little retreat.

The largest room, the Master Suite, occupies one corner of the upstairs. The sleigh bed seems larger than the queen size it is. The double whirlpool bath has a reputation for comfort. The softly upholstered love seat provides room to spread out. This room wants to pamper its occupants. Like the other rooms, it has a private bath; this one showcases an antique commode.

Breakfast consists of a faultless presentation of tempting food on lace, china, and a huge antique table, all lit by a chandelier. The meal is served family-style, and our morning started with large, fresh fruit salad supplemented with baked goods and pastries. The main course was an airy yet satisfying ham and vegetable frittata. Breakfast was a casual affair with a full table of lively conversation with topics ranging from the previous day's nuptials of one couple to the day's plans in Rochester, all interspersed with contented murmurings about the meal itself. In addition to breakfast, Jane and Robert serve afternoon tea by request. Fresh fruit and non-alcoholic beverages are also available throughout the day.

Aside from the ample and unique urban cycling in the city, Rochester offers a wealth of other activities. In the center of town is Silver Lake, which, in addition to hosting a large flock of Canadian Geese, has hiking and biking trails, small boat rentals, and an activity center. Rochester offers 63 other public parks, eight golf courses, and 37 public tennis courts. Near the inn is the Quarry Hill Nature Center, with an informative set of displays and a number of hiking trails highlighting the local flora and fauna. Here, we came upon a happy wood snake warming himself in the middle of one path on a cool morning.

Rochester is a big enough city to host a thriving cultural life as well. The Mayowood Mansion, the Plummer House, and the Olmsted County History Center provide a window into Rochester's history. Symphony performances, art galleries, and theatrical productions will appeal to your high art sensibilities. In a more pedestrian vein, Rochester offers antique shops, shopping centers (malls and downtown areas), seasonal farmer's markets and a variety of craft shows. Between the choices in the city and the retreat at the inn you can plan a day full of activities or nothing but relaxation—whichever you please.

Rides from Inn at Rocky Creek

We enjoyed our ride on the Douglas Trail just outside of Rochester, but the truly unique part of this stay was the city trails within Rochester. Madison, Wisconsin, is the other bike-friendly urban area that we've included in this book. Rochester and Madison are a lot alike. Rochester has a slightly different approach to their bike paths, however, taking them under bridges and overpasses for most roads. We rode from the center of town almost out to the western edge of town, crossing only one or two roads in the process. It made for a very enjoyable urban ride, well worth the time spent.

Terrain: The Douglas Trail is a rails-to-trails path, so the inclines are not steep. In town, you'll find yourself going up and down on the city trails, but only for short distances as you go under street bridges or up to sidewalk access points.

Road Conditions: The city paths are all nicely paved, though on a few occasions you have to ride diagonally across train tracks, a somewhat risky proposition. The Douglas Trail is a smooth and easy riding surface.

Traffic: The city paths are popular, and even though we were out early in the morning, we still had to keep an eye out for other trail users. We saw far fewer people on the Douglas Trail, especially once we cleared the city.

Best Time to Ride: We wouldn't so much pick a season as a time of day for riding. We were out on the Douglas Trail just towards sunset and had a beautiful ride. On the other hand, we rode the city trails earlier in the morning and it was a nice ride, watching the city wake up.

Nearest Bike Shop
Bicycle Sports
1409 South Broadway
Rochester, MN 55904
(507) 281-5007

Douglas State Trail (26 miles)
This out-and-back ride to Pine Island provides a pleasant cruise through Southern Minnesota farmland. There are several places where the trail cuts deep through stands of trees and one beautiful cut of rock as well. This is a well-serviced trail with restrooms at all the trailheads and, somewhat oddly, a soda machine at one rest area out in the middle of the countryside. To reach the trailhead via automobile, follow these cues:

Pt.-Pt.	Cume	Turn	Street/Landmark
0.0	0.0	L	Left out of Inn at Rocky Creek driveway
0.2	0.2	**L**	**Rt. 22**
1.1	1.3	S	Cross Rt. 63
0.3	1.6	S	Cross East River Rd.
0.7	2.3	S	Cross West River Pkwy.
0.8	3.1	S	Cross 18th Ave. NW
0.3	3.4	S	Cross 21st Ave. NW
0.1	3.5	**R**	**Entryway to Highway 52. Don't get on, just take it over to 41 St. NW.**
0.2	3.7	**L**	**41st St. NW**
0.2	3.9	S	Cross West Frontage Rd.

Pt.-Pt.	Cume	Turn	Street/Landmark
1.1	5.0	**L**	**Rt. 22**
0.4	5.4	**L**	**High Valley Rd.**
0.3	5.7	**L**	**Parking lot for Douglas State Trail**

Douglas State Trail Cue Sheet

0.0	0.0	-	**High Valley Rd. Tailhead**
0.2	0.2	-	Trail access from right
0.0	0.2	-	Bridge over 41st NW
0.8	1.0	-	Trail access from right
0.0	1.0	-	Bridge over Rt. 22
0.7	1.7	**S**	Cross 55th St. NW
0.3	2.0	**S**	Cross unmarked road
0.3	2.3	**S**	Cross unmarked dirt road
1.2	3.5	**S**	Cross unmarked dirt road
1.2	4.7	**S**	Cross Major Road (and **Douglas Trailhead**)
1.9	6.6	**S**	Cross 90th St. NW
0.9	7.5	-	Bridge over river
0.1	7.6	**S**	Cross Rt. 3
1.0	8.6	**S**	Cross unmarked dirt road
1.3	9.9	**S**	Cross unmarked dirt road (*caution:* **loose gravel**)
0.3	10.2	**S**	Cross 85th Ave. NW
0.7	10.9	**S**	Cross unmarked dirt road
0.1	11.0	**S**	Cross unmarked dirt road
0.6	11.6	**S**	Cross unmarked dirt road
0.0	11.6	-	**Soda machine** to side of trail
0.7	12.3	**S**	Cross unmarked paved road
0.7	13.0	**TA**	**Pine Island Trailhead** and park
0.7	13.7	**S**	Cross unmarked paved road
0.7	14.4	**S**	Cross unmarked dirt road
0.6	15.0	**S**	Cross unmarked dirt road
0.1	15.1	**S**	Cross unmarked dirt road
0.7	15.8	**S**	Cross 85th Ave. NW
0.3	16.1	**S**	Cross unmarked dirt road

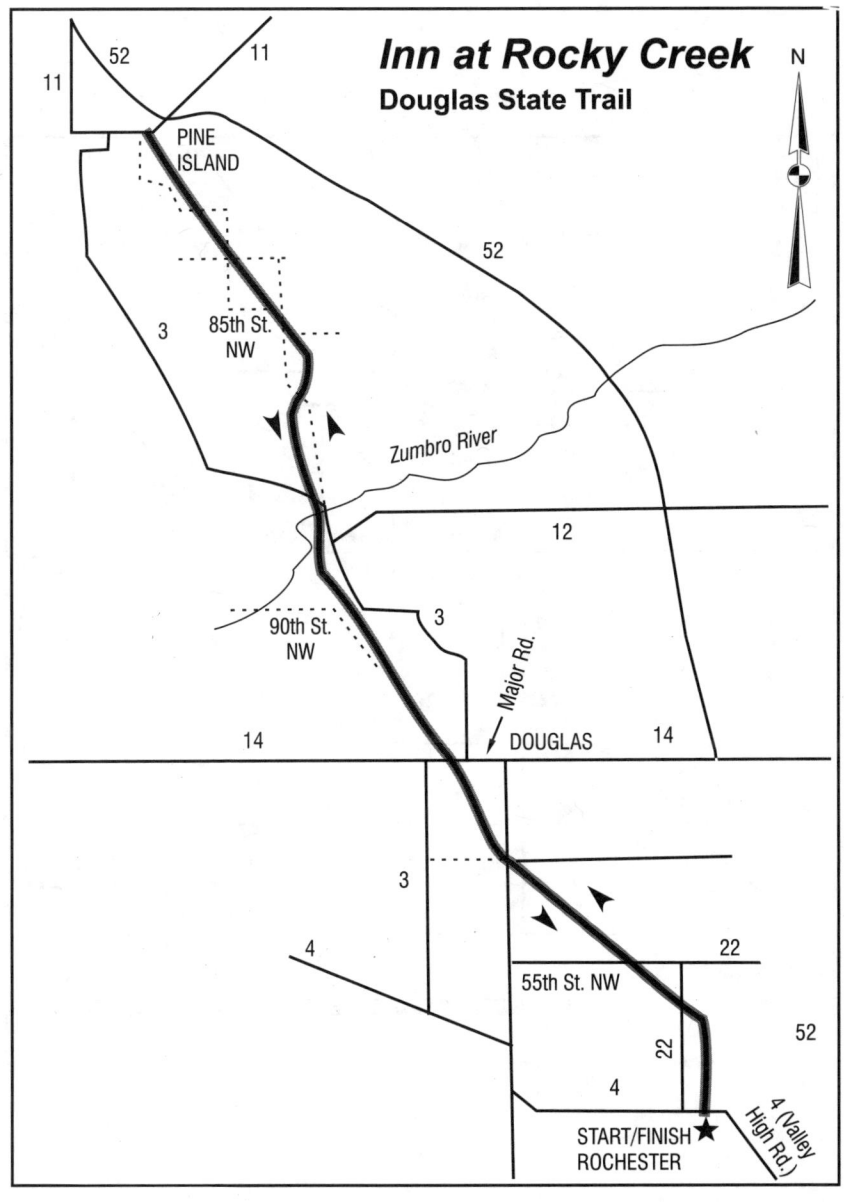

Inn at Rocky Creek
Douglas State Trail

N

52
11
11

PINE
ISLAND

52

3

85th St.
NW

Zumbro River

12

90th St.
NW

3

Major Rd.

14

DOUGLAS

14

3

4

22

55th St. NW

22

52

4

4 (Valley
High Rd.)

START/FINISH
ROCHESTER

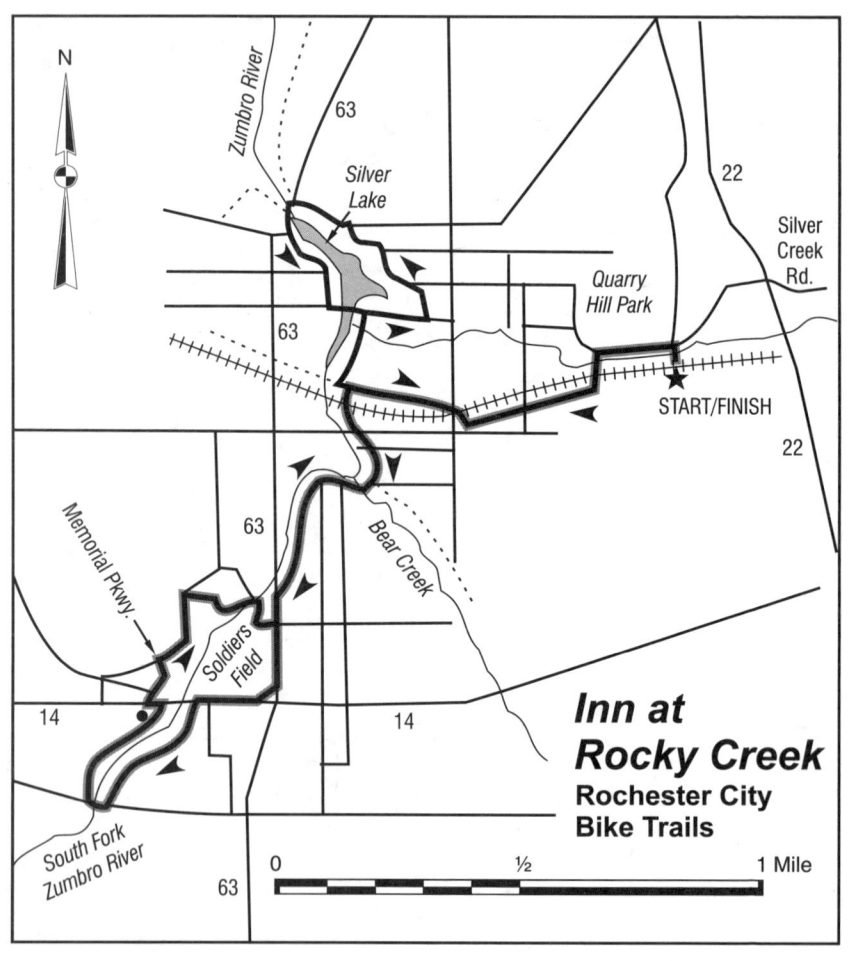

N

Zumbro River

63

Silver Lake

63

22

Silver Creek Rd.

Quarry Hill Park

START/FINISH

22

Memorial Pkwy.

63

Bear Creek

Soldiers Field

14

14

Inn at
Rocky Creek
Rochester City
Bike Trails

South Fork Zumbro River

63

0   ½   1 Mile

Pt.-Pt.	Cume	Turn	Street/Landmark
1.3	17.4	S	Cross unmarked dirt road
0.9	18.3	S	Cross Rt. 3
0.1	18.4	-	Bridge over river
1.0	19.4	S	Cross 90th St. NW
1.9	21.3	S	Cross Major Road at **Douglas Trailhead**
1.2	22.5	S	Cross unmarked dirt road
1.2	23.7	S	Cross unmarked dirt road
0.3	24.0	S	Cross unmarked road
0.3	24.3	S	Cross 55th St. NW
0.6	24.9	-	Bridge over Rt. 22
0.8	25.7	-	Bridge over 41st St. NW
0.3	26.0	-	**High Valley Rd. Tailhead**

Rochester City Bike Trails Ride (12.3 miles)

This ride gives you a little bit of everything urban and a few things not so urban. It was at the start of this ride that we came across the wood snake sunning itself on the Quarry Hill Nature Preserve path. From the Preserve, the ride becomes steadily more urban, though the ride around Silver Lake definitely has a park-like feel to it. To reach the trailhead by car, follow these cues:

0.0	0.0	L	Left out of Inn at Rocky Creek Driveway
0.2	0.2	R	**Rt. 22**
0.5	0.7	S	Cross Viola Rd.
1.1	1.8	R	**Silver Creek Rd.**
0.4	2.2	-	Enter **parking lot for nature conservancy**

Rochester City Bike Trails Cue Sheet

0.0	0.0		Quarry Hill Nature Park Parking Lot
0.0	0.0	BL	Trail almost immediately forks, **take left fork**
0.1	0.1	S	Trail to right, continue straight
0.3	0.4	L	Trail continues straight but **turn left**
0.1	0.5	-	Trail turns left under bridge, then makes a quick right to parallel the train tracks ("S" turn). Follow it.

Pt.-Pt.	Cume	Turn	Street/Landmark
0.3	0.8	**S**	Cross city street
0.3	1.1	**S**	Cross city street
0.1	1.2	**S**	Cross city street; trail jogs to right across railroad tracks
0.2	1.4	**S**	Cross city street
0.2	1.6	**S**	Paved trail T's from left; continue straight
0.3	1.9	**BL**	**Trail crosses bridge**; trail to pool goes right
0.1	2.0	**S**	Trail access from right; continue straight under bridge
0.1	2.1	**L**	Trail curves up to street level, **turn when trail T's with another trail**
0.2	2.3	**BL**	Sidewalk goes straight
0.3	2.6	-	Path to park pavilion
0.4	3.0	**L**	Trail ends at a street, turn left **onto sidewalk**
0.3	3.3	**L**	**Onto bridge across river**
0.1	3.4	**L**	**Bike path** resumes to left
0.4	3.8	-	Pavilion to rent pedal boats and feed geese
0.1	3.9	**L**	**Trail turns left**
0.1	4.0	**L**	Turn **onto path looping under bridge** (this is how we came out)
0.2	4.2	**BR**	**Up over bridge**
0.3	4.5	**R**	Straight heads back to Quarry Hill; turn right
0.4	4.9	-	Base point for Rochester city trails. Pavilion and pedestrian bridge to right
0.1	5.0	**L**	Turn **left onto the South Fork Zumbro Trail** via a short access trail. What appears to be the main trail continues straight beneath a bridge and becomes the Bear Creek Trail.
0.0	5.0	**R**	Turn **onto sidewalk and cross bridge** over Bear Creek and Bear Creek Trail
0.1	5.1	**R**	**Onto trail** back up along river
0.1	5.2	**BR**	Continue **under the bridge**
0.1	5.3	**BR**	Very confusing intersection. As you come in there are three options to go right, **take the least severe, going almost straight across the intersection**, continuing up along the river

Pt.-Pt.	Cume	Turn	Street/Landmark
0.3	5.6	-	Gated trail comes in from right
0.1	5.7	**BR**	**Under bridge**
0.2	5.9	**S**	Straight through intersection of trails at entrance to Soldiers Field
0.8	6.7	**BR**	**Under bridge** (a sharp left after staying right)
0.0	6.7	**BR**	After the bridge there's a triangle of trail intersections, **keep right**
0.7	7.4	**BL**	**Fork in trail, keep left**
0.1	7.5	**R**	**Take sidewalk over bridge**
0.2	7.7	**R**	**Onto sidewalk** past Apache Mall
0.2	7.9	**R**	**Leave sidewalk for bike path**
0.4	8.3	**SL**	Sharp left (**only option**, just after bridge)
0.0	8.3	**R**	Onto neighborhood street, **7th Ave. SW**
0.2	8.5	**R**	**Memorial Parkway**
0.0	8.5	**S**	Continue straight on **Memorial** despite dead-end sign
0.1	8.6	-	Trail picks up again at end of Memorial (by golf course)
0.2	8.8	-	Sidewalk merges in from left
0.3	9.1	-	Not marked as a stop, but is a golf cart crossing—*use caution*
0.0	9.1	**R**	**Turn right over bridge to return to the trail used coming out**
0.2	9.3	**L**	**Return on same trail used coming out**
0.3	9.6	**BR**	Gated trail goes straight
0.1	9.7	**BL**	**Under bridge**
0.1	9.8	**BR**	Goofy intersection, continue **almost straight across, staying a bit right**
0.4	10.2	**L**	**Onto sidewalk across bridge**
0.0	10.2	**L**	**Just across bridge turn onto path**
0.1	10.3	**R**	Access from bridge T's with path, go right
0.4	10.7	**R**	Trail T's, turn right **back to Quarry Hill Nature Park**
0.2	10.9	**S**	Cross city street
0.2	11.1	**S**	Cross city street, trail jogs right across tracks

Pt.-Pt.	Cume	Turn	Street/Landmark
0.1	11.2	**S**	Cross city street
0.3	11.5	**S**	Cross city street
0.3	11.8	-	"S" turn under bridge to cross tracks
0.1	11.9	**R**	Trail T's, turn right **back to Quarry Hill Nature Park parking lot**
0.3	12.2	-	Trail joins from left
0.1	12.3	-	**Quarry Hill Nature Park** parking lot

JailHouse Inn, Preston, Minnesota

JailHouse Inn

Jeanne & Marc Sather
109 Houston St. N.W.
Preston, MN 55965
Rates: Budget – Deluxe

Phone: (507) 265-2181
Fax: (507) 765-2558
E-mail: sbinjail@rconnect.com
Web: www.jailhouseinn.com

Have you ever been on vacation and wanted to be locked up so you couldn't go home? The JailHouse Inn bed and breakfast just might be able to accommodate you. Located in Preston, Minnesota, the county courthouse and jail were built in 1869. Things have changed since Jeanne and Marc Sather took over the property and opened an inn. The old cellblock has been retained, but it and the other 11 guestrooms have been done over for your comfort.

The cellblock has been made over into a suite with two queen-size beds and a whirlpool bath. The beds are located in the old cells complete with the original iron bar cell doors. All the access halls around the cells are part of the suite so there's ample space to spread out. There's also a private entrance off the side porch. If you didn't bring the gang on vacation, you might prefer doing time in the drunk tank. This room has a king-size bed resting on the original pine flooring, as well as a large claw-foot tub and a private entrance across a sun porch. Other oversized rooms include the Court Room, with a beautiful brick patio just out its back door, and the Bridal Suite, with all the accommodations one might expect.

There are several other rooms as well, each sporting some small delight or distinctive feature. The Sun Room is as bright as its name with a white and yellow color scheme, cottage furnishings, and a handmade quilt. The Amish Room features an antique copper bathtub, game table, and spoon-carved bed. The Oriental Room lives up to its moniker with Eastlake furnishings and an antique slate fireplace. Every room has a private bathroom, some with whirlpools.

The public areas of the inn are no less delightful than the guestrooms. Expertly renovated to serve as an inn, many features of the original building have been retained. The walnut banister curving up the stairs is original, as are the seven-foot paneled doors found in several rooms. Though you have to go to the basement for breakfast, the curved glass along one end of the atrium-like space makes the dining room feel light yet cozy.

Speaking of breakfast, the previous occupants probably didn't fair so well as those who spend the night in modern times. The obligatory coffee and juice await you when you first are seated. Our first course was a fruit cup followed by a main course of French toast. Saying the

French toast was excellent fails to do it justice. All the breakfasts are made from scratch, and we think Marc must have some secret ingredient to make such hearty and delicious fare.

Once you've finished Marc's magic breakfasts you can step out into Preston, a place one could call enchanted—if only because the locals claim it never has any mosquitoes. Preston's charms go way beyond a low insect count, however. The town was established in 1853 and named after the its first postmaster, Luther Preston. It has an authentic air that many more touristy small towns can only try to recreate. It nestles like a refuge in the bluff country formed 350 million years ago as the runoff from glaciers cut through the high plateau of southeastern Minnesota. The high sandstone and dolomite cliffs make for some steep hills on the local roads. Though you'll be grateful for the gentle 3% railroad grades on the Root River State Trail, it's worth hopping in the car and going for a ride to catch the spectacular scenery along the roller coaster country roads. In the area around Preston you'll find a wealth of activities besides the Root River State Trail. Naturalists can enjoy canoeing, hiking, and birding. Sportsmen can golf or fish. Those more interested in arts and crafts can shop, go antiquing, or take in a play in the summer theatre. The area's geology has also given rise to a number of caves, and there are cave tours available to escape the summer heat if need be.

From the old jailhouse we went to the Old Village Hall in Lanesboro. Now a restaurant, it serves a menu of American cuisine perfectly suited to the old building. A little closer at hand is the Branding Iron on a hill just outside of Preston. The sunsets are spectacular and the steaks are a delicious fuel for the hungry cyclist. The JailHouse has a collection of menus from other local restaurants to choose from as well.

Rides from The JailHouse Inn
The two trail rides documented here are just a small portion of the riding available in the Root River Trail System. The state has plans to expand and connect these trails to make a large loop of southeastern Minnesota. The resulting system would include several hundred miles of riding. If you're addicted to road riding, there are some road-based out-and-back rides, but many roads aren't paved.

Terrain: The Root River Trail follows the river pretty closely and consequently is relatively level. The Harmony Valley Trail, on the other hand, climbs out of the river valley up to Harmony. When this was a train route, they employed "pusher" engines to help get trains up the slopes. You might wish on occasion for some kind of similar help.

Road Conditions: Both of these rides are on well-paved and well-maintained trails. There are some road intersections, but these are well marked and not generally a distraction.

Traffic: The only traffic you'll encounter here is other cyclists and hikers.

Best Time to Ride: The fall. These trails beg to be ridden when the leaves are changing and the days are crisp. That said, there really isn't a bad time to ride these trails once the snow melts.

Nearest Bike Shop: In Preston and in nearby Lanesboro, there are a number of bike shops that will be able to handle basic repairs. However, when we broke a derailleur on our tandem, finding an appropriate replacement required a trip to Bicycle Sports in Rochester, Minnesota.

Bicycle Sports
1409 South Broadway
Rochester, MN 55904
(507) 281-5007

In terms of other bicycle services, Overland Touring (507/467-2623) is tops. They provide excellent shuttle service anywhere along the trail system and—by the way—have a wonderful restaurant right beside the trail. Ask Dave Harrenstein to tell you what pies are available while he's moving you to one end of the trail or the other, and by all means stop by and sample these delicious mid-ride pick-me-ups.

Harmony-Preston Valley Ride (25.3 miles)

Leaving from Preston, this is one long uphill out and one long downhill back. In some areas, the grades are too steep to be part of a rails-to-trails conversion, but at no point was the ride unpleasant. If you want to do a road loop back, there are some all-pavement options (mainly on County 22 and 17) that provide some wonderful ridge views and an amazing downhill back into Preston.

Pt.-Pt.	Cume	Turn	Street/Landmark
0.0	0.0	**R**	Out of the JailHouse Inn parking lot onto **Preston St.**
0.0	0.0	**R**	**Houston St.**
0.0	0.0	**L**	**Fillmore St.**
0.1	0.1	**S**	Cross St. Paul Street
0.1	0.2	**S**	Cross St. Anthony

Pt.-Pt.	Cume	Turn	Street/Landmark
0.0	0.2	-	Pleasant St.
0.1	0.3	-	Center St.
0.1	0.4	-	Cross Root River Bridge
0.1	0.5	-	Fillmore Pl.
0.4	0.9	**R**	Onto **Harmony-Preston Valley Trail**
0.8	1.7	-	Turnout to creek on right
1.2	2.9	**S**	Cross unmarked road
1.7	4.6	**S**	Cross unmarked road
0.5	5.1	**S**	Cross unmarked road
0.8	5.9	**S**	Cross unmarked road
0.6	6.5	**S**	Cross unmarked road
3.6	10.1	**S**	Cross unmarked road
0.5	10.6	-	Shelter and picnic table
0.6	11.2	**BL**	Trail comes up Rt. 17 and curves left, not crossing immediately
0.4	11.6	**S**	Trail crosses Rt. 17, beneath the crest of a hill— *use caution*
0.8	12.4	**S**	Cross unmarked road
0.1	12.5	**S**	Cross unmarked paved road
0.1	12.6	**TR**	**Harmony Trailhead**
0.1	12.7	**S**	Cross unmarked paved road
0.0	12.7	**S**	Cross unmarked road
1.0	13.7	**S**	Trail crosses Rt. 17, beneath the crest of a hill— *use caution*
0.9	14.6	-	Shelter and picnic table
0.6	15.2	**S**	Cross unmarked road
3.5	18.7	**S**	Cross unmarked road
0.6	19.3	**S**	Cross unmarked road
0.8	20.1	**S**	Cross unmarked road
0.5	20.6	**S**	Cross unmarked road
1.7	22.3	**S**	Cross unmarked road
1.2	23.5	-	Path to river
0.8	24.3	**L**	**Rt. 12** (Also **Fillmore St.**)
0.5	24.8	-	Fillmore Pl.
0.1	24.9	-	Center St.

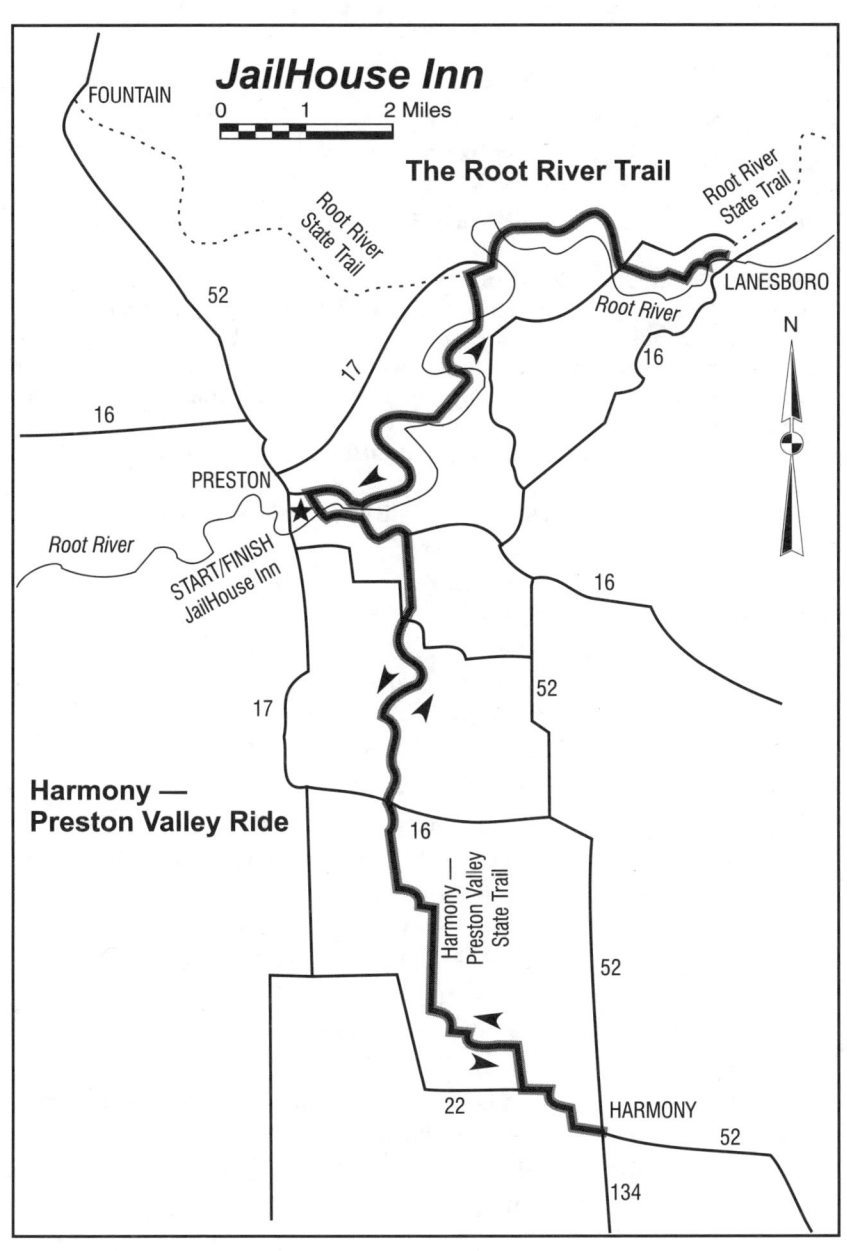

JailHouse Inn

0   1   2 Miles

The Root River Trail

FOUNTAIN

Root River State Trail

Root River State Trail

LANESBORO

52

17

Root River

16

16

PRESTON

Root River

16

START/FINISH
JailHouse Inn

17

52

**Harmony —
Preston Valley Ride**

16

Harmony —
Preston Valley
State Trail

52

22

HARMONY

52

134

N

Pt.-Pt.	Cume	Turn	Street/Landmark
0.1	25.0	-	Pleasant St.
0.1	25.1	S	Cross St. Anthony
0.0	25.1	S	Cross St. Paul St.
0.1	25.2	R	**Houston St.**
0.1	25.3	L	**Preston**
0.0	25.3	-	**JailHouse Inn**

The Root River Trail (22.2 miles)

If we had to pick one recreational trail as the best trail we've ever ridden, this would probably be the one. It's well maintained and strongly supported by the small towns along the way. The scenery is beautiful and the trail itself is a stimulating but not overbearing ride. We saw deer, golden eagles, and a variety of other wildlife. The combination of this wonderful trail and the outstanding JailHouse Inn is a hard to beat.

0.0	0.0	R	Out of the JailHouse Inn parking lot onto **Preston St.**
0.0	0.0	R	**Houston St.**
0.0	0.0	L	**Fillmore St.**
0.1	0.1	S	Cross St. Paul St.
0.1	0.2	S	Cross St. Anthony
0.0	0.2	-	Pleasant St.
0.1	0.3	-	Center St.
0.0	0.3	L	**Root River Trailhead**
0.1	0.4	S	Entrance to trail from back of parking lot
5.7	6.1	R	Trails T's, go right **to Lanesboro**
0.5	6.6	S	Cross unnamed gravel road
2.7	9.3	S	Cross unnamed gravel road
1.8	11.1	TR	Just past old bridge, **Lanesboro ride board**. Town is up to left
1.9	13.0	S	Cross unnamed gravel road
2.7	15.7	S	Cross unnamed gravel road
0.4	16.1	L	Can go straight, but left is **back to Preston**
5.7	21.8	-	Trailhead parking lot
0.1	21.9	R	**Fillmore St.**
0.0	21.9	-	Center St.

Pt.-Pt.	Cume	Turn	Street/Landmark
0.0	21.9	-	Pleasant St.
0.1	22.0	S	Cross St. Anthony
0.1	22.1	S	Cross St. Paul St.
0.0	22.1	**R**	**Houston St.**
0.1	22.2	**L**	**Preston St.**
0.0	22.2	-	Back at the **JailHouse Inn**

The Park Street Inn, Nevis, Minnesota

The Park Street Inn

Irene & Len Hall　　　　　**Phone: (218) 652-4500**
106 Park Street　　　　　　　　　**(800) 797-1778**
Nevis, MN 56467
Rates: Budget — moderate

The Park Street Inn was built in 1912 as a residence for Justin Halvorson, banker and owner of the Nevis Land Company. Fittingly, the house contains some of the grandeur of a bank. The entryway is framed by built-in oak lampposts, which are situated underneath a massive wooden archway intricately carved in roses and other floral designs. This monumental style of woodwork continues in the living room, with a substantial mission-style fireplace and another wooden arch leading into the dining room. Expertly crafted doorjambs and a plate rail pick up the theme in the dining room.

In the midst of all this well-kept grandeur, Irene and Len Hall have created an at-home space, relaxing and comfortable. A hardwood staircase winds up from the entryway to three rooms upstairs. The Blue and Red Rooms, part of a recently finished (and seamlessly integrated) addition, feature private baths and share a spacious second-story deck. The Blue Room has a canopy bed wrapped in blues and whites and a double wedding ring quilt on the bed. It also has the house's original clawfoot tub with a shower. The Red Room has an antique brass bed with a radiant star quilt. Situated on the east side of the house, this room lights up each day with morning sun.

Across the front of the house is The Suite. This set of rooms has a private bath with shower. In addition to a queen-size bed, the main room features an air-jet two person Jacuzzi. Placed in the old oak nook of a cabinet bed, this Jacuzzi provided a most relaxing soak and immediately hatched plans in our minds for a similar addition at home. Just off the main room is a sleeping porch with a wicker couch and chair and a second bed. The entire south face of the porch is enveloped by windows, and on a sunny breezy summer day, there's no place nicer to linger. On the landing outside the rooms is a huge antique bookcase filled with books, including some of the original *Tom Swift* series, with a little *Tarzan* thrown in for good measure.

The inn's complement of rooms is rounded out by The Grotto. Located in the basement, The Grotto is reached by a separate entrance. This room is a jungle adventure, with rain forest murals on all four walls and a rock waterfall in one corner. The king bed and two-person water-jet jacuzzi complete the room's appointments.

Breakfasts at the inn are the result of a discussion between guests and Irene. She doesn't cook from a set menu, but if our breakfasts were any indication, she can make things up on the fly anytime she wants to. Thirty minutes before breakfast, coffee, hot chocolate, or hot cider are set outside your door. Our first day there, breakfast started out with a rich, decadent chocolate bread. To ease our guilty conscience, that was followed by an exceptional fresh cup of locally grown fruits and berries. Our entrée the first day was thick waffles slathered with maple or blueberry syrup. Slices of smoked baked turkey breast rounded out the meal. On the second day we had a light egg and cheese soufflé with oven baked potatoes and turkey sausage patties as sides.

In addition to the Heartland Trail just a block behind the Inn, there are a number of activities within easy driving distance from the house. Perhaps the most notable is Lake Itasca State Park, which contains the headwaters of the Mississippi River. Here, you can splash around and hop across on a few stones without getting your feet wet—it's a far cry from the vast expanse of water at the mouth of the river where it empties into the Gulf of Mexico. Besides this park, the Chippewa National Forest and Paul Bunyan State Forest offer ample wilderness opportunities. If you are looking for something a little more civilized, there are numerous golf courses, casinos, and antique shops scattered nearby. The inn also looks out over Lac de Belle Taine and the Nevis City Park with swimming and picnic spots.

You can come for adventure or quiet time. The surrounding area supports a wide variety of activities or you can sit on the porch and talk philosophy with Len. Or if you'd rather just sit on the deck and watch the squirrels and blue jays at the feeder, that's okay too. Whatever choice you make, The Park Street Inn is ready to accommodate you.

Rides from The Park Street Inn
There are many other riding opportunities around Nevis besides the two rides we've included here. The Heartland Trail is paved for more than 50 miles of its length. There are also numerous snowmobile trails maintained through the summer as mountain biking trails. Check in with the Forestry Service Office in Park Rapids (218/732-3309). Ron Norneberg, a park forester, was very helpful in discussing all the various local options.

Terrain: The Heartland Trail and the roads we included in that loop are relatively flat. The loop weaves among many lakes, and while you'll find some ups and downs, they won't take your legs out from under you. The Bear Tracks ride has a little more diversity but it's more the sand than the hills that your legs will be working on.

Road Conditions: The Heartland Trail was just recently resurfaced and the associated roads are in pretty good shape as well, though there are not extensive shoulders. The forest roads in the Paul Bunyan are just that, forest roads, so you need to be on the lookout for deadfalls, puddles, and other obstacles. On the day we were riding, the intermittent sandy patches were the biggest challenge.

Traffic: Though we rode the Heartland Trail in the late afternoon and were out on the roads on the way back during "rush hour," we saw only a few cars and nobody else on the trail itself. The forest roads of the Paul Bunyan are driveable by a suitably-equipped car or truck but we only saw two motocross motorcycles and two ATVs during our ride.

Best Time to Ride: This part of Minnesota is far enough north that the whole summer season provides pleasant riding.

Nearest Bike Shop
Gurney's Repair and Bike Shop
Park Rapids, MN
(218) 732-9816

Bear Tracks Ride (12.3 miles)
The Martineau Recreation Area is a set of trails created for mountain bikes, motorcycles, and ATVs. Lest you worry about sharing the trails with mechanized equipment, we found the trails and roads to be wide enough for comfortable passage and, in any event, saw more evidence of animals than people. At one stop near a sandy stretch of the ride, we spotted large tracks which, upon describing them to a ranger later, we learned were bear tracks. There were also rumors of giant beavers, a rumor backed up by the evidence of some rather large trees that had been gnawed down along the road. To reach the trailhead by car, follow these cues:

Pt.-Pt.	Cume	Turn	Street/Landmark
0.0	0.0		Head **east on Park Street**
0.0	0.0	**R**	**Paul Bunyan Trail**
0.1	0.1	**L**	**Highway 34** (towards Akley)
5.0	5.1	**L**	**County 25**
3.0	8.1	**L**	**State 64**
4.5	12.6	**L**	**Dirt road to Martineau Recreation Parking**
0.3	12.9	-	**Parking lot** and map board

Bear Tracks Cue Sheet

Pt.-Pt.	Cume	Turn	Street/Landmark
0.0	0.0		From the map board at the back of the parking lot, head back out towards Rt. 64.
0.2	0.2	S	Cross Rt. 64 and pick up the **Blue Trail Forest Road**
0.1	0.3	-	Motocross trail off to left
0.9	1.2	-	Unmarked trail to left
0.3	1.5	L	**Parkway Forest Road**
0.6	2.1	-	Unmarked trail to left
0.3	2.4	-	Unmarked trail to left
0.7	3.1	S	Kabekona Forest Road to left, continue straight
0.3	3.4	-	Unmarked trail to right
0.4	3.8	-	Unmarked trail to right
0.5	4.3	S	Lester Lake Trail to left, continue straight
0.2	4.5	R	**East Steamboat Forest Road**
0.5	5.0	-	Unmarked trail to right
0.7	5.7	-	Here is where we spotted the bear tracks
0.4	6.1	S	Paul Bunyan Trail to the left, continue straight
0.4	6.5	-	Unmarked road to right
0.4	6.9	-	Ambiguous trail to right
0.2	7.1	-	Ambiguous trail to left
0.4	7.5	-	Blocked trail to right
0.0	7.5	-	Unmarked singletrack
0.5	8.0	-	Unmarked singletrack
0.4	8.4	-	Unmarked road to right
0.2	8.6	-	Unmarked road to right
1.1	9.7	R	**Parkway Forest Road** (not well marked)
0.5	10.2	-	Unmarked trail to right
0.6	10.8	L	**Blue Trail Forest Road**
1.2	12.0	S	Cross Route 64 and back to parking lot
0.3	12.3	-	**End of ride** at map board

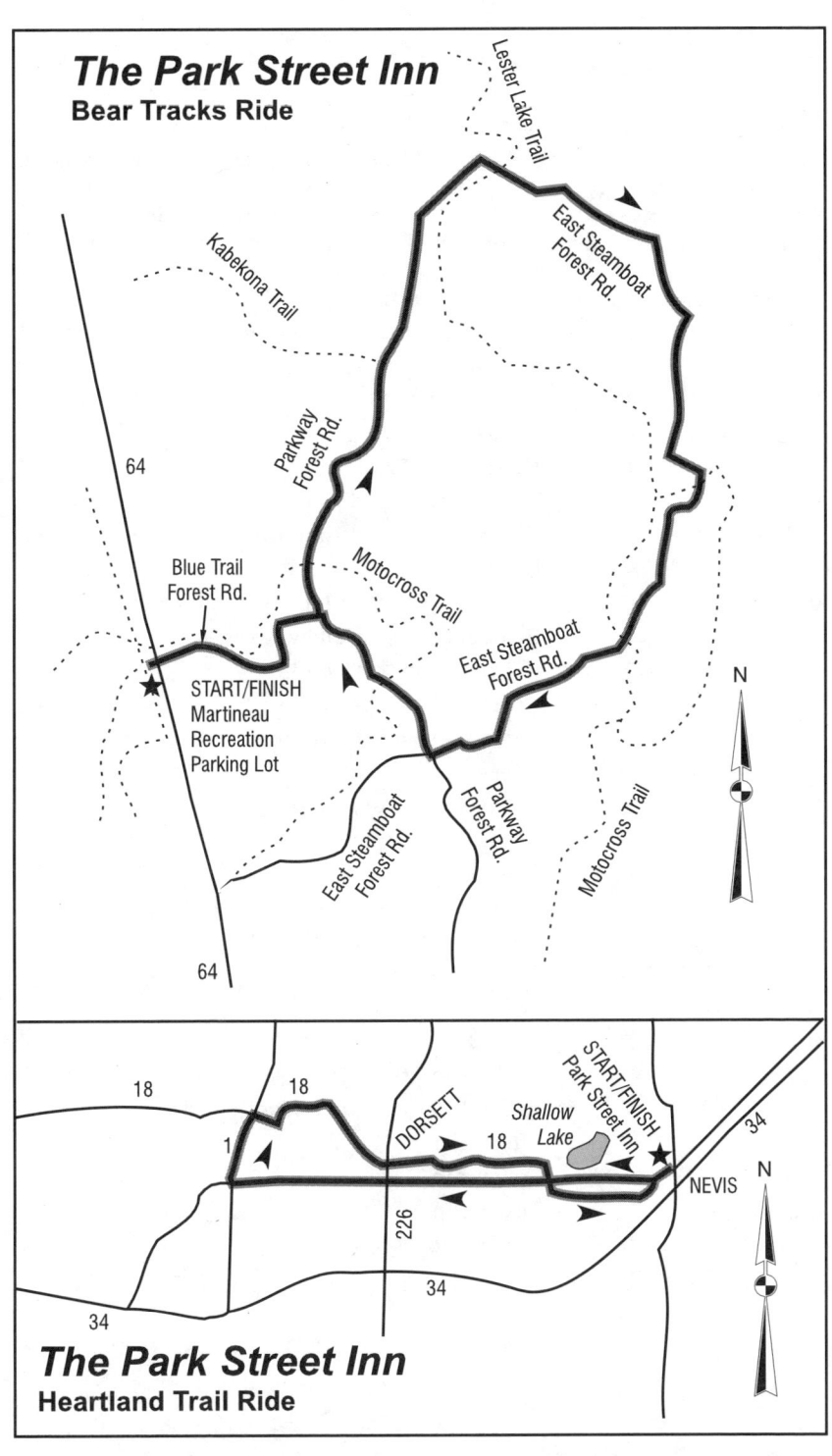

Heartland Trail Ride (22.7 miles)

The Heartland Trail is the oldest rails-to-trails conversion in Minnesota. The trail has aged gracefully without a lot of development along its length. Given it's recent resurfacing, you could easily imagine this was a new trail, recently laid down among the lakes and stands of trees.

Pt.-Pt.	Cume	Turn	Street/Landmark
0.0	0.0	L	In the alley behind the inn head west **(left out of the driveway)**
0.0	0.0	R	**Third Ave.**
0.0	0.0	S	Cross Rt. 18
0.1	0.1	L	**Heartland Trail**
0.4	0.5	S	Cross unmarked road
1.0	1.5	S	Cross unmarked road (Shallow Lake is to the right)
0.6	2.1	S	Rt. 18 crosses trail, continue straight
0.2	2.3	-	Bridge across Shallow River
1.0	3.3	S	Cross unmarked road
2.0	5.3	S	Cross Rt. 226 (downtown Dorsett is just off the path; there are restrooms here as well)
1.0	6.3	S	Cross unmarked road
0.6	6.9	S	Cross unmarked road
1.6	8.5	S	Cross major road (unmarked)
1.5	10.0	R	**Rt. 1**
0.3	10.3	-	Unmarked road to right (Headwater Village)
0.3	10.6	-	Headwaters Country Club
0.9	11.5	-	Township KK
0.9	12.4	-	Township LL to left
0.5	12.9	R	**Rt. 18**
0.2	13.1	-	Township 16 to left
0.7	13.8	S	Cross Rt. 4, a major road; continue straight after stop
0.2	14.0	-	Township T
0.5	14.5	-	Township 14A
2.1	16.6	-	Rt. 112 to right
0.5	17.1	S	Cross Rt. 7, a major road; continue straight after stop

Pt.-Pt.	Cume	Turn	Street/Landmark
0.5	17.6	-	Township 0
1.5	19.1	-	Township 7
1.5	20.6	-	Heartland Trail
0.0	20.6	**BL**	**Follow Rt. 18 to left** immediately after trail (Township 8-1 goes straight)
0.6	21.2	-	Township 8
0.7	21.9	-	Township 9-1
0.3	22.2	-	Township 9 to left
0.3	22.5	-	McCurnin Place
0.1	22.6	**R**	**Third Ave.**
0.0	22.6	**L**	**Alley behind inn**
0.1	22.7	-	**End of ride**

Pincushion Mountain Bed and Breakfast, Grand Marais, Minnesota

Pincushion Mountain Bed and Breakfast

Scott & Mary Beattie
968 Gunflint Trail
Grand Marais, MN 55604-9707
Rates: Budget — Moderate

Phone: (218) 387-1276
(800) 542-1226
E-mail: pincushion@boreal.org
Web: www.pincushionbb.com

If you have ever driven up California's Highway 1 along the Pacific Ocean or along U.S. Highway 1 on the Atlantic coast of Maine, you'll feel right at home driving up U.S. Highway 61 along Minnesota's north shore of Lake Superior. It helps that Lake Superior, often called an inland sea, is the largest body of fresh water in the world. Having the Sawtooth Mountains just across the road in the Superior National Forest doesn't hurt the impression either. By the time you've passed through the route's two tunnels, many switchbacks, and numerous overlooks on your way to the Pincushion Mountain Bed and Breakfast, you'll know you're "Up North."

Scott and Mary Beattie ended up in Grand Marais after a journey in search of perfect snow. Having worked many years in the ski resorts of Arizona, they began looking around the U.S. for a place where they might open a cross-country ski lodge. The large annual snowfalls of Minnesota's Arrowhead region drew their attention and in the mid-1980s they bought several acres of land on the shoulder of the Sawtooth Mountain ridgeline and built the Pincushion Mountain Bed and Breakfast a thousand feet above the shores of Lake Superior. They groomed 25 kilometers of ski trails starting right at the inn's door. Several summers later Scott discovered that ski trails make excellent mountain biking trails after the snow melts. The trails provide some spectacular biking and matching views of Lake Superior.

The inn has four guestrooms decorated in what could be called the "American Ski Lodge" style—light wood paneling, thick comforters on the beds, and pegs in the walls for hanging all your gear. The inn sits away off the road so every room has windows looking out into the surrounding woods. The lightness and Scandinavian sparseness of the rooms was a refreshing change from the more ornate style typical of many Victorian bed and breakfasts, and we didn't feel like we lacked for any comfort in these roomy but cozy accommodations. Each room has a private bath, and if you ask in advance you might even get private time in the sauna, probably a good idea after a day spent on these hilly trails in the woods. The Birch Room has a king bed, while the Pine, Maple, and Aspen all have queen beds. The Pine is more spacious than the other rooms, with a sitting area and a sofa sleeper in addition to the queen bed.

Though the inn seems to be focused on getting you out into the gorgeous surrounding countryside, Scott and Mary won't push you out the door with an empty stomach. We've eaten a lot of breakfasts in our travels, but Scott and Mary have the distinction of starting us on a culinary quest. They served a delicious chilled fruit soup as a starter for breakfast that we've been trying to recreate ever since. It has a crispness, texture, and flavor that will wake up your palette and conjure dreams of summer—and that was just the first course. In addition to the obligatory coffee and juice, we had muffins and a wild rice and mushroom frittata that gave us all the get up and go we needed to tackle the trails outside. If that's not enough to keep you going, the innkeepers can prepare a trail lunch for you with a little advance notice.

If you decide to leave the bike behind you still have a number of recreational options. There's hiking on the Superior Trail, which connects with the inn's trails. Nearby you'll find golf courses, lake and stream fishing, and just 30 minutes up the road, the National Boundary Waters Canoe Area offers hundreds of miles of streams and lakes where even the simplest mechanical beasts—such as bikes—are not permitted. There are a number of outfitters ready to prepare you for any adventure and even to serve as guides.

Grand Marais also has the range of diversions one might expect to find in a considerably larger city. Playing host to a thriving artist community, the town has a number of galleries, an active theatre, a collection of folk, jazz, blues, and classical concerts, and an annual arts festival. It also has a variety of shops, cafés, and restaurants. The Angry Trout is perhaps the most popular local restaurant, and while you can expect to spend some time on the deck overlooking the lake before you're seated, the food is worth the wait. Just up the road is the Nanniboujou Lodge. The dining room's art deco and Egyptian decorations and spectacular food are well worth the drive.

Almost as soon as we started down the driveway to our next destination we were plotting when we could return to the Pincushion. The excellent mountain biking, the comfort and welcome created by Scott and Mary, and the range of adventures left unexplored on our first visit all encouraged a return visit.

Rides from Pincushion Mountain Bed and Breakfast

The rides documented here are right out the back door of the inn on its private trails. It's great mountain biking with beautiful wooded scenery and a couple of fantastic lake views throw in for good measure. You could easily spend a few days and not wander from this set of varied and challenging trails, but if you want to wander farther afield, there are plenty of opportunities. Scott can get you started on other opportunities and Mark and Melinda Spinler at the Superior North Outdoor Center can supply you with maps, gear, and the complete inside scoop on biking in the area. There's also an inn-to-inn biking service available.

Terrain: Hilly. The outer ring of these trails is fairly easy, even for a novice, as long as you're in decent shape. The inner trails? Well, they're a bit more of a challenge, both in the climbing and in the basic composition of the trails, with more rocks, roots, and other obstacles to deal with. We're still a bit amazed that people can actually go up some of these hills once they're covered with snow.

Road Conditions: These are ski trails that are lightly maintained for mountain biking. There's no pavement out here, and that's a good thing if serious mountain biking is what you're after. We were, and had a fantastic time.

Traffic: In all our riding we ran into precisely one other rider.

Best Time to Ride: Picking a best time seems to imply that other times might not be good; therefore, we're reluctant to do that in this case. Perhaps once it really snows and the trails are groomed, one could consider it a not-so-great time to ride. The only real factor here is how far north the Pincushion is (just shy of the Canadian border), so the riding season is a little shorter than it is further south.

Nearest Bike Shop
Superior North Outdoor Center
P.O. Box 177
Grand Marais, MN 55604
(218) 387-2186

The Lookout (5.5 miles)
The Lookout ride sticks to the outer ring of trails. It does have some challenging surfaces and a few climbs, but nothing that will be beyond most riders' skill or endurance levels. There's access to the Superior Hiking Trail and a little hike up to a crest overlooking the town of Grand Marais and Lake Superior.

*(**Note:** In the following cue sheets, an "X intersection" is a trail junction where two trails approach as almost parallel, share a single track for a short distance, and then separate again.)*

PtPt.	Cume	Turn	Street/Landmark
0.0	0.0	R	B&B Loop in front of inn; **head north on the loop** (**right** if you're facing the inn)
0.1	0.1	R	Turn onto **Pincushion Mountain Loop**
0.2	0.3	-	Spur to left
0.7	1.0	**BL**	One of three options; avoid the hard right and hard left
0.3	1.3	L	**Pincushion Mountain Loop**
0.7	2.0	-	Link to the Superior Hiking Trail (no bikes)
0.4	2.4	-	Pincushion Mountain Overlook
0.9	3.3	S	Trail to left, continue straight
0.4	3.7	R	**X intersection, stay right**
0.1	3.8	R	**X intersection, stay right**
0.3	4.1	R	Multiple options, go **far right**
0.0	4.1	L	trail forks; **go left**
0.6	4.7	**BL**	**X Intersection, take center left exit.**
0.3	5.0	L	Turn left
0.1	5.1	-	Another trail running parallel
0.3	5.4	R	Multiple route intersection; **stay right**
0.1	5.5	-	**End of ride**

No Mercy with a Few Downhills (5.5 miles)

There were times when we wondered if this ride was all uphill. We half expected to come to a sharp precipice overlooking the inn far below when we came to the end of the ride. That said, it was a great ride with fairly technical climbs and few rocketing downhills.

0.0	0.0	L	B&B Loop in front of inn; **head south on the loop** (**left** if you're facing the inn)
0.0	0.0+	**BL**	**Stay left** as you head into the woods
0.0+	0.0	R	**Intersection #12**
1.3	1.3	R	**Intersection #3; stay right**
0.0	1.3+	R	**At fork**
0.1	1.4	L	**Turn left**; straight ahead goes to a trailhead with restrooms and a great view
0.1	1.5	-	Sponsor board
0.1	1.6	-	Trail to right, continue straight
0.1	1.7	R	**X intersection; stay right**
0.2	1.9	L	**X intersection; stay left**
0.2	2.1	-	Parallel trails; stay left
0.1	2.2	-	Parallel trails; stay right
0.3	2.5	-	Parallel trails; stay left

PtPt.	Cume	Turn	Street/Landmark
0.2	2.7	R	**X intersection; stay right**
0.4	3.1	-	Parallel trail, stay left
0.4	3.5	L	**X intersection; stay left**
0.4	3.9	SR	**Hard right**
0.1	3.9+	SR	**Hard right**
0.7	4.6	SR	**Hard right**
0.1	4.7	L	**X intersection; stay left**
0.3	5	SL	**Hard left**
0.2	5.2	-	Parallel trails; stay right
0.2	5.4	R	**Right turn towards B&B**
0.1	5.5	-	**Back at starting point**

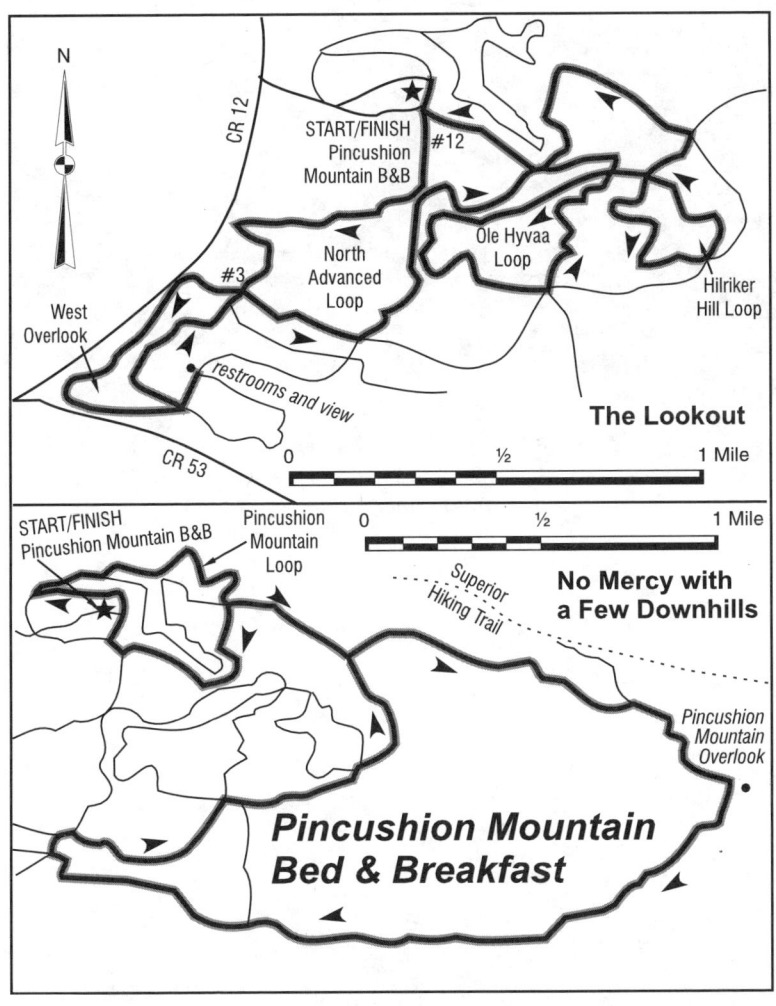

The Spicer Castle, Spicer, Minnesota

The Spicer Castle

Allen & Marti Latham, Owners
Mary Swanson, Manager
P.O. Box 307
Spicer, MN 56288
Rates: Budget – Moderate

Phone: (320) 796-5870
(800) 821-6675
Fax: (320) 796-4076
Email: spicercastle@spicercastle.com
Web: www.spicercastle.com

Calling this inn a castle is a bit of a fisherman's hyperbole, but then again that's probably closer to the truth than calling it a cottage which is what John Spicer called it when he built Meydato Cottage around the turn of the last century. The castle moniker arose in the 1930s when fishermen on Green Lake began using the cottage as a landmark, calling it Spicer Castle. Seen from the lake, situated on a rise of land with its turret and gables projecting up into the trees, you can see the fishermen's point.

Built in 1893 as country lake home for the Spicer family, the Castle is still owned by the grandson of John Spicer. The transition from family resort to lakeside bed and breakfast was gently made. The gracefully rustic original furnishings and the wooded grounds seemed to have absorbed the ease of many summers, inviting you to relax, all the while whispering of the great Adirondack camps of the last century.

The Castle has eight guestrooms and two cabins, all as delightfully eccentric as you might expect from a turn-of-the-century cottage. Some are tucked up under the eaves, peaking out on the lake. Others are reconstructed sleeping porches with more windows than walls. Each has a bit of the personality of the members of the original Spicer clan that occupied them. Several of the daughters were painters, and you'll find their works scattered throughout the Castle. One adventurous son brought home mementos from the Spanish American War and from ranching in Colorado.

We stayed in Jessie's Room, which overlooks the lake from the octagonal tower. It was Jessie's idea to remodel the exterior of the cottage in the Tudor style, so it's appropriate that her room was in the tower. Frances' Room was originally the master bedroom and has a commanding view of the gardens and woods through French windows. The wife of John Spicer, Frances was the first artist in the family, inspiring her daughters in all the arts—including culinary. If you want a bit more space and privacy, you might consider John's cabin. He had it built to create some space for his business that was not quite so embedded in the ebb and flow of family activities taking place throughout the Castle. Today it will provide you with an intimate getaway.

The main floor of the Castle has several spacious dining rooms, a lovely enclosed porch overlooking the lake, and a central gathering room stocked with games and other diversions. Should you be looking for more structured entertainment, the Castle hosts Murder Mystery Evenings on most weekends and the Spicer Castle Belle offers fine dining as you cruise on Green Lake, perhaps spotting a loon as evening falls.

If you could somehow manage to forget your stay at the Spicer Castle, you'd still remember the food. The breakfasts are reminiscent of hearty logging camp fare, with added refinement. You'll start with juice, fresh fruit, and a spread of breads, cakes, and muffins that will force a few early morning decisions. That's followed by a main entrée of traditional breakfast items, including pancakes, waffles, or eggs with a side of sausage. Whatever the menu holds for a particular day, you'll leave the breakfast table satisfied and ready for a day of riding or exploring.

The Castle is just a short drive outside the small resort town of Spicer on the southwestern edge of Green Lake. The town is set up to support recreation with a public beach right downtown and all the boating, fishing, skiing, and swimming that a good-sized lake suggests. There are several golf courses within easy reach as well as an interpretative nature center at Sibley State Park. You might want to stop at one of the small shops for an ice cream cone or to look over the local crafts. Just along the edge of town is the Glacial Lakes State Trail, with a paved surface that provided portions of the rides for our visit.

All in all, you'll feel like you've found summertime when you arrive in Spicer, and the impression will only be reinforced by your stay at the Spicer Castle.

Rides from the Spicer Castle
These rides among the lakes and farms surrounding Spicer are pleasant pastoral diversions. Between the country roads and the bike path, the biker is well taken care of on these rides.

Terrain: The trail, being a true rails-to-trails, has no significant grades as it winds its way between lakes and meadows. The roads have some high rolling hills that present some degree of challenge, but nothing that can't be handled by your granny gear if need be.

Road Conditions: The roads included in these rides are all country roads, except where you pass through Spicer. There are not significant shoulders in most cases, but we never felt crowded while riding.

Traffic: These roads don't carry significant traffic. On many stretches we did not see a single car despite being in the area during high tourist season. It seems that much of the local activity centers on the larger lakes and when you get away from them, there is a noticeable drop in traffic of all kinds.

Best Time to Ride: Early summer or early fall will be the most comfortable times to ride this area, though it is fairly unusual to reach the upper, unbearable end of the thermometer around these parts.

Nearest Bike Shop: The nearest full-service bike shop is just down the road in Willmar, Minnesota:

Rick's Schwinn & Sports Center
320 West 3rd St.
Willmar, MN 56201
(320) 235-0202

The Freight Train (18.1 miles)

This road and trail ride is named for the excellent tail wind we had on a rolling section of hills on State Route 26. After a number of no-effort uphills followed by long downhills, it felt as if the tandem might grab some air over the top of the last few hills. This ride starts with a short stretch along Green Lake and then crosses over to Diamond Lake before heading for home on Route 26. The last section of the ride is along the Glacial Lakes State Trail.

Pt.-Pt.	Cume	Turn	Street/Landmark
			From the Spicer Castle
0.0	0.0		Abreast of the small cabin
0.0+	0.0+	**R**	**Indian Beach Rd.**
0.6	0.6	**L**	**County Road 10**
1.3	1.9	-	120th N.E
1.0	2.9	**R**	**County Road 4**
1.6	4.5	-	82nd N.E.
0.5	5.0	-	County Road 28 to left
0.3	5.3	-	Diamond Lake to left; public park with concessions and bathrooms
0.7	6.0	**R**	**County Road 26**
0.6	6.6	-	County Road 134 to left
1.5	8.1	-	97th N.E.
1.1	9.2	**S**	Cross County Road 8
1.5	10.7	-	County 127
0.7	11.4	**R**	**Glacial Lakes Trail**
1.4	12.8	-	Unnamed dirt road

Pt.-Pt.	Cume	Turn	Street/Landmark
0.7	13.5	-	Bench overlooking lake
0.7	14.2	-	Unnamed dirt road
0.6	14.8	-	Driveway intersection
0.1	14.9	**S**	Cross South St.
0.3	15.2	**S**	Cross Progress Way
0.2	15.4	-	Spicer Trailhead of Glacial Lakes Trail
0.0	15.4	**R**	**Agnes St.**
0.0	15.4	**S**	Cross Highway 23. *Careful*—busy road
0.1	15.5	**R**	Lake Street (Also County Rd. 10)
0.1	15.6	**S**	Cross intersection with Ruth
0.2	15.8	-	Beach St. to right (despite the actual beach being to the left)
0.3	16.1	-	County Rd. 8 to right
1.3	17.4	-	Green Lake Bible camp
0.1	17.5	**L**	**Indian Beach Road, County Rd. 95** (This is a blind corner behind you, so turn *carefully*)
0.6	18.1	**L**	**Spicer Castle Driveway**

North of Spicer (16.1 miles)

The North of Spicer ride heads out on the Glacial Lakes Trail and then cuts across some wetlands and back down to Green Lake. It's a happy little rustic ride for that portion just off the trail and then alternates between little lake cottages and cattails once you get back on Green Lake.

			Spicer Castle to New London
0.0	0.0		Abreast of the small cabin
0.0+	0.0+	**R**	**Indian Beach Rd.**
0.6	0.6	**R**	**County Road 10 (also 105th Ave.)**
1.4	2.0	-	County Rd. 8
0.5	2.5	**S**	Cross Ruth St.; 4-way stop
0.1	2.6	**L**	**Agnes**
0.0	2.6	**S**	Cross Highway 26 *carefully*—busy road
<0.1	2.6	**R**	**Glacial Lakes Trail**
0.3	2.9	**S**	Cross Manitoba
0.1	3.0	-	Driveway
0.5	3.5	**S**	Cross Woodcock Rd.
0.1	3.6	-	Driveway; you'll encounter driveways approximately every tenth of a mile for the next half mile
0.5	4.1	-	County Rd. 32
0.6	4.7	-	Unmarked through road

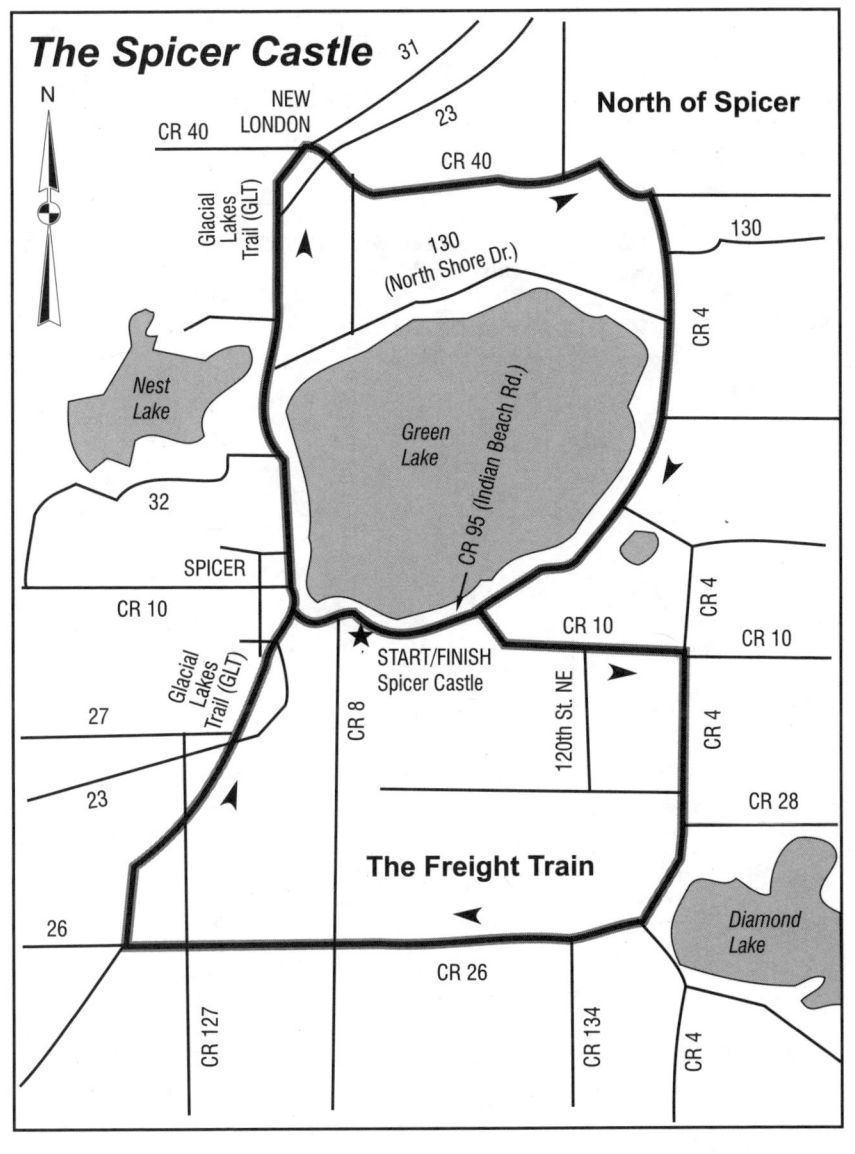

The Spicer Castle

N

NEW LONDON

31

23

CR 40

CR 40

130
(North Shore Dr.)

North of Spicer

130

CR 4

Glacial Lakes Trail (GLT)

Nest Lake

Green Lake

CR 95 (Indian Beach Rd.)

32

SPICER

CR 10

CR 10

CR 4

CR 10

CR 4

★ START/FINISH
Spicer Castle

Glacial Lakes Trail (GLT)

27

23

CR 8

120th St. NE

CR 4

CR 28

26

The Freight Train

Diamond Lake

CR 127

CR 26

CR 134

CR 4

Pt.-Pt.	Cume	Turn	Street/Landmark
0.3	5.0	-	Crow River, seat and scenic path
0.5	5.5	S	Cross 155th N.E.
1.5	7.0	-	New London Trailhead
0.3	7.3	R	**County Road 40**
<0.1	7.3	S	Cross Highway 23 *carefully*
1.2	8.5	-	92nd N.E.
2.0	10.5	-	120th N.E.
0.7	11.2	R	**County Road 4**
0.8	12.0	-	County 130
0.5	12.5	BL	**CR 4 merges with CR 30 from right**
0.7	13.2	R	**Indian Beach Rd.**
0.5	13.7	-	134th
2.4	16.1	R	**Spicer Castle Driveway**
0.0	16.1	-	End of ride

Wander Inn Bed and Breakfast

Andrea & Mark Smith
2590 Vega Avenue
P.O. Box 1127
Watertown, MN 55388
Rates: Budget – Moderate

Phone: (612) 955-2230
Fax: (612) 955-2230
E-mail wanderin@winternet.com
Web: www.wander-inn.com

If you've ever traveled in Europe and stayed in the guesthouses, you'll immediately recognize the brand of family hospitality that Andrea, Mark, and their kids serve up at the Wander Inn. Andrea was born in Germany and brings that generous sense of hosting to this one-building melting pot, designed and decorated in an American West idiom. Just a short drive down a gravel road off County Road 20, this small horse farm is a wonderful getaway, whether exploring the Luce Line Trail, soaking in the hot tub, or just sitting on one of the wide, sheltered porches.

The guestrooms are around back along one of those porches. You enter through a common area that has a large stone fireplace across from a plush maroon leather couch. There's a rustic pine table and chairs, a satellite-connected television, and a set of leather chairs with an ottoman to match the couch. The walls are filled with shadow boxes, paintings, and artifacts from Andrea and Mike's western art collection. Though the addition that houses the inn was built only two years ago, it has the comfortable fit and feeling of an old pair of blue jeans.

The three guestrooms are arrayed down one long hallway from the common area. The Roses and Lace is the most traditional room with antiques, a fourposter bed, and Victorian clothing displayed on the walls. It has a private half bath and a shared tub. The other half of that sharing equation is the Tack Room, which, as the name indicates, is decorated for the horse lover. Bridles and other kinds of horse paraphernalia decorate this room along with various horse scenes. It has a sleigh bed and private half bath in addition to the shared tub. The Winchester Room is decorated in a woodsy tone. A local craftsman built the beautiful pine and birch log furniture. The Alpaca fur quilt on the bed begs to be petted. Hunting scenes, antique traps and rifles (all non-functioning) complete the decoration scheme. The private bath has an old clawfoot tub with a pipe and rod shower. The only other space in the guest side of the lodge is a small alcove off the common room that has local information and—perhaps more importantly—a refrigerator that Andrea keeps stocked with snacks, drinks, and her amazing desserts. Unable to resist, we finished off a complete blueberry, whipped cream, and angel food cake during our stay.

We should have known about the desserts. One of Andrea's daughters greeted us upon arrival and showed us to our room. "Mom loves to cook, and loves to cook a lot," she said when telling us about breakfast. To our good fortune that turned out to be true. Breakfast started with coffee and juice set out a half-hour before we'd asked for breakfast. When the table was set right on schedule we were served Belgian waffles, an egg and cheese casserole, and sides of sausage and fresh fruit. The whipped cream on the Belgian Waffles was a gourmet delight all by itself—light and fluffy, yet intensely flavorful. The waffles were perfectly browned and crisp, in excellent counterpoint to the topping. A few blueberries and some maple syrup completed the plate. The egg casserole has onions and spices baked in with a rich cheese sauce laid down the center. Either one would have made a complete and delightful meal. We were left completely satisfied, if perhaps wanting just a bit more stomach space so we could continue appreciating these wonderful tasty dishes. We almost didn't eat supper that first night so we'd have more room the next morning. The lightly spiced scrambled eggs, rich vanilla pancakes, and perfectly crisp-on-the-outside, steamy-soft-on-the-inside hash browns didn't disappoint. We didn't have enough advance time to ask for one of Andrea's home-cooked suppers (she asks for two days notice) and have been trying to figure out our schedule so we can go back ever since.

Though the Wander Inn is out in the country, you won't be roughing it. There are golf courses, movie theaters, and antique shops within a short drive. If you're really feeling urban withdrawal symptoms, the Twin Cities and the Mall of America are a little over half an hour away. We didn't feel that temptation too strongly, though. With the welcoming and casual hospitality of the Smith family, the western air of space and quiet and serenity, and the Luce Line Trail just out the side door, we were entirely content to spend our time within walking and riding distance of the wide and sheltered porches of the Wander Inn.

Rides from Wander Inn

The Luce Line Trail is the mainstay of riding in this immediate locale. There are a number of paved country roads for road bikers, but this is on the edge of the western part of Minnesota where more country roads are gravel than paved, so be sure of your route if you go exploring that way.

Terrain: Though this trail is laid out along an old railroad corridor, it seems that some of the old roadbed was not preserved. There are no long, steep grades, but there are numerous abrupt uphills and downhills, all of which are rideable.

Road Conditions: Unlike many other Minnesota trails, the Luce Line is a compacted limestone trail, which gives it a slightly more rustic feeling. One word of caution: those short, abrupt up- and downhills sometimes have gravel washes in them which are noticeably looser.

Traffic: The only traffic you'll encounter here is other trail users. This is a shared trail with horses and hikers; in an almost surreal touch, we encountered cadre of unicyclists on the day we rode the trail. We only had to dismount and walk our bikes by one set of horses. The riders thanked us, and the horses let us pet their soft warm noses.

Best Time to Ride: The snowmobile maps we found for this trail said it's open for that use from December through the end of March, so you probably don't want to plan an early spring riding trip here. We visited in mid-August and found the weather to be comfortable, aided by the generally well-shaded character of the trail.

Nearest Bike Shop
Gear West
Long Lake, MN
(612) 476-0093

A Picnic at Winstead Ride (10.7 miles)
After we got back from this relaxing little ride down to Winstead, Andrea and Mike told us that they often do that same ride on horseback, packing a picnic lunch for the quaint little town park in the center of Winstead. In general, the trail to Winstead is groomed well enough that you could take a hybrid or road bike on the trail. If you plan to extend this ride to the portion of the trail that picks up on the other side of Winstead, however, you'll need to be on a mountain bike.

Pt.-Pt.	Cume	Turn	Street/Landmark
0.0	0.0	R	Headed down the driveway from the bell, turn **right on Vega Ave.**
0.0	0.0	R	**Onto Luce Line Trail**
1.1	1.1	S	Cross County 33
1.5	2.6	S	Cross Yancey Ave.
0.5	3.1	S	Cross Zebra Ave.
0.7	3.8	S	Cross unmarked road
0.3	4.1	-	Trestle collapse site
0.6	4.7	R	Winstead Trailhead, **onto Kingsley St.**
0.1	4.8	-	Arthur Ave.
0.1	4.9	-	South Shore Dr. on right

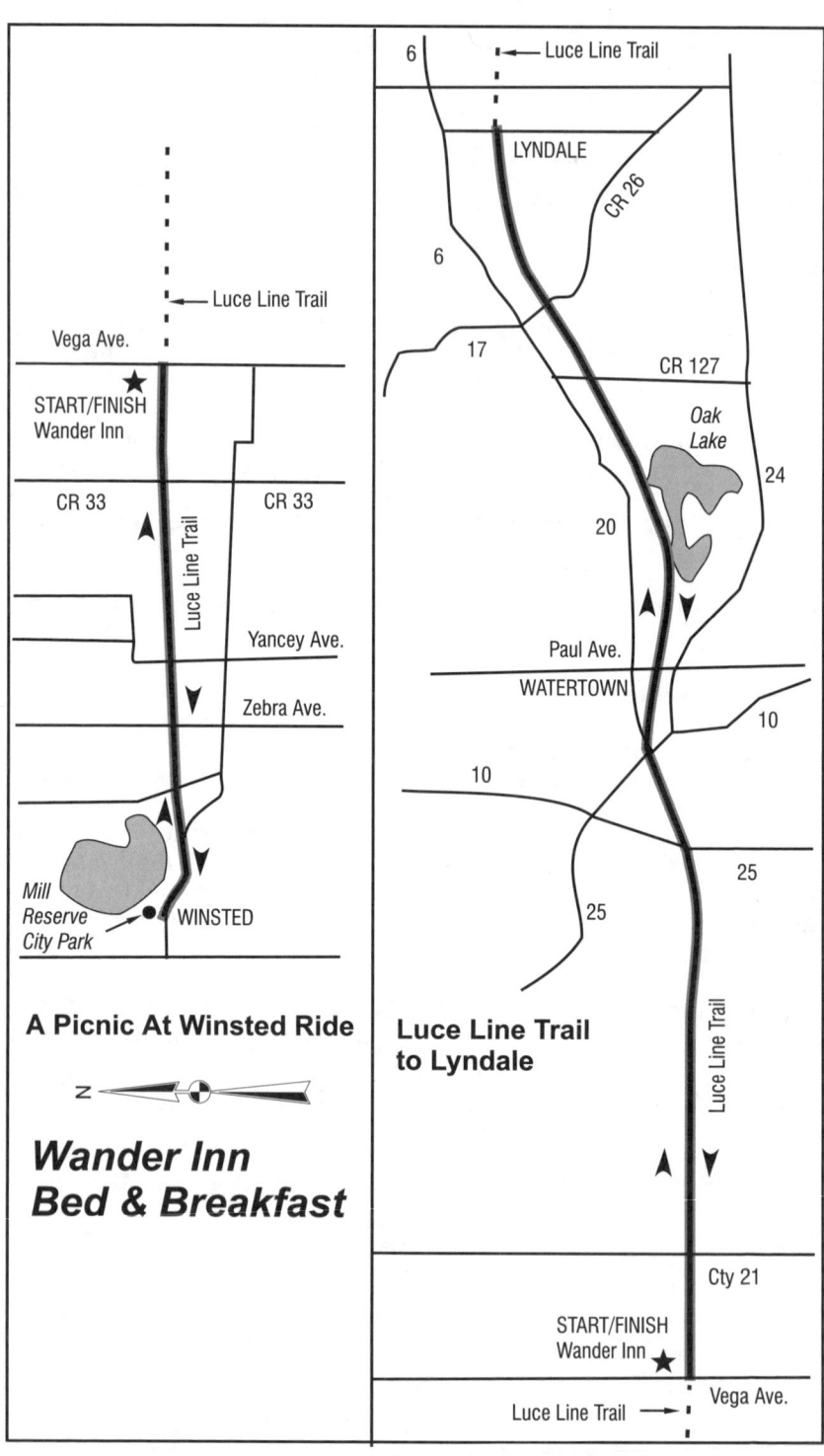

A Picnic At Winsted Ride

**Wander Inn
Bed & Breakfast**

**Luce Line Trail
to Lyndale**

Pt.-Pt.	Cume	Turn	Street/Landmark
0.0	4.9	-	Sherman Ave.
0.1	5.0	-	Rosalie Ave.
0.1	5.1	-	Lewis Ave.
0.1	5.2	L	**McLeod Ave.** (Kingsley St. ends)
0.0	5.2	R	**First St.**
0.1	5.3	TR	**Mill Reserve City Park** on lake; restrooms, picnic site
0.1	5.4	L	**McLeod Ave.**
0.0	5.4	R	**Kingsley St.** (McLeod Ave. ends)
0.1	5.5	-	Lewis Ave.
0.1	5.6	-	Rosalie Ave.
0.1	5.7	-	Sherman Ave.
0.0	5.7	-	South Shore Dr.
0.1	5.8	-	Arthur Ave
0.1	5.9	L	**Onto Luce Line Trail**
0.6	6.5	-	Trestle collapse site
0.3	6.8	S	Cross unmarked road
0.7	7.5	S	Cross Zebra Ave.
0.5	8.0	S	Cross Yancey Ave.
1.6	9.6	S	Cross County 33
1.1	10.7	L	**Vega Ave.**
0.0	10.7	L	**Wander Inn driveway**

Lyndale (23.2 miles)

This ride follows the trail east through Watertown to a turnaround point at Lyndale. Lyndale is one of those wide spots in the road that will be disappointing if you're looking for fast food or a strip mall, but otherwise is kind of comforting and quietly delightful. The Ox Yoke Inn is just up the road from the trailhead if you need a snack or other refreshments.

0.0	0.0	R	Headed down the driveway from the bell, turn **right onto Vega Ave.**
0.0	0.0	L	**Onto Luce Line Trail**
1.0	1.0	S	Cross County 21
3.5	4.5	S	Cross Hutchinson Rd.
0.1	4.6	-	Tunnel under Highway 25 (coming into Watertown)
0.3	4.9	S	Cross unnamed road (trail jogs a bit left as it crosses road)
0.3	5.2	S	Cross parking lot

Pt.-Pt.	Cume	Turn	Street/Landmark
0.1	5.3	**S**	Cross unnamed road (trail jogs a bit right and picks up into park)
0.1	5.4	**S**	Cross unnamed road
0.1	5.5	-	County Rd. 10 underpass
0.8	6.3	**S**	Cross Paul Ave.
0.8	7.1	-	Oak Lake
2.0	9.1	**S**	Cross County Rd. 127
0.1	9.2	**S**	Cross unnamed dirt road
0.5	9.7	**S**	Cross County Rd. 26
1.9	11.6	**TR**	**Lyndale Trailhead**
1.9	13.5	**S**	Cross County Rd. 26
0.5	14.0	**S**	Cross unnamed dirt road
0.1	14.1	**S**	Cross County Rd. 127
2.0	16.1	-	Oak Lake
0.8	16.9	**S**	Cross Paul Ave.
0.8	17.7	-	County Rd. 10 underpass
0.1	17.8	**S**	Cross unnamed road (and enter park)
0.1	17.9	**S**	Cross unnamed road (at exit of park)
0.1	18.0	**S**	Cross parking lot
0.3	18.3	**S**	Cross unnamed road (trail jogs a bit left as it crosses road)
0.3	18.6	-	Tunnel under Highway 25
0.1	18.7	**S**	Cross Hutchinson Rd.
3.5	22.2	**S**	Cross County 21
1.0	23.2	**R**	**Vega Ave.**
0.0	23.2	**L**	**Wander Inn driveway**

Wisconsin

Wisconsin boasts the first rails-to-trails conversions in the United States and one of the most bike-friendly cities as well. The state bike path system includes hundreds of miles of trails in all kinds of environments and topographies, and there are many well-paved but lightly-traveled country roads throughout the state.

Much of the riding was shaped by forces of nature thousands of years ago. If you visit the Hamilton House in Whitewater, the associated mountain bike riding through Kettle Moraine State Park is a little glacial geography lesson. If you ride in Governor Dodge State Park while visiting the Hill Street Bed and Breakfast, you can see what mountain biking is like on the other side of the glacial line; this is known as the "driftless area," a region untouched by the glaciers. You just might wish the glaciers would come back and smooth things out a little bit as you're pushing up some of the hills on the road ride around Frank Lloyd Wright's Taliesin. For yet another view of glacial topography, visit the Fargo Mansion Inn and the Glacial Drumlin Trail. A little further east and north, the Blacksmith Inn sits on a dolomite projection that split the glaciers and now stands out as a peninsula in Lake Michigan. The gentle rise and fall of the road ride and the sand and pine trail of Newport State Park hint that both the glaciers and the ridge gave a little bit when they met.

Not all of the Wisconsin riding is glacier-centric. The Arbor Inn in Madison is the starting point for a ride around several lakes and a spin in the country among the famous black and white cows. North of Madison, you'll find the Wisconsin River Valley and some of the most beautiful road riding in this book. The beauty of the rides is matched by the Victorian Treasure in Lodi, a perfect home base for these rides. The Strawberry Lace Inn in Sparta is on the Elroy-Sparta Trail, the rails-to-trails conversion that started it all, with its interesting history and three railroad tunnels. Further north, the St. Croix River Inn celebrates the river history of the region acting as home base for a mountain bike ride through the ancient river bottoms and the Gandy Dancer Trail, which takes you up though the north woods. For pure north woods exposure, the Lumberman Mansion Inn is an access point to hundreds of miles of mountain bike trails in the Chequamegon National Forest as well as a woodsy road ride. A little to the east, the Inn at Pinewood provides similar riding in the Nicolet National Forest.

If you travel as far north as Wisconsin goes, you'll end up on the shores of Lake Superior in Bayfield. The Old Rittenhouse Inn perches on a hillside overlooking the lake and an easy ride around Madeline Island, the largest of the Apostle Islands. Riding out of town behind the inn, you'll climb those hills all the way out and then coast all the way home on a wonderful one-hill roller coaster of a ride.

The excellent state bike trail system is partially supported by fees. You'll need trail passes to ride on the state trails and there are occasionally wardens out checking for passes. Seasonal passes can be purchased from the State Department of Natural Resources; visit www.dnr.state.wi.us/wiparks/fees/fees.html or call (608) 266-2181. Day passes can be purchased at trailheads and other local outlets.

For general tourist information you can contact the Wisconsin Department of Tourism at:

(800) 432-TRIP
http://travelwisconsin.com/

Arbor House—an Environmental Inn, Madison, Wisconsin

Arbor House, an Environmental Inn

John & Cathie Imes
3402 Monroe St.
Madison, WI 53711
Rates: Budget — Deluxe

Phone: (608) 238-2981
Fax: (608) 238-1175
Web: www.arbor-house.com

Built in 1853, the Arbor House has the distinction of being one of the oldest houses in Madison. John and Cathie have maintained the charm and character that a house acquires only after many years while adding additional space in the newly constructed annex in 1996. Old or new, the public spaces and guestrooms of Arbor House provide a serene and comfortable welcome to weary bikers.

The innkeepers set out to create an inn that supports sustainable tourism. From the site itself to many of the interior fittings and furnishings, the Imeses have focused on resource efficiency without sacrificing modern amenities and convenience. The newer annex features hardwood floors recycled from the old Sears Building in Chicago and massive recovered Douglas fir timbers in the great room. Bathroom tiles, natural stone fireplaces, and a host of other fixtures have also been given new life in both the annex and the original house. All of these elements have been carefully blended and lovingly restored to ensure that anywhere you cast your gaze, you'll find something to delight the eye.

Named for prominent Madisonian environmentalists, the three rooms in the annex all have luxury accommodations with whirlpools, stereos, and TVs and feature natural furnishings with much exposed wood and a relaxed, organic feel. The rooms in the main house are spread across three floors, offering a wide variety of options. Each has a distinct history and personality; some have a fireplace, others have a whirlpool—one even has a fish tank. The first floor Tap Room once served as a popular tavern when the historic Plough Inn operated on the same premises. The expansive Studio, a two-room suite, once housed the art studio of a University of Wisconsin-Madison art professor.

Breakfast mirrors the general ambiance of Arbor House, with a variety of healthy light options. A number of cereals including strawberry oatmeal and kashi are set out in jars along with juice, milk, and soymilk. English muffins and bagels sat on a sideboard along with some wonderful raspberry jelly. In addition to these continental breakfast fixings, we had a light scrambled egg dish with tomatoes and scallions added in and brioche with orange marmalade. The bagels, lox, and cream cheese that accompanied this main course were almost too beautiful to eat. In addition to this breakfast fare, some sweets are usually set out each evening in the main house. John claims Cathie's caramel corn is good enough to warrant a business all on its own.

A taste of the diverse entertainment in Madison is available within easy walking distance from the inn. Just down Monroe Street are cafés, bakeries, small shops, and a number of restaurants. Beyond Monroe Street, situated on the isthmus between Lakes Mendota and Monona, you'll find a beautiful town square with majestic shade trees framing the state capitol. On any summer Saturday morning you'll find a lively farmers market on the square, which also hosts other events such as bike races and an art fair. Connecting the square with the grounds of the University (or The UW as locals call it) is State Street, a stroller's delight which has something to offer most everyone.

If you're looking for a little more organic experience, Olbrich Botanical Gardens on the near-east side of town has a rich selection of both indoor and outdoor gardens. You might also want to stroll down past the University's Memorial Union to the path that runs out along Lake Mendota towards Picnic Point. Bikes are allowed on the path and out on Picnic Point as well. The richest outdoor experience is just across the street from the Arbor Inn: the University Arboretum. The lake route described below takes you on the only roads that allow bikes, but there are a number of footpaths running through the arboretum, which are well worth exploring. If you feel like a long hike, find the connector to the South Arboretum and explore even further.

When it's suppertime, Madison presents a host of options. We've heard it said that Madison has the most restaurants per capita of any town in the U.S. (We've also heard the same thing about bookstores). The Arbor Inn maintains an extensive list of restaurants ranging from indigenous beer and brats all the way to escargot. One of our personal favorites is La Paella, a Spanish restaurant on the south side of town run by Tomas Ballesta cooking authentic cuisine from his homeland. If you're after pasta, there's none better in town than Pasta Per Tutti on the near-east side. If you're in the mood for diner food, Monty's Blue Plate Diner is just down the street from Pasta Per Tutti. Housed in a renovated gas station, the home-style menu—and especially the Oreo milkshakes—will satisfy any hunger. Campy southwestern décor, gourmet southwestern cuisine, and a great list of margaritas will entertain and satisfy at the Eldorado just east of downtown.

Rides from Arbor House
We'd originally decided not to include any larger towns in this guide on the theory that real biking vacations don't involve cities. Madison, Wisconsin, and Rochester, Minnesota, changed our minds on that account. Madison has a number of bike paths running through the city and despite its size (300,000+ in the metropolitan area), it's relatively simple to hop on your bike, get out of town, and be riding country lanes lined

by those famous Wisconsin Oreo cows showing off their black and white markings. Other cycling destinations in or near town include Picnic Point and the Military Ridge State Trail.

Terrain: The Lake Monona Ride is almost flat. There are a few hills here and there, but all of the riding is pretty recreational. The Paoli ride has a little more up and down to it, but is still not an alpine ride. The variations in altitude provide interest rather than dread.

Road Conditions: The trails in town are well maintained and smooth. Where the Lake Monona Ride passes through Madison on city streets you'll find some rougher pavement here and there, but nothing that can't be navigated. The roads on the Paoli Ride are in good shape and will allow for unconcerned high-speed cruising if you so desire.

Traffic: The Lake Monona Ride is through the heart of town so some caution when on the roads is advised, though Madison drivers are used to seeing cyclists on this route. The city bike path past the Monona Convention Center is one of the city's most popular and is shared with walkers, joggers, and rollerbladers. All in all, the in-town ride is more recreational just because the route requires a slower pace. As for the Paoli Ride, once across McKee Road on the way to Paoli, traffic is hardly an issue. Seminole Highway has an excellent surface and well-marked bike lanes to get you to that point.

Best Time to Ride: Our personal favorite time is in late September and early October. The temperature is right and the colors set off against the lakes can be quite spectacular. July and August can get a bit hot, though rarely for long stretches of time.

Nearest Bike Shop
Budget Bicycle
1230 Regent Street
Madison, WI 53706
(608) 251-8413

The Lake Monona Ride (22 miles)
The Lake Monona Ride takes a combination of city bike paths and neighborhood streets around the second-largest of four lakes in the Madison area. In going from the inn to the lake you'll also ride through the University Arboretum and through Vilas Park on the way back for a good sampling of some of Madison's best scenery.

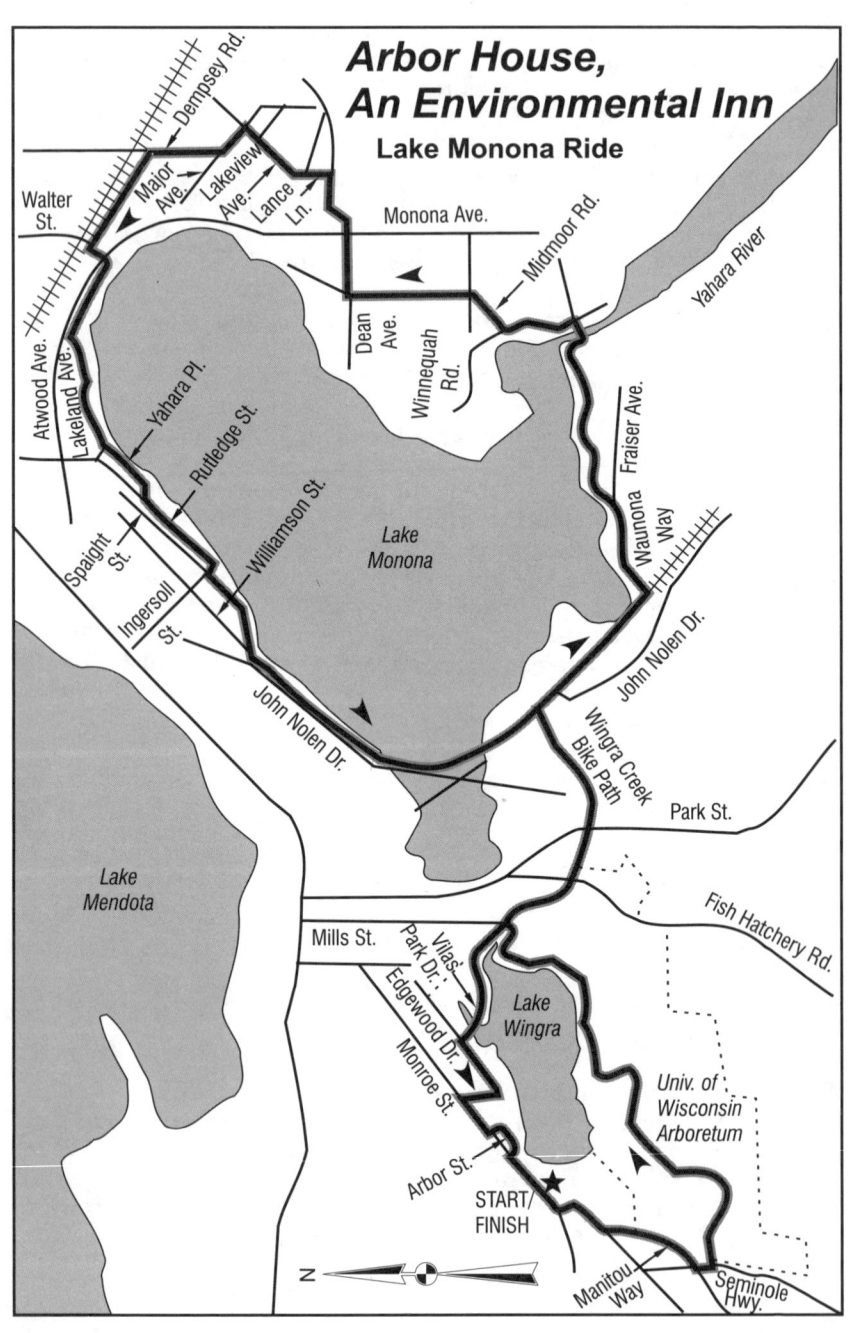

Arbor House,
An Environmental Inn
Lake Monona Ride

Walter St.

Dempsey Rd.

Major Ave.

Lakeview Ave.

Lance Ln.

Monona Ave.

Midmoor Rd.

Yahara River

Atwood Ave.

Lakeland Ave.

Dean Ave.

Winnequah Rd.

Yahara Pl.

Rutledge St.

Williamson St.

Lake Monona

Fraiser Ave.

Waunona Way

John Nolen Dr.

Spaight St.

Ingersoll St.

John Nolen Dr.

Wingra Creek Bike Path

Park St.

Lake Mendota

Fish Hatchery Rd.

Mills St.

Vilas Park Dr.

Edgewood Dr.

Lake Wingra

Monroe St.

Univ. of Wisconsin Arboretum

Arbor St.

START/ FINISH

N

Manitou Way

Seminole Hwy.

PtPt.	Cume	Turn	Street/Landmark
0.0	0.0	**R**	Across Monroe Street from inn on sidewalk at stoplight. (**Turn right after crossing street**)
0.4	0.4	**L**	**Manitou Way**
0.2	0.6	**S**	Cross Mandan Crescent
0.1	0.7	**S**	Cross Tumalo Tr.
0.3	1.0	**S**	Cross Iroquois Dr.
0.0	1.0	**L**	**Seminole Highway**
0.0	1.0	**L**	**University Arboretum**
0.8	1.8	**L**	**Onto paved walking path**
0.0	1.8	**S**	Walking path almost immediately rejoins road from right
1.1	2.9	-	Covall to right
1.1	4.0	**R**	Exit arboretum and **turn right onto city bike trail**
0.6	4.6	**S**	Stop light at Fish Hatchery Rd., go straight across **on trail**
0.3	4.9	**S**	Stop light at Park St., go straight across and **continue on trail**
0.1	5.0	**S**	Cross Beld St.
0.0	5.0	-	Train tracks
0.5	5.5	**S**	Trail ends, cross Olin Ave. and **continue on Colby St.**
0.1	5.6	**R**	**Van Dueson**
0.1	5.7	**R**	**City bike trail** (in middle of road curving to left)
0.2	5.9	**R**	**Olin-Turville Ct.**
0.2	6.1	**R**	**Stub of city bike trail up to an intersection**
0.0	6.1	**S**	Cross Olin Ave.
0.4	6.5	**S**	Cross Rimrock Rd.
0.4	6.9	-	Railroad tracks; trail ends at a cul de sac of Waunona Way
0.3	7.2	-	Greenleaf St.
0.3	7.5	-	Ester Beach Rd.
0.0	7.5	-	Woodley Rd.
0.0	7.5	**BL**	**Winona Way** goes left, Fraiser goes to right
0.3	7.8	-	Raywood
0.1	7.9	-	Fayette
0.2	8.1	**S**	Hoboken (There's a dead end sign on Waunona, ignore it and continue straight)
0.3	8.4	**S**	Cul de sac with bike path starting up at far end
0.2	8.6	-	Blind turn to the right, go slow

Pt.-Pt.	Cume	Turn	Street/Landmark
0.1	8.7	L	**Cross bridge** over Yahara Waterway on side walk
0.1	8.8	L	**Sidewalk curves around to left and Winaqua Rd.** Follow it to first driveway and then cross to get on right side of road.
0.4	9.2	-	Frost Woods Rd.
0.0	9.2	R	**Allen Rd.**
0.1	9.3	L	**Midmoor Rd.**
0.1	9.4	-	Moygara Rd.
0.1	9.5	-	Panther Tr.
0.3	9.8	S	Cross Nichols Rd.
0.2	10.0	-	Greenway Rd.
0.2	10.2	R	**Dean Ave.**
0.2	10.4	-	Schoefield Rd.
0.1	10.5	-	Wallace Rd.
0.0	10.5	-	Gordon Ave.
0.0	10.5	S	Cross Monona Ave.
0.2	10.7	-	Tyre Ave.
0.2	10.9	L	**Lance Lane**
0.1	11.0	L	**Lakeview Ave.**
0.1	11.1	-	Coldspring
0.1	11.2	-	Dean Ave.
0.1	11.3	S	Cross Buckeye Rd.
0.2	11.5	L	**Major Ave.**
0.1	11.6	R	**Davies St.**
0.1	11.7	-	Drexel Ave.
0.1	11.8	BL	**Dempsey Rd.,** (not the hard left onto Mayer Ave.)
0.2	12.0	-	Park Ct.
0.0	12.0	-	Davidson St.
0.1	12.1	S	Cross Cottage Grove Rd.
0.1	12.2	L	Just across railroad tracks turn **onto city bike path**
0.6	12.8	-	Cross Margaret St.; **trail jogs to left across railroad tracks and then continues on to the right**
0.1	12.9	L	**Walter St.**
0.1	13.0	-	Johns Street
0.1	13.1	-	Cross Atwood Ave. at stoplight and **pick up trail (on sidewalk) to right**
0.3	13.4	-	Cross bridge and trail curves left away from road
0.2	13.6	L	Climb hill on dead end street to **Welch Ave.**
0.1	13.7	L	**Lakeland Ave.**

Pt.-Pt.	Cume	Turn	Street/Landmark
0.1	13.8	-	Elm St.
0.1	13.9	-	Miller Ave.
0.1	14.0	**BL**	**Stay on Lakeland Ave.** to left, Hudson Ave. goes right
0.1	14.1	-	Schiller Ct.
0.1	14.2	**L**	**Dining St.**
0.0	14.2	**R**	**Yahara Pl.**
0.4	14.6	**R**	**Riverside Dr.**
0.0	14.6	**L**	**Rutledge St.**
0.1	14.7	-	Thorton Ave.
0.1	14.8	-	Rogers St.
0.1	14.9	-	Dickenson St.
0.1	15.0	-	Baldwin St.
0.1	15.1	-	Ortin Ct.
0.0	15.1	-	Few St.
0.2	15.3	**R**	**Ingersol St.**
0.1	15.4	**L**	**Spaight St.**
0.1	15.5	-	Brearly St.
0.1	15.6	-	Patterson St.
0.1	15.7	**L**	**Jennifer St.**
0.1	15.8	**L**	**Bike path picks up on sidewalk** before crossing Williamson St.
0.2	16.0	**BL**	**Path curves left at stop light** of John Nolan Dr.
0.4	16.4	-	Monona Convention Center
1.3	17.7	**S**	Path empties onto **Olin-Turville Ct.**
0.1	17.8	**R**	**Wingra Creek Bike Path** under John Nolan
0.2	18.0	**L**	**Van Dueson**
0.1	18.1	**L**	**Colby St.**
0.1	18.2	-	Cross Olin Ave.; **path picks up to left** across Olin
0.5	18.7	**S**	Cross railroad and Beld St.
0.1	18.8	**S**	Cross Park St.
0.3	19.1	**S**	Cross Fish Hatchery Rd.
0.6	19.7	**S**	Cross Arboretum Rd., continue straight on path
0.2	19.9	**S**	Path empties onto **Vilas Park Dr.** and the **Vilas Zoo**
0.6	20.5	**L**	Just across small bridge turn **left onto Edgewood Dr.**
0.4	20.9	**R**	**Woodrow St.**
0.1	21.0	-	Entrance to Edgewood College
0.2	21.2	**L**	**Onto Monroe St. sidewalk**

Pt.-Pt.	Cume	Turn	Street/Landmark
0.0	21.2	-	Terry Pl.
0.1	21.3	**L**	**Bike path picks up through park to left at bottom of hill**
0.1	21.4	**S**	Path empties into **Arbor St.** cul de sac
0.1	21.5	**S**	Cross Knickerbocker St.
0.2	21.7	**L**	**Path picks up to left** as Arbor curves to right
0.3	22.0	-	**Arbor House**

The Paoli Ride (27.2 miles)

If the Lake Monona ride is almost completely urban, the Paoli ride is just the opposite. There are two climbs out of the city, and once you pass the second one as you cross McKee Road at just short of three miles, you're in the country. You'll skirt a few neighborhoods as you ride near Verona, but the rest of the ride—even through the little village of Paoli at the far point of the ride—looks, feels, and sounds like a day in the country.

Pt.-Pt.	Cume	Turn	Street/Landmark
0.0	0.0	**R**	Across Monroe St. from inn on sidewalk at stoplight. **(Turn right after crossing street)**
0.0	0.0	**BL**	**Path veers to left,** sidewalk goes straight
0.3	0.3	**L**	**Manitou Way**
0.3	0.6	-	Mandan Crescent
0.1	0.7	-	Tumalo Tr.
0.3	1.0	-	Iroquois Dr.
0.0	1.0	**L**	**Seminole Highway**
0.0	1.0	-	Arboretum Entrance
0.1	1.1	-	Wanetah Tr.
0.1	1.2	-	Winslow Ln./Mohawk Dr.
0.1	1.3	-	Beverly Rd.
0.0	1.3	-	Doncaster Dr.
0.1	1.4	-	Warwick Way
0.0	1.4	**S**	Cross Beltline Frontage Rd.; entrance to South Arboretum is diagonally across the road
0.1	1.5	-	Lumley Rd.
0.1	1.6	-	Sheffield Rd.
0.0	1.6	-	Milford Rd.
0.1	1.7	-	Windflower Way
0.1	1.8	-	Lilac Ln.
0.0	1.8	-	Daisy Dr.
0.1	1.9	-	Clover Court
0.1	2.0	-	Sentinel Pass
0.3	2.3	-	Capital City Trail

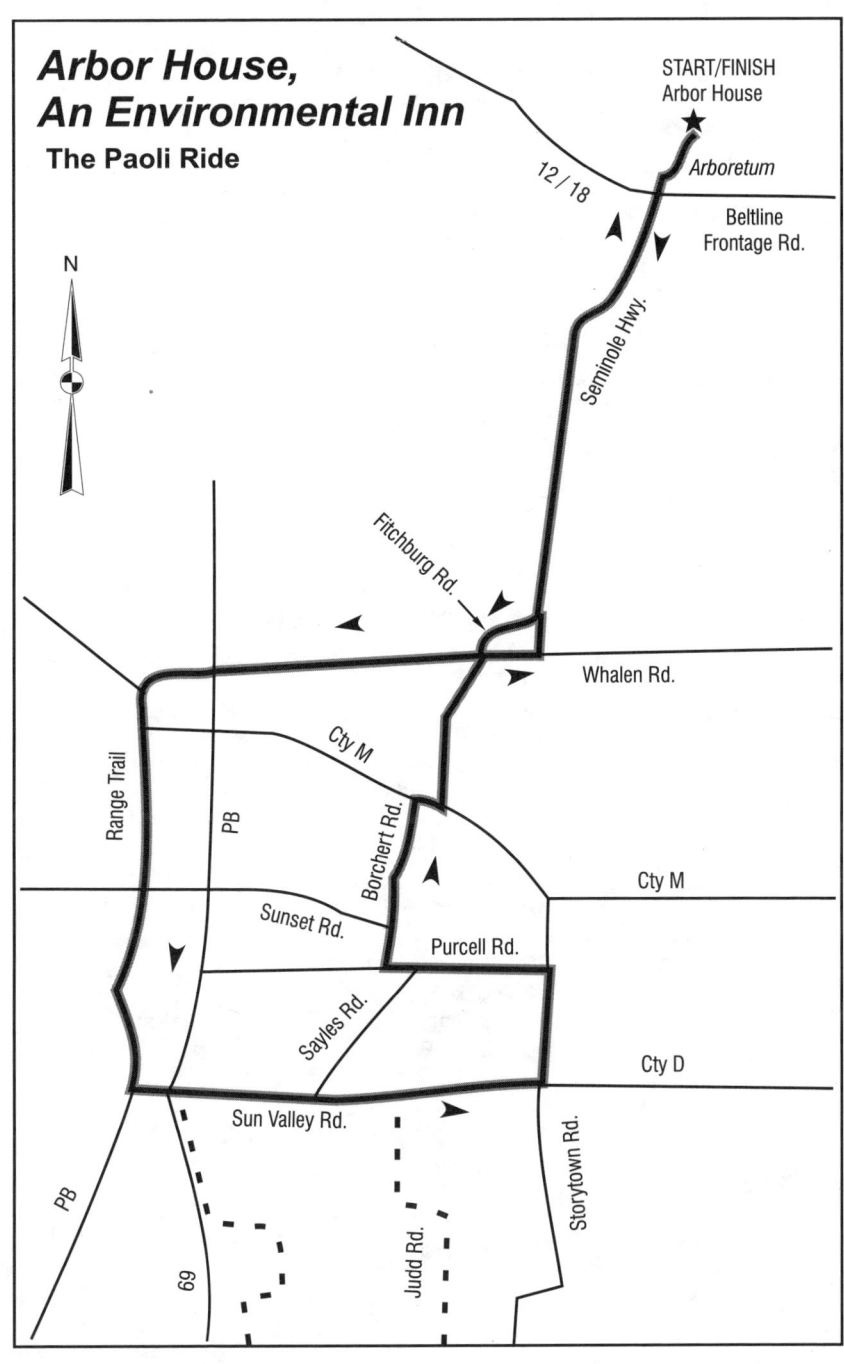

Arbor House,
An Environmental Inn
The Paoli Ride

N

START/FINISH
Arbor House

Arboretum

Beltline
Frontage Rd.

12 / 18

Seminole Hwy.

Fitchburg Rd.

Whalen Rd.

Cty M

Range Trail

PB

Borchert Rd.

Cty M

Sunset Rd.

Purcell Rd.

Sayles Rd.

Cty D

Sun Valley Rd.

Storytown Rd.

PB

69

Judd Rd.

Pt.-Pt.	Cume	Turn	Street/Landmark
0.5	2.8	-	Croix Dr.
0.1	2.9	**S**	Cross McKee Rd.
0.1	3.0	-	Seminole Central Court
0.3	3.3	-	Schumann Dr.
0.7	4.0	**R**	**Lacy Rd.**
0.0	4.0	-	Train tracks
1.3	5.3	**L**	**Fitchrona Rd.**
0.0	5.3	-	Pheasant Ln.
0.3	5.6	-	Tonto Tr.
0.5	6.1	-	Grandview Dr.
0.6	6.7	**R**	**Whalen Rd.**
1.4	8.1	**S**	Cross Old PB
0.5	8.6	-	Harvest Ln.
0.1	8.7	-	Fairview Tr.
0.1	8.8	-	Eastview Rd.
0.1	8.9	**L**	**County M**
0.4	9.3	**R**	**Range Trail**
1.5	10.8	**S**	Cross Sunset Drive
1.6	12.4	**L**	**County PB;** we're in **Paoli**
0.2	12.6	**S**	County PB turns left, go **straight on Sun Valley Rd.**
1.1	13.7	-	Sayles Rd.
0.8	14.5	-	Judd Rd.
0.2	14.7	-	Ravenoaks Tr.
0.2	14.9	-	Hampton Hills Rd.
0.1	15.0	-	Conamarra Rd.
0.5	15.5	-	HobbyHorse Tr.
0.2	15.7	-	Pinon Tr.
0.2	15.9	**L**	**Storytown Rd.**
0.8	16.7	-	Arbor Rd.
0.2	16.9	**BL**	Storytown becomes **Purcell Rd.**
0.2	17.1	-	Blizzard Rd.
1.1	18.2	-	Sayles Rd. (followed by train tracks)
0.2	18.4	**R**	**Borchert Rd.**
0.4	18.8	-	Sunset Dr.
0.8	19.6	**R**	**County M**
0.3	19.9	**L**	**Fitchburg Rd.**
0.4	20.3	-	Adams Rd.
1.1	21.4	**R**	**Whalen Rd.**
0.4	21.8	**L**	**Seminole Highway**
0.3	22.1	-	Vroman Rd.
1.2	23.3	-	Lacy Rd.

PtPt.	Cume	Turn	Street/Landmark
0.6	23.9	-	Schumann Dr.
0.2	24.1	-	Seminole Court
0.2	24.3	S	Cross McKee Rd.
0.1	24.4	-	Croix Dr.
0.5	24.9	-	Capital City Trail
0.3	25.2	-	Sentinel Pass
0.1	25.3	-	Clover Court
0.1	25.4	-	Daisy Dr.
0.0	25.4	-	Lilac Ln.
0.1	25.5	-	Windflower Way
0.1	25.6	-	Milford Rd.
0.0	25.6	-	Sheffield Rd.
0.1	25.7	-	Lumley Rd.
0.1	25.8	S	Cross Beltline Frontage Rd.; entrance to South Arboretum is diagonally across the road
0.0	25.8	-	Warwick Way
0.1	25.9	-	Doncaster Dr.
0.0	25.9	-	Beverly Rd.
0.1	26.0	-	Winslow Ln./Mohawk Dr.
0.1	26.1	-	Wanetah Tr.
0.1	26.2	-	Arboretum entrance
0.0	26.2	R	**Manitou Way**
0.0	26.2	-	Iroquois Dr.
0.3	26.5	-	Tumalo Tr.
0.1	26.6	-	Mandan Crescent
0.3	26.9	R	**Turn onto sidewalk along Nakoma Dr.**
0.2	27.1	BR	**Path leaves Nakoma Dr.**
0.1	27.2		Across Monroe Street from **inn** on sidewalk at stoplight.

The Blacksmith Inn, Baileys Harbor, Wisconsin

The Blacksmith Inn

Bryan Nelson & Joan Holliday
8152 Highway 57
P.O. Box 220
Baileys Harbor, WI 54202
Rates: Deluxe

Phone: (920) 839-9222
(800) 769-8619
Fax: (920) 839-9356
Email: relax@theblacksmithinn.com
Web: www.theblacksmithinn.com

From the time it was first used as a safe harbor for a cargo ship, Baileys Harbor has been a working town. This practical ambience carries through to The Blacksmith Inn, where you'll find all of the comfort but none of the high formality of a historic Victorian establishment. The Inn is a 1912 stovewood and timber structure built by August Zahn to house his family on the shores of Lake Michigan. Zahn was a working blacksmith and his shop, built in 1905, is still in operation as part of the inn.

Lest images of heavy industry spring to mind, rest assured this Inn has the comfortable feeling of a fine lodge. In several of the rooms you'll find exposed beams and see the ends of stovewood emerging from stuccoed walls. Quilts, antique furniture, and other historical pieces also contribute to the ambiance of an earlier era. Expertly blended into the period decorations are all the modern conveniences, including private baths with whirlpools, CD/cassette stereos, gas fireplaces, and air conditioning.

Complementing the rustic yet polished interior are the spectacular natural resources just out the back door. The room rates rise with every flight of stairs as you get better and better lake views the higher you climb. The inn provides both a kayak and a sailboat for the more nautically inclined, or perhaps you'll just want to sit on the spacious decks which adorn every floor and watch the birds float on the lake breezes. The inn also has 400 feet of sandy beach. A short walk up the road is the Ridges Sanctuary, a wildflower preserve that draws a variety of small wildlife as well. If you're after more man-made entertainment, golfing, horseback riding, charter fishing, shopping, and dining are either a short walk or drive away.

Bryan and Joan serve as excellent hosts, available to provide local information and history, but never intruding. This light touch carries over to morning repast, which is an expanded continental breakfast set out for guests to serve themselves and perhaps carry out onto the deck to enjoy lakeside.

Bryan is a good resource for the abundant local biking opportunities. We've included one road ride and one mountain bike ride as samples, but there are a number of other rides available and Bryan will be happy to talk to you about them. The area hosts a century ride each fall (which brings faithful riders back to the Blacksmith each year) as well as a metric century in mid-June. In addition to the mountain biking at Newport Beach State Park, the Peninsula State Park across the peninsula also has some excellent trails.

All this is set in the middle of a small northern Door County town that is reminiscent of an old seaside resort. Northern Door County, especially the interior and Lake Michigan shore, has a rural feeling without being remote. Every road is different and offers surprises like a little gem of a farm or village tucked around the next corner. There are three lighthouses, including Cana Island, near Baileys Harbor, along with two designated Wisconsin Rustic Roads.

Northern Door County starts at Sturgeon Bay. If you follow Highway 42 up the bayside you'll find the traditional pleasures of a vacation destination, including a blend of craft and specialty shops, antique stores, and a number of unique dining experiences. Al Johnson's Swedish Restaurant, for example, has the best in Swedish fare served up under a real sod roof complete with grazing goats. More traditional fine dining is available in villages along the way. Peninsula State Park offers some wonderful high bluff views of the bay.

The Lake Michigan side provides a more rural experience, with cherry orchards and dairy herds scattered among the small villages, shops, and eating establishments. Highway 57 breaks off from Highway 42 just north of Sturgeon Bay and cuts across to Jacksonport, Baileys Harbor, and other lakeside destinations like the Whitefish Dunes State Park before it rejoins Highway 42 near the tip of the peninsula. Both Whitefish Dunes and Newport State Park provide ample Lake Michigan access and views.

Rides from the Blacksmith Inn
In addition to this road ride and mountain bike ride there are plenty of other opportunities, including mountain biking in Peninsula State Park on the bayside and a great deal of road riding as well.

Terrain: While there are some long assents when leaving the coast (lakeside or bayside), none are extremely steep—and the land always pays back. Portions of the rides along the shore will give occasional lake vistas through the trees, and inland dairy farms and apple and cherry orchards make for pleasant riding scenery.

Road Conditions: The roads are in good condition. These are mainly backcountry roads without shoulders or bike lanes, but portions are well-marked bike routes.

Traffic: The roads on the Over Niagra Falls route are all country roads and will have less traffic. During high tourist season (June-August) be careful crossing Route 57. If you take the optional longer ride to Ephraim be very careful on Route 42. It is very heavily traveled in season.

Best Time to Ride: The weather will be most hospitable from mid-May to mid-September. On the other hand, orchards may blossom a bit earlier (depending on the weather), and the fall foliage reaches it peak in late September or early October. Door County earned the moniker "New England of the Midwest" on the strength of its colorful fall leaves.

Nearest Bike Shop
Nor-Dor Sport & Cyclery
4007 Highway 42
Fish Creek, WI
(920) 868-2275

Over Niagra Falls (19.2 miles)
This road ride isn't nearly as tumultuous as the name implies, but you will ride over the same dolomite ridges that a little further to the east form Niagara Falls. The ride takes you from the Lake Michigan side almost over to the Green Bay (the bay, not the city) side. It's uphill most of the way out and downhill most of the way back, with farms and orchards providing a pleasing backdrop. If you go in May you will also have the pleasure of seeing the orchards in bloom. In July or early August, you can stop at one of the you-pick cherry orchards for a mid-ride pick-me-up.

Pt.-Pt.	Cume	Turn	Street/Landmark
			From the Blacksmith Inn
0.0	0.0	**R**	**Rt. 57**
0.5	0.5	**R**	**County Rd. Q**
0.9	1.4	**BR**	**Stay on Q** at unmarked fork
2.1	3.5	-	Small beach with view of Baileys Harbor
0.1	3.6	-	Moonlight Bay Dr. on right
0.3	3.9	-	Old Logging Terrace
0.1	4.0	-	Rustic Road 38 (Cana Island Rd.) on right
0.2	4.2	-	Cana Island Rd. on right
0.9	5.1	-	Birch Dr. on left
0.6	5.7	-	Pine Dr. on right
0.3	6.0	-	Goodnow Rd.
0.1	6.1	-	Sunset
0.3	6.4	-	North Bay Dr. on right

Pt.-Pt.	Cume	Turn	Street/Landmark
1.2	7.6	-	North Bay Dr. on right
0.3	7.9	-	Winding Ln.
0.5	8.4	-	Mueller Ln. on left
0.4	8.8	-	Mueller Ln. on left
0.6	9.4	**S**	Cross Woodcrest Rd. (gravel to left)
0.5	9.9	-	Orchard Dr. to right
0.5	10.4	**S**	Cross Rt. 57 (potentially busy intersection)
1.1	11.5	**L**	**Town Line Rd.** (going straight leads you to Ephraim in about a mile with Peninsula State Park just beyond). Town Line Rd. becomes **Sumac** somewhere before mile 14.2.
0.3	11.8	-	German Rd.
0.7	12.5	-	Pioneer Rd.
0.5	13.0	-	Lime Kiln Rd. to left
0.6	13.6	-	Unmarked road to left
0.6	14.2	**R**	**Meadow**
0.6	14.8	**BL**	Gravel road to right
0.4	15.2	-	Unmarked road on right
1.2	16.4	-	Cedar Rd. on left
0.2	16.6	**L**	**Maple Grove Rd./County F** (Not marked but major road)
0.1	16.7	-	Triangle Road on right
0.4	17.1	**BL**	Highland Rd. to right
0.2	17.3	-	Schultz Lane on left
1.0	18.3	**L**	**County EE/F** (F turns left and merges with EE which comes in from right)
0.2	18.5	-	Juniper Ridge Rd. on right
0.5	19.0	**L**	**Park Rd.**
0.2	19.2	**L**	**Highway 57**
0.0	19.2	-	**Blacksmith Inn**

Newport State Park

On the site of the now defunct village of Newport, Newport State Park has over 28 miles of woodland trails with 15 of those miles open to mountain bikers. These trails are somewhere between forest service roads and true singletrack, so a mountain bike is the best equipment. A hybrid or cross bike might survive the roots and rock outcroppings but will leave you walking through soft sand at points on the trails. Riding on state park trails requires a trail pass available at the park office (a daily pass is $3.00; $10.00 for a season pass). The Park is about 20 minutes north of The Blacksmith Inn and we recommend you drive due to potential heavy traffic on Highways 57 and 42. To reach the trailhead, follow these cues:

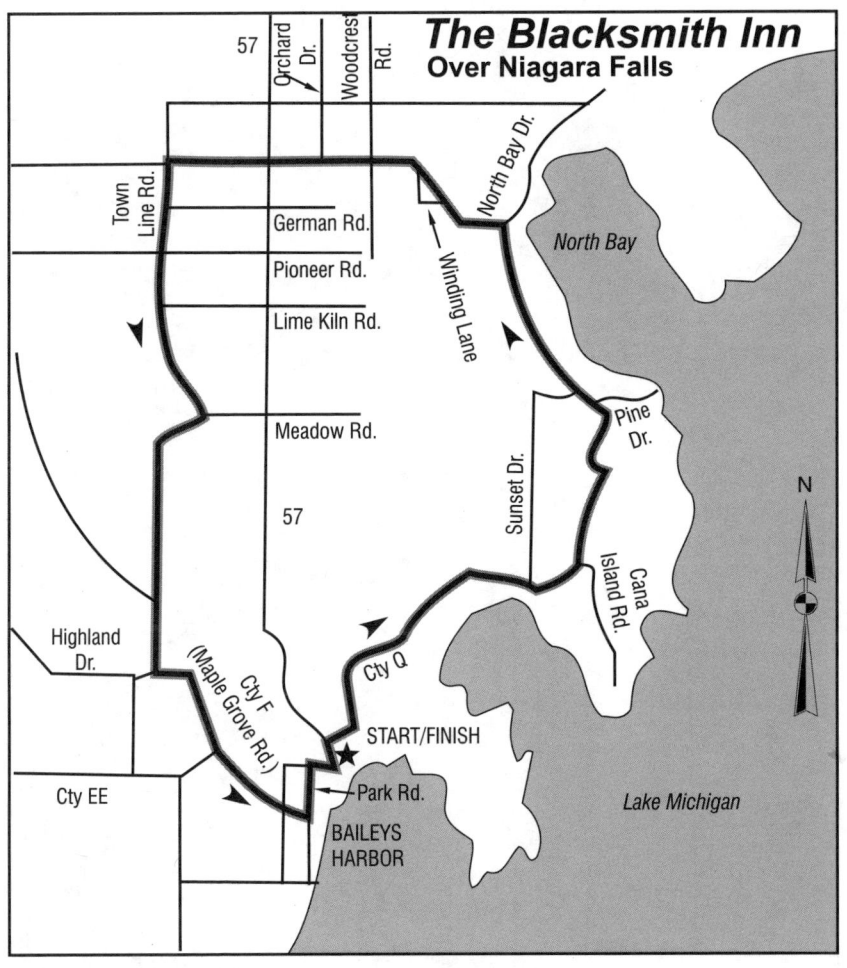

The Blacksmith Inn
Over Niagara Falls

57
Orchard Dr.
Woodcrest Rd.
North Bay Dr.
Town Line Rd.
German Rd.
Pioneer Rd.
Lime Kiln Rd.
Winding Lane
North Bay
Meadow Rd.
57
Sunset Dr.
Pine Dr.
Cana Island Rd.
N
Highland Dr.
Cty F (Maple Grove Rd.)
Cty Q
START/FINISH
Cty EE
Park Rd.
BAILEYS HARBOR
Lake Michigan

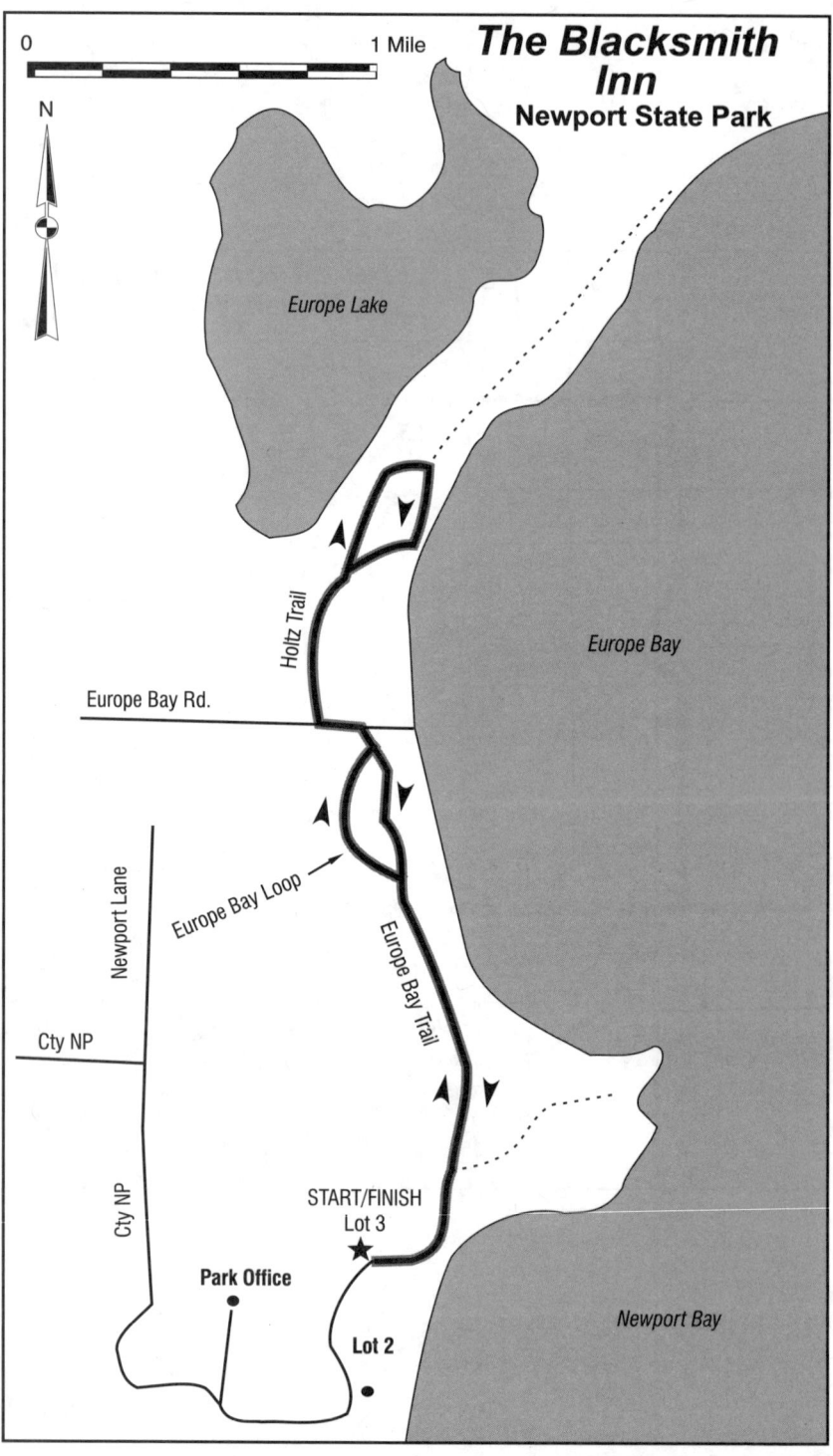

Pt.-Pt.	Cume	Turn	Street/Landmark
			From the Blacksmith Inn
0.0	0.0	R	**Rt. 57**
8.6	8.6	R	**Rt. 42** (Rt. 57 ends)
0.4	9.0	-	Look out for the goats on the roof of Al Johnson's Swedish restaurant.
5.1	14.1	-	Town of Ellison Bay
2.3	16.4	R	**County NP**
1.1	17.5	-	Sharp left turn!
1.0	18.5	-	Timberline Rd. on left
0.4	18.9	BR	While apparently a "T" intersection, **NP continues right** and Newport Lane goes off to left
0.6	19.5	-	**State Park entrance**
0.4	19.9	-	**Park Office** to left
0.7	20.6	-	**Lot 3**—ride starts from here

Fern Corners Ride (6.5 miles)

This out-and-back ride on the Europe Bay and Holtz Trails has a little bit of everything except water, from sand to rocks and roots to hills. With the exception of the first tenth of a mile, the entire ride is through the woods with Lake Michigan or Europe Bay occasionally sparkling between the trees. While not extremely technical, the trail will require your attention. While it takes about 50 minutes to ride the 6.2 miles, we took over an hour as we had to stop to admire the lake views, ferns and other flora, and one snake that was sunning himself beside the trail. There are two loops in the middle of this out and back ride. The cue sheet goes left at these opportunities both out and back in order to give the maximum diversity.

			From Lot 3 to Europe Bay and Newport trail markers
0.0	0.0	S	**Europe Bay Trail**
0.1	0.1	-	Beach sand!
0.1	0.2	-	Linde Point Trail (hiking only)
0.2	0.4	-	Bike camping site
0.2	0.6	-	Fern Trail to left, Linde Point to right (both hiking only)
0.5	1.1	L	**Beginning of Europe Bay Loop**
0.5	1.6	-	Europe Bay loop rejoins trail from right
0.2	1.8	L	**Europe Bay Rd.** (end of Europe Bay trail)
0.1	1.9	R	**Holtz Trailhead** (watch for rocks/roots going through gate)

PtPt.	Cume	Turn	Street/Landmark
0.2	2.1	**BL**	**Onto Holtz Trail loop** (beware of the false trail which is a hard left)
0.3	2.4	-	Foot trail to lake and hand pump with water fountain
0.1	2.5	**R**	Trails going straight and left are footpaths only. **Turn right and go down hill**
0.0	2.5+	-	Other half of Holtz Trail loop comes back in from right; we'll visit this on the way back
0.7	3.2	**TA**	Hiking only trail to right, **turn around and head back**
0.7	3.9	**L**	**Onto Holtz Trail loop** (*note:* this is a different portion of the loop than the one you rode on the way in)
0.1	4.0	**R**	Hiking-only trail goes straight. This grove of ferns gave this ride its name.
0.2	4.2	**BL**	Other portion of Holtz Trail loop comes in from right
0.3	4.5	**L**	**Europe Bay Rd.** (End of Holtz trail)
0.1	4.6	**R**	**Europe Bay Trail**
0.1	4.7	**L**	Other side of **Europe Bay loop**
0.6	5.3	**BL**	End of loop
1.0	6.3	-	Out of woods, into sand
0.2	6.5	-	**End of Fern Corners ride**

Fargo Mansion Inn

Barry Luce & Tom Boycks
406 Mulberry St.   Phone: (920) 648-3654
Lake Mills, WI 53551   Web: www.innsite.com/inns/A000065.html
Rates: Budget — Deluxe

In the second half of the 19th century Lake Mills was a mecca for wealthy vacationers riding the trains up from Chicago. The trains don't run to Lake Mills from Chicago anymore. Instead, the Glacial Drumlin State Bicycle Trail follows the old train lines. The trail, along with other recreational opportunities such as Rock Lake, keeps the resort atmosphere alive in Lake Mills. An older town than the nearby state capitol, Madison, it has not grown the way Madison has and retains a country village charm. From the large park with a bandstand in the center of town to small businesses and cafes lining the main street, Lake Mills feels instantly familiar and comfortable.

In 1836, Joseph Keyes began construction of two mills—on land which was probably not his—near the shores of what is now Rock Lake. Fortunately for today's travelers, the Fargo brothers came to town a few years later and made their fortunes, building their houses on land they owned along Mulberry Street. While you may not be able to find the original mills, E.J. Fargo's home is still standing as the Fargo Mansion Inn.

Many gables and rooflines rise above the Queen Anne-style inn's broad wraparound porch. If you choose to arrive by horse-drawn coach, pull under the porte-cochere and dismount to a set of steps that starts at carriage level so the ladies will not have to sully their petticoats (which should probably be removed anyway before a long bike ride). The inn has one of the grandest entryways we've seen in a bed and breakfast, rising through all three stories of the corner tower and showcasing a stunning oak staircase. As the staircase seemingly floats up through the open space of the tower, it beckons the traveler to the guestrooms on the second and third floors.

When we visited the inn there were five rooms on the second floor with a few more under construction on the third floor. The eleven-foot ceilings that seem standard on the first floors of many Victorian houses were carried through to the mansion's second floor. The size of the rooms seems to be calculated to match the height of the ceilings. All the rooms have private baths—two have a Jacuzzi.

The E.J. Fargo room is the mansion's equivalent of the presidential suite. The main area is dominated by an 8½-foot antique bed set off by floor-to-ceiling windows overlooking the grounds. There's also a marble fireplace, a sitting room, and a private balcony. Don't be dismayed if you can't find the bathroom at first. Behind a bookcase lies marble tile, a Jacuzzi, and an oversized shower, creating a room more akin to a Sybaritic bath than a simple bathroom. Though not quite as extravagant in its square footage, the Eljia Harvey room has many of the same fine appointments.

One could be tempted to spend the entire visit on the second floor. But aside from missing some pleasant bike rides, you'd also miss the enchanting first floor. Every room—and there are several—seems to realize one preconception or another of Victorian luxury. In the library, tucked away behind the staircase, you can almost hear the murmured voices of the gentlemen wrapped in the smoke of fine cigars. The dining room, the sitting room, and the music room all hint at stories of their own. The rich exposed trim, the fine wood inlays, and the polished antiques are all part of an atmosphere of comfort and beauty that we'd like to experience again and again. If your imagination needs a little jump-start, ask to see some of the pictures taken in and around the house by its original occupants.

Breakfast lives up to the surroundings. It is usually served in the Music Room, which fills up with morning light. The courses start off with baked goods, coffee, tea, and juice. Gourmet interpretations of eggs and other breakfast favorites follow, served on antique china with real silver. Tom and Barry have several different sets so check out your place setting from day to day. Our breakfast finished off with delicious sweets. All in all, you'll be well prepared for a day of riding or other activities.

Rides from the Fargo Mansion Inn

Each of these loops mix road and trail riding. Both include portions of the Glacial Drumlin Trail, which follows the old train lines that brought vacationers to the area from Chicago over a century ago.

Terrain: The countryside around Lake Mills is some of the most fertile farmland in the U.S. Whether riding on the roads or the Glacial Drumlin Trail, you'll be gazed at by cows as you cross gently rolling terrain smoothed thousands of years ago for your riding pleasure by the retreating glacier.

Road Conditions: The roads are in good condition. In Dane County the roads have a well-marked, paved, and generous shoulder. In Jefferson County (Lake Mills) the roads do not have a marked shoulder, but are in good condition. The Glacial Drumlin Trail is packed crushed limestone. It was easily navigable with our tandem road bike and should present no problems for either hybrids or mountain bikes.

Traffic: County B and BB west of Lake Mills are used only for local travel (an interstate covers the same territory just a few miles north). Traffic is generally light, though the speed limit is 55 mph. On the Glacial Drumlin Trail, motorized vehicles are prohibited, though you meet a mix of cyclists, joggers, and walkers.

Best Time to Ride: Any time from May to October will have its share of nice riding weather. August can get a little steamy, but provides the best local sweet corn as a tradeoff. There are a number of special events both in Lake Mills and on the Glacial Drumlin Trail including a moonlight trail ride, usually under June's full moon.

Fargo Mansion Inn, Lake Mills, Wisconsin

Nearest Bike Shop: There is no bike shop in Lake Mills, but Tom and Barry can direct you to local service stations for flats. Budget Bicycle (one of our sponsors) in Madison is about a half-hour away.

Budget Bicycle
1230 Regent Street
Madison, WI 53706
(608) 251-8413

Glacial Drumlin – West (35 miles)

This road and trail ride is a loop running through the trailhead in Cottage Grove. On the road ride to Cottage Grove you pass dairy farms and cornfields the whole way. By and large the cows are as friendly as the terrain. While there are a number of hills, they tend not to be too long or too steep. We shifted into our lowest gear range only twice. At Cottage Grove you get on the Glacial Drumlin Trail and head back east, passing through Deerfield on the way. The trail is on an old railroad bed so you'll never have a grade steeper than 3%. Be careful where the trail crosses roads out in the country—visibility is not always the best.

Pt.-Pt.	Cume	Turn	Street/Landmark
			From the Fargo Mansion Inn
0.0	0.0	**R**	**Mulberry St.**
0.0+	0.0+	-	Washington St.
0.1	0.1	-	Oak St.
0.1	0.2	**R**	**Madison**
0.1	0.3	**S**	Cross intersection with Main St.; continue on **Madison**
0.1	0.4	-	Church St. on left
0.0	0.4	-	College St. on left
0.1	0.5	-	Freemont
0.1	0.6	-	Margarite St.
0.0	0.6	-	Pleasant St.
0.1	0.7	-	Prospect St.
0.1	0.8	-	Pine St.
0.0	0.8	-	Highland Rd.
0.0	1.0	-	Shore Acres on left
0.1	1.1	-	County V on right; Main turns into **County Route B**
0.2	1.3	-	Baid Ln.
0.0	1.3	-	Rock Lake on left
0.4	1.7	-	Rock Lake Rd.
0.2	1.9	-	Lakeview Ln.
0.0	1.9	-	Delores Lane on left
0.4	2.3	-	Shorewood Hills Rd.
0.9	3.2	-	Newville Rd.
0.3	3.5	-	County Route S
1.3	4.8	-	Kreoughville Rd.
0.6	5.4	-	Stoney Creek Rd.
0.9	6.3	-	County Rt. O; **as the road crosses this intersection, Rt. B becomes Rt. BB**
1.6	7.9	-	Goose Lake Wildlife Refuge

Pt.-Pt.	Cume	Turn	Street/Landmark
0.6	8.5	-	Kreuger Rd.
0.2	8.7	-	Missouri Rd.
0.9	9.6	-	Rod and Gun Rd.
0.2	9.8	**S**	Cross Highway 73 *(use caution);* continue on County BB
1.3	11.1	-	Gotzion Ln.
0.4	11.5	-	Oak Park Rd.
0.2	11.7	-	Smith Dr.
0.6	12.3	-	Wire Ln.
0.4	12.7	-	Wagner Rd.

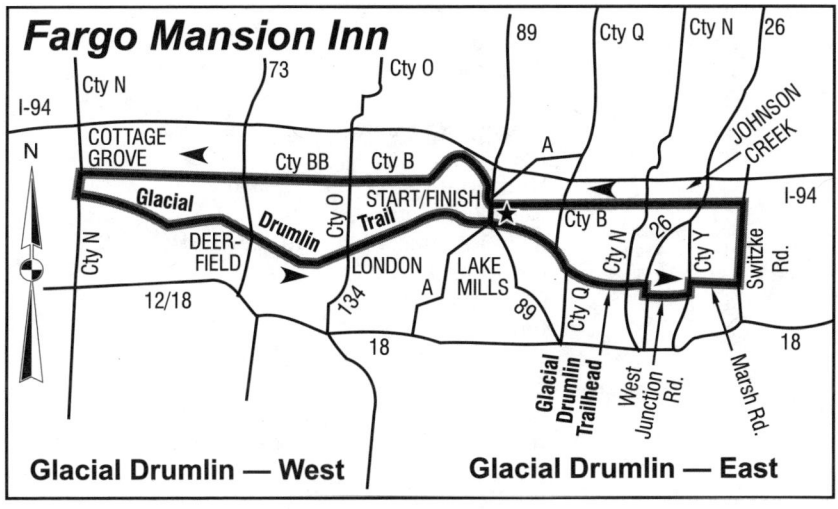

1.3	14.0	-	Ridge Rd. on left
0.5	14.5	-	Rathert Rd.
0.7	15.2	-	Baxter Rd.
0.1	15.3	-	American Way on left
0.4	15.7	-	Kennedy Dr.
0.5	16.2	-	Meyer Rd.
0.4	16.6	-	Oak St.
0.2	16.8	**L**	**County Rt. N**
0.3	17.1	-	Vista Dr.
0.4	17.5	**L**	**Glacial Drumlin Trail**, just past railroad tracks
0.5	18.0	-	Unmarked road

Pt.-Pt.	Cume	Turn	Street/Landmark
1.3	19.3	S	Cross Koshgenon Bridge and stop at Ridge Rd. *Caution:* blind intersection. Stop and listen for traffic before proceeding straight.
1.9	21.2	-	Dvorak Rd. following a bridge
0.5	21.7	-	Driveway
0.8	22.5	-	Oak Park Rd.
0.9	23.4	-	Tractor crossing
0.6	24.0	-	Zechner Rd.
0.4	24.4	S	Trail comes out on **Rt. 73**. Town of Deerfield; water, shelter
0.2	24.6	-	Unmarked road
0.9	25.5	-	Tractor crossing
0.4	25.9	-	London Rd.
0.5	26.4	-	Prairie Rd.
1.3	27.7	-	Spur Dr.
0.2	27.9	-	Unmarked road
0.1	28.0	-	County Route O
1.9	29.9	-	Farm crossing
0.5	30.4	-	Unmarked road
1.9	32.3	-	Rock Lake on right
1.1	33.4	L	At Lake Mills Trailhead, **turn left on 89** (will turn into **Main St.**)
0.1	33.5	-	Columbus Rd.
0.1	33.6	-	Pinnacle
0.2	33.8	-	Tyrenna Golf Course on right
0.1	33.9	-	Catlin Dr.
0.1	34.0	-	Lake Park Rd.
0.5	34.5	-	Water St. followed by Lake St. and Commons Park on right
0.1	34.6	R	**Madison St.**
0.1	34.7	L	**Mulberry St.**
0.1	34.8	-	Oak St.
0.1	34.9	-	Washington St.
0.1	35.0		**Fargo Mansion Inn**

Glacial Drumlin East (24.3 miles)

0.1	0.0	L	**Turn left on Mulberry** out of Fargo Mansion Inn
0.1	0.1	-	Washington
0.1	0.2	-	Oak St.
0.1	0.3	R	**Madison St.**

Pt.-Pt.	Cume	Turn	Street/Landmark
0.1	0.4	**L**	**Main St.**
0.1	0.5	-	Water St. followed by Lake St. and Commons Park on right
0.5	1.0	-	Lake Park Rd.
0.1	1.1	-	Catlin Dr.
0.2	1.2	-	Tyrenna Golf Course on right
0.1	1.4	-	Pinnacle
0.1	1.5	-	Columbus Rd.
0.1	1.6	**L**	**Glacial Drumlin Trailhead**
0.5	2.1	**R**	**Right at fork**; left branch goes to Atzalan Park
1.5	3.6	**S**	Cross Harvey Rd.
0.6	4.2	**S**	Cross Mansfield Rd.
0.4	4.6	**S**	Cross County Q
1.0	5.6	**S**	Cross Popp Rd.
1.7	7.3	**S**	Cross County N
0.5	7.8	**BR**	Rt. 26 on bridge over trail; **trail curves right** immediately after bridge
0.3	8.1	**L**	**West Junction Rd.;** trail ends
0.7	8.8	-	Road to granary to left and railroad tracks
0.0	8.8	-	North Dewey Rd. to right
1.1	9.9	**L**	**County Y**
0.2	10.1	**R**	**Marsh Rd.**
0.8	10.9	**S**	Cross Christberg Rd.; trail picks up to right, but stay on **Marsh Rd.**
1.0	11.9	**L**	**Switzke Rd.**
1.0	12.9	-	Krenze Rd. to right
2.0	14.9	**L**	**County B**
0.4	15.3	-	Christberg Rd.
0.6	15.9	-	Spring Rd.
0.1	16.0	-	Hunter's Glenn Dr.
0.2	16.2	-	Wright Rd.
0.1	16.3	-	Deer Crossing Rd. (in Johnson Creek, County B is **Milwaukee St.** in town)
0.1	16.4	**S**	Cross Highway 26
0.1	16.5	-	Grell Ln.
0.1	16.6	-	South St.
0.1	16.7	**S**	Cross South Watertown
0.1	16.8	-	Depot St. followed by rail bridge
0.0	16.8	**L**	**Union Street** (traffic from left doesn't stop)
0.1	16.9	-	Atzalan St.
0.0	16.9	-	Jefferson St.
1.0	17.9	-	Boat landing on left

Pt.-Pt.	Cume	Turn	Street/Landmark
0.6	18.5	-	County N to right
0.1	18.6	-	County N to left
0.4	19.0	-	Seigmenn Rd.
1.0	20.0	-	Pirkel Ln.
0.6	20.6	-	Ziebell Rd.
0.8	21.4	-	County Q
0.2	21.6	-	Gomoll Rd.
0.6	22.2	-	Wollin Rd./Harvey Rd.
0.2	22.4	-	County D
0.2	22.6	-	Harold St.
0.2	22.8	-	Industrial Rd., East Mills Drive
0.3	23.1	-	Wakeman
0.2	23.3	-	CP Ave.
0.1	23.4	-	Ashland Ave.
0.2	23.6	-	Grove St.
0.1	23.7	-	Owen St.
0.0	23.7	-	Washington
0.1	23.8	-	Oak St.
0.1	23.9	**R**	**Madison St.**
0.1	24.0	**R**	**Mulberry St.**
0.1	24.1	-	Oak St.
0.1	24.2	-	Washington St.
0.1	24.3	-	**Fargo Mansion Inn**

Hamilton House Bed and Breakfast

Claudia Anderson
328 West Main St.
Whitewater, WI 53190
Rates: Budget – Moderate

Phone: (414) 473-1900

E-mail: hamhouse@idcnet.com

If you're especially impressed with the mountain biking in the Kettle Moraine State Forest, it may be because the trails took about 90,000 years to construct and then had to be aged for another 10,000 years before they were open to the general public. The topography of the state forest was shaped by four distinct periods of glacial activity starting about 100,000 years ago. As the glaciers melted, gargantuan rivers laid down silt, gravel, and even gigantic boulders, forming the long ridges known as moraines.

In addition to the moraines, the trails of the forest lead by or through a number of other glacial features including deep kettles. The kettles were formed when huge chunks of glacial ice were buried and then slowly melted, leaving deep, steep-sided bowls in the landscape. Eventually, ice was replaced by seemingly endless oak savannas until settlement once again began to reshape the landscape. The Kettle Moraine State Forest has the largest oak savanna still in existence in Wisconsin.

The Hamilton House Bed and Breakfast, listed on the National Register of Historic Places, is a relative newcomer on the scene when compared with the geological features of the state forest. Nonetheless, at almost 140 years old, it has had time to settle into its surroundings comfortably. Built in the Second Empire style with mansard rooflines and intricately detailed Queen Anne porches, the house is a solid, upstanding member of the community.

Inside, the rich detailing includes ornate woodwork, massive pocket doors, and high rounded windows. Within this Victorian structure, Claudia Anderson has brought her interpretation of Renaissance flair to the interior decoration. Each of the four rooms on the second floor is named after a Renaissance figure. The King Henry VIII Chamber Room is the most luxurious, with a fireplace, sitting area, and private bath. The William Shakespeare room includes a fourposter cherry bed, a fireplace, and three-sided bay window. It shares a double whirlpool bath with the Queen Katherine of Aragon room. The Queen Elizabeth I Amber room, decorated in ivory and gold, is tucked up under slanting rooflines. With an original built-in bookshelf and a private whirlpool bath, the combined effect is a cozy space. The morning of our stay, Claudia served a traditional hearty egg and bratwurst breakfast. Complemented by coffee and juice, breakfast is served by candlelight.

Whitewater is the site of the University of Wisconsin-Whitewater, and also a center for the surrounding farming communities. Whitewater has a long agricultural heritage, having been founded in 1837 with a Hamilton family listed among the early settlers. In addition to the various offerings at the University, Whitewater is home to the Fireside Dinner Theatre and is within easy reach of rich antique shopping at either Cambridge or Milton.

Rides from Hamilton House Bed and Breakfast

The Southern Unit of Kettle Moraine State Forest contains two sets of mountain bike trails: The John Muir Trails and the Emma Carlin Trails. Spread out over the geological and topographical footprints left by glaciers, both sets of trails provide interesting rides. You will need trail passes which can be purchased at local bike shops, and you will also need to pay for parking, which can be done at the parking areas. Trail maps are sometimes available at the trailhead and at many local establishments. As mentioned in the state introduction, you can purchase both park permits and trail passes in advance from the Wisconsin Department of Natural Resources.

Terrain: Carved by the passage of the glaciers, there are many ups and downs on these rides. You will most likely use every gear you have in every range. Most of the trails are packed dirt. However, on the John Muir Green Trail, there is one extended section of beach-like sand, left as a special favor by the glaciers.

Trail Conditions: Given that we're talking forest trails here, trail conditions vary with the weather. Some portions of the trail pass through deep shade, so even after several bright sunny days you may find some mud here and there. Overall, the trails are well maintained with erosion control pads and good signage.

Traffic: Weekdays the trails can be almost empty, but on weekends or summer weekday evenings you'll be sharing the trails with many enthusiasts.

Best Time to Ride: The John Muir Trails can get quite busy on weekends during the summer, with riders from Madison, Milwaukee, and Chicago. If you can catch these trails during the week you'll encounter less traffic. Or you can just go over to the Emma Carlin Trail and its connector to the John Muir trails. These rides are significantly more difficult and as a result are much less congested. On both sets of trails, the routes are mostly one-way, making congestion less of an issue. The rides in from the trailheads and the connector between John Muir and Emma Carlin (five beautiful—if very hilly—miles) are two-way sections. If you ride in mid- to late summer be sure to bring insect repellant.

Nearest Bike Shop
LaGrange General Store
Highway 12 and H
LaGrange, Wisconsin
(414) 495-8600
Rental bikes, provides minor repairs, and also trail passes.

The John Muir Orange Trail (5.3 miles)
The John Muir mountain bike trails are some of the most popular in Southern Wisconsin. The trails range in difficulty from a short ride in the park, so to speak, to fairly difficult trails that will challenge even the most experienced hill climber. Though the trails do overlap, you'll have to ride over twenty-five miles to ride all combinations. If you choose to, you'll sleep well that night but may be a bit stiff and sore the next morning. A word of warning: These trails seem to make bikes feisty. On one occasion, one of us found himself being chased through the woods by his own bike for several paces before it ran him over and continued off into the bush. Interesting trails, these.

To drive to the John Muir Trails, leave the Hamilton House headed east on Route 12/Main Street. After 7.7 miles, turn left onto County H in the town of LaGrange. Follow H for 1.5 miles and turn left into the John Muir Trails parking lot.

Pt.-Pt.	Cume	Turn	Street/Landmark
0.0	0.0		At the John Muir Map Board
<0.1	0.0	**L**	**T in trail**
0.4	0.4	**L**	**Left following the White Trail**
0.5	0.9	-	Fast downhill followed by hard right
1.9	2.8	**S**	**White Trail** continues straight, Blue Trail goes left
<0.1	2.8	**S**	**Onto Orange Trail** straight up hill, White Trail goes right
0.1	2.9	**BR**	Blue Trail comes in from left, **Orange continues right**
0.5	3.4	-	Long downhill with turns; *maintain control*
0.7	4.1	**R**	**Orange Trail turns right,** Blue/Green to left

Pt.-Pt.	Cume	Turn	Street/Landmark
0.2	4.3	**R**	**Intersection with doubletrack**
0.5	4.8	**BL**	Red/White rejoin from right after long uphill
0.2	5.0	**R**	**T intersection** with Blue/Green. Watch for fast traffic from left
0.3	5.3	**L**	**Turn left to John Muir Map Board**

The Emma Carlin Green Trail (4.0 miles)

This is easily the most difficult—some might even say extreme—set of publicly-maintained trails in Southern Wisconsin. If you are looking for a challenge, the Emma Carlin green trail is it: steep twisting climbs, boulder fields, and flying downhills punctuated with tree-induced turns. It's only four miles long if you do the loop, but it's easily twice as difficult as anything John Muir has to offer. To reach Emma Carlin from the John Muir Trails, follow these cues:

0.0	0.0	**L**	Leaving John Muir parking lot
5.5	5.5	**S**	**County H joins SR 59** coming in from left
1.4	6.9	**S**	County H goes left; continue on **SR 59**
1.0	7.9	**R**	**County Z**
0.7	8.6	**R**	**Parking lot for Emma Carlin Trails**

The Emma Carlin Green Trail Cue Sheet

0.0	0.0		Emma Carlin ride board
0.2	0.2	**SR**	Four-way intersection, turn hard right
0.3	0.5	**L**	**T intersection**
0.4	0.9	**R**	**Green goes right**, Red/Orange go left
0.8	1.7	**L**	**Green goes left;** John Muir Connector goes straight
0.8	2.5	-	Monstrous curvy downhill, *be careful*
0.6	3.1	**S**	**Continue straight** as Orange trail comes in from left
0.3	3.4	-	Rocky section ahead
0.4	3.8	**R**	Back **at four-way intersection** and path to trailhead
0.2	4.0	-	**Emma Carlin ride board**

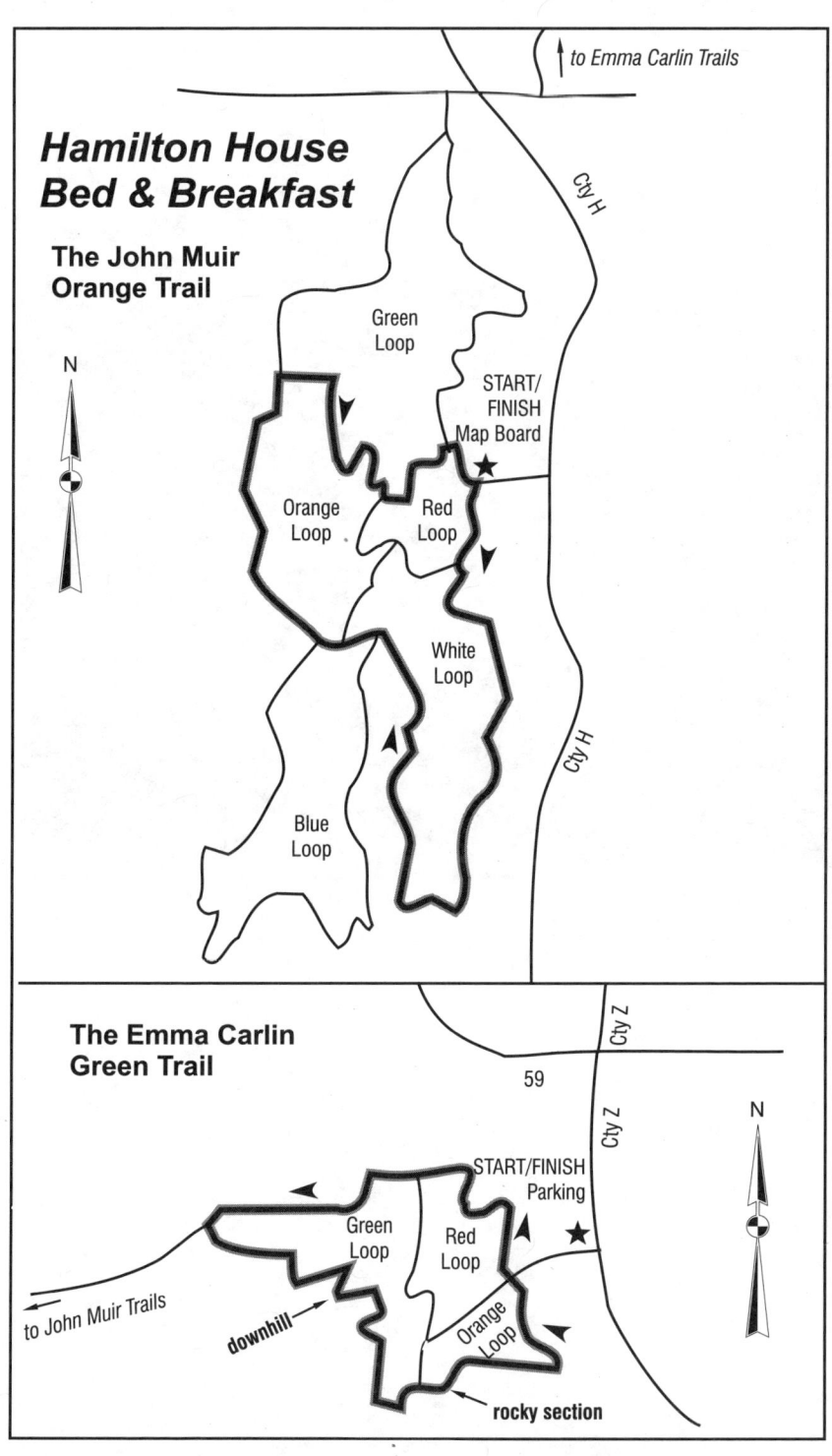

The Hill Street Bed and Breakfast, Spring Green, Wisconsin

The Hill Street Bed and Breakfast

Kelly & Jay Phelps   **Phone: (608) 588-7751**
353 W. Hill St.
Spring Green, WI 53588   **E-mail: hillstbb@execpc.com**
Rates: Budget   **Web: www.hillstreetbb.com**

Don't be surprised if you find yourself thinking of Garrison Keillor or Thornton Wilder when you first visit The Hill Street Bed and Breakfast in Spring Green, Wisconsin. It does seem as if everything in this sweet little town really is above average. That trend probably started several thousand years ago when the last glaciers to visit the region pulled up short of this part of the state, leaving it with some of the most beautiful and diverse topography in the Midwest. It gathered strength when noted architect Frank Lloyd Wright returned to his boyhood neighborhood to set up his professional studio and residence, Taliesin. That above-average ambience is carried forward today by the high number of artists residing in the area, the American Players Theatre, and any number of other area attractions and activities.

Just a few easy-to-walk blocks from downtown you'll find The Hill Street Bed and Breakfast, a Queen Ann Victorian built in 1904 for Thomas Hill, Senior. The building itself welcomes you in off the sidewalk with a broad porch well-stocked with comfortable wicker furniture. It seems to present a standing invitation to come in, sit down, relax, and enjoy. Innkeepers Kelly and Jay Phelps deliver on that promise from the moment you step through the door until you push back from the breakfast table for the last time, utterly satisfied.

Inside, the high ceilings and open doorways on the first floor provide a perfect backdrop for the beautiful woodwork, including several intricate examples of carpenter's lace in the doorway to the parlor and living room. There are four guestrooms on the second floor, one off the living room on the main floor, and two recently-added guestrooms off a common room on the lower level.

The Harry Gray Room is the showcase of the inn. Across from the top of a rich wooden staircase, it takes advantage of the mandatory Queen Anne turret to provide a comfortable sitting nook off the room itself. This is the largest guestroom and seems full of light on sunny days. It has a queen bed and a private bath (shower only).

The Wright Room is a delightfully eccentric room tucked under the eaves across the back end of the second floor. Spreading out in three directions, it has three twin beds and a private bath. The Bossard and Kanouse Rooms off the upstairs hallway complete the second floor. Both have queen beds (with a pullout couch in the Kanouse) and share a bath.

The Hill Room is a spacious guestroom on the main floor with a beautifully-appointed tiled private bathroom. The recently updated Green and the Rose Rooms on the lower level are modern constructions done in the Victorian idiom. Both have queen beds with private baths.

Kelly and Jay do an admirable job of making their guests comfortable, whether serving cookies and tea in the afternoon or sharing their knowledge of the area's arts scene. They are ably assisted by Sparky, Tigger, and Roo, the family cats, who are more than willing to share their deep understanding of getting comfortable.

Jay puts on a scrumptious breakfast. We shared the breakfast table with a delightful extended family up for the weekend from Chicago. We all "oohed" and "ahhed" over the several courses, culminating in a French toast which made all moan with delight. Suffice it to say that cyclists' engines will be well stoked for a day of riding. For early risers, coffee is available before the full breakfast spread.

Even the most hardcore riders will be tempted by other activities and sites in and around Spring Green. Most notable is Taliesin, the lovingly preserved estate of Frank Lloyd Wright, which provides several structural examples of his work as well as a wealth of information about both the man and his architectural legacy at the visitor's center. A summer art fair and fall art tour provide access to local artists in residence, and the American Players Theatre provides delightful open-air Shakespeare through the summer and into the fall. There are several other art fairs and tours throughout the summer and fall. Other activities include a championship golf course, canoeing on the Wisconsin River, and several nearby state parks.

For a town its size, Spring Green provides several good dining options. The Post House is the oldest continuously-operating restaurant in the state and serves up traditional American cuisine with a strong Wisconsin rural flavor. You won't go away hungry. Around the corner from the Post House is a place called the General Store. It provides café-style dining among arts and crafts with a hip menu that includes vegetarian options and spicy choices. Jay and Kelly can point you to a number of other restaurants within an easy drive.

Rides from The Hill Street Bed and Breakfast

In addition to the rides documented below, there are any number of routes one can choose on the country roads in and around Spring Green. The Spring Green Traveler (http://www.execpc.com/~spring) contains maps of several rides, as well as a wide variety of local information.

Terrain: The most telling fact about this terrain is that it does not have a history of being scrubbed by the glaciers. Consequently, both the road ride around Spring Green and the mountain bike ride at Governor Dodge State Park have some significant changes in elevation. The upside of the ups is that you do get some spectacular views of the Wisconsin River Valley and the areas surrounding the State Park.

Road Conditions: The Taliesin Tour is all on paved roads with one short, packed gravel exception (Limmex Hill Road). After an opening stretch on Highway 23, most of the ride is on country roads that are relatively well maintained. They do not have shoulders, and sometimes sight lines are not extensive, but we never felt in danger.

Traffic: Highway 23 is a main artery between Dodgeville and Spring Green and experiences relatively heavy traffic for being as rural as it is. The good news is that it has generous shoulders. The only other place traffic might be of concern is in the middle of the ride for a 1.7-mile stretch on County 130. In practice, however, this road is not heavily traveled and has very good sight lines after the first curve or two.

Best Time to Ride: In May or June, expect balmy weather (assuming it's not raining), with hotter temperatures later in the summer. If you do go earlier in the summer for the mountain biking, check with the State Park first (608/935-2315) as to the conditions of the trails. They can get a bit muddy from the spring rains. This area is one of our regular routes in the fall because of the beautiful color prominent here.

Nearest Bike Shop: While there are some rentals available, there is not a full-service bike shop available in Spring Green. Among other options, Budget Bicycle is a full-service shop located in Madison, about 45 minutes away.

Budget Bicycle
1230 Regent Street
Madison, WI 53706
(608) 251-8413

Governor Dodge State Park (6.8 miles)

The 500 acres that make up the park are a prime example of the "Driftless Area" left untouched by the glaciers, with sandstone bluffs that are almost 500 million years old. Governor Dodge State Park offers several variations on the ride documented below as well as connection to the 39 miles of the Military Ridge State Bicycle Trail. This ride starts out with a steep climb and then runs through meadows, along ridges above wooded valleys, and finally descends to ride along the shoreline of Twin Valley

Lake. You'll find a variety of surfaces from loose gravel to packed dirt to sandy singletrack. Be aware that parts of this trail are shared with both hikers and horses.

The park does have an entrance fee ($5/day for state residents, $7 for non-residents) and a trail pass requirement ($3/day). To get to the park from the Hill Street Inn, follow these cues:

Pt.-Pt.	Cume	Turn	Street/Landmark
0.0	0.0	-	Hill St. East
0.0	0.0	R	**Cincinnati St.**
0.1	0.1	L	**Daley St.**
0.4	0.5	R	**Winstead/Rt. 23**
13.8	14.3	L	**Governor Dodge State Park Rd.**
0.2	14.5	-	Park offices
0.1	14.6	-	Trail crossing
0.0	14.7	R	**To Cox Hollow Lake and Meadow Valley Trailhead**
1.9	16.6	-	Access to Cox Hollow Lake on right
0.5	17.1	BR	Road to left, but **head right up to parking**
0.1	17.2	-	Cox Hollow Lake and Dam
0.1	17.3	-	**Back of parking lot**

Governor Dodge State Park Cue Sheet

0.0	0.0	-	From back corner of parking lot opposite restrooms and lake, heading uphill on **Meadow Valley Trail**
0.1	0.1	S	Trail leads onto pavement, **go straight**
0.1	0.2	S	Pavement goes left, go **straight onto trail**
0.4	0.6	BR	As another trail comes in from left
0.1	0.7	L	Four-way intersection of trails; **left up hill**
0.1	0.8	S	Cross unnamed road; **trail picks up on other side**
0.1	0.9	BR	As another trail comes in from left
0.6	1.5	S	Turning right onto the Goldmine Trail shortens this ride by about 2 miles; cue sheet is for longer ride
0.0	1.5	R	**Trail forks, go right**
0.2	1.7	BR	Right as the **trail curves right** there's a footpath to the left. Leads to a nice overlook across a small valley
0.1	1.8	S	**Go straight.** There is a trail off to the left to Wellspring

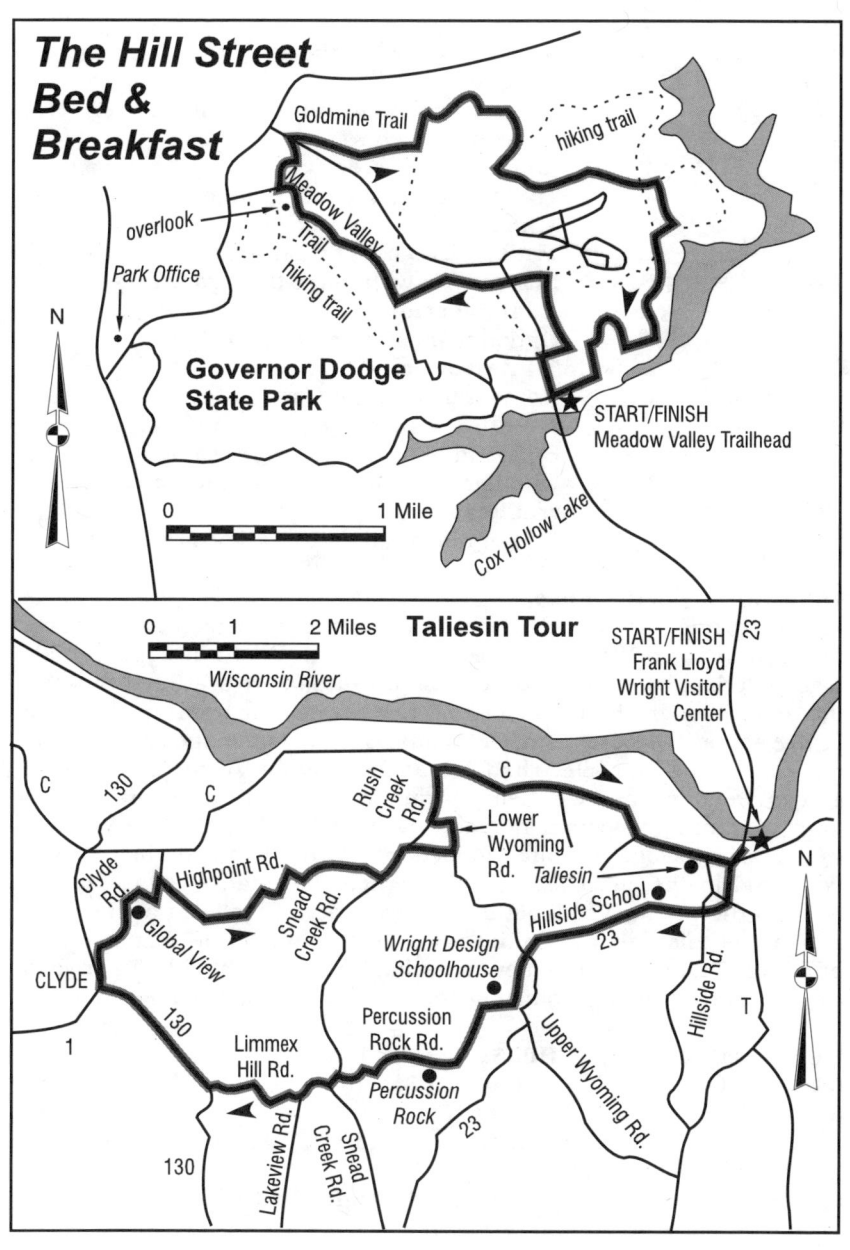

The Hill Street Bed & Breakfast

Goldmine Trail

hiking trail

Meadow Valley Trail

overlook

Park Office

hiking trail

N

Governor Dodge State Park

START/FINISH
Meadow Valley Trailhead

0   1 Mile

Cox Hollow Lake

0   1   2 Miles   **Taliesin Tour**

Wisconsin River

START/FINISH
Frank Lloyd
Wright Visitor
Center

23

C   130

C

Rush Creek Rd.

C

Lower Wyoming Rd.

Taliesin

Clyde Rd.

Highpoint Rd.

Snead Creek Rd.

Hillside School

Global View

23

CLYDE

Wright Design Schoolhouse

Hillside Rd.

N

130

Percussion Rock Rd.

Upper Wyoming Rd.

T

1

Limmex Hill Rd.

Percussion Rock

Lakeview Rd.

Snead Creek Rd.

23

130

Pt.-Pt.	Cume	Turn	Street/Landmark
0.4	2.2	**BR**	Another overlook to the left, with bubbling brook at bottom of valley
0.5	2.7	**R**	**T intersection**, with hiking only to left
0.2	2.9	**S**	Cross unnamed road
0.1	3.0	**R**	Another **T intersection**
0.5	3.5	-	Trail to right is the other end of the Goldmine Trail mentioned earlier
0.6	4.1	**R**	**Trail forks, go right**; straight is horses only
0.8	4.9	**S**	Intersection with horse trail, **go straight**
0.1	5.0	**R**	**T intersection**
0.1	5.1	**R**	Option to go straight, but **go right**
0.1	5.2	**L**	**T intersection**
0.3	5.5	**L**	Horse trail goes right, **we go left**
0.2	5.7	-	A tenth of a mile of beach sand
0.7	6.4	-	Still kind of muddy/sandy/swampy
0.3	6.7	**R**	Uphill to parking lot, **turn right to return to trailhead**
0.1	6.8	-	End of ride at **Meadow Valley Trailhead**

Taliesin Tour (21.4 miles)

This road ride journeys through a part of the Wisconsin River Valley that Frank Lloyd Wright called home. Several Wright-designed buildings including his home and workshop, Taliesin, are scattered through the area. Though the roads for this ride are not far from the Inn, one bridge across the Wisconsin River with no shoulders makes it a dangerous ride to the tour site. The folks at the Taliesin Visitor Center were gracious enough to offer their parking lot as a starting point for this tour. We strongly recommend you drive there (and take in the Visitor's Center and one of the estate's guided tours) and then bike the route as described in the cue sheet below. Though the estate's roads are not open to the public, you'll get a wonderful view of Taliesin at the start and end of this ride. In addition, you'll see a number of Wright's other buildings, including an elementary school, a bit into the ride. To drive to the Visitor's Center, the starting point of this ride, follow these cues:

0.0	0.0	-	**Hill St. East**
0.0	0.0	**R**	**Cincinnati St.**
0.1	0.1	**L**	**Daley St.**
0.4	0.5	**R**	**Winstead/Rt. 23**
2.5	3.0	**L**	**County C**
0.1	3.1	**R**	**Frank Lloyd Wright Visitor's Center parking lot**

Taliesin Cue Sheet

Pt.-Pt.	Cume	Turn	Street/Landmark
0.0	0.0	-	**Trail picks up from back of parking lot**
0.1	0.1	S	Path access from right, go straight
0.7	0.8	S	Cross County T
0.4	1.2	S	**Hillside School Rd.**, path ends; cross Rt. 23 and continue on shoulder
0.5	1.7	-	Hilltop Rd.
1.5	3.2	-	Lower Wyoming Rd.
0.5	3.7	-	Frank Lloyd Wright School to right
0.2	3.9	R	**Percussion Rock Rd.**
0.5	4.4	-	Cook Hill Rd
2.3	6.7	L	Percussion Rock ends; **Snead Creek comes in from left and goes on straight. Take it left across a creek**
0.0	6.7	S	Lake View road to the left; stay right/straight
0.4	7.1	R	**Limmex Hill Rd.** (Gravel for a short stretch)
1.4	8.5	R	**Rt. 130**
1.7	10.2	-	Rt. I to left
0.0	10.2	R	**Clyde Rd.**
1.8	12.0	R	**Highpoint Rd.**
3.1	15.1	L	**Snead Creek Rd.**
1.1	16.2	L	**Lower Wyoming Rd.**
0.5	16.7	BR	**Stay on Lower Wyoming** as Rush Creek Rd. merges from left
0.7	17.4	R	**County C**
3.9	21.3	L	Cross Highway 23; **turn left on trail back to parking lot**
0.1	21.4	-	Back at parking lot

Inn at Pinewood, Eagle River, Wisconsin

Inn at Pinewood

Bill & Jane Weber, Owners   **Phone: (715) 477-2377**
Page & Mike Keck, Innkeepers   **Fax: (715) 477-0040**
1820 Silver Forest Lane   **Web: www.inn-at-pinewood.com**
Eagle River, WI 54521
Rates: Budget — Luxury

In 1934, a log cabin was put up on the shores of Carpenter Lake to serve as a hunting and fishing lodge. Over the years, that simple cabin was expanded left and right, front and back, up, and even a bit down. New cabins were built in close proximity. The grounds became the site of a boy's school for awhile. Today, even though you might not be able to see it from the outside, that log cabin is still the heart and soul of the Inn at Pinewood. You can see the actual cabin walls in the center sitting room of the building.

While Bill and Jane Weber have done a good job of preserving the rustic Americana charm of the cabin, they've also done a good job of eliminating any sense of roughing it during your stay at the inn. Even the standard rooms are spacious with king-sized beds, private baths, and balconies overlooking the lake, the woods, or the grounds. The inn also offers two suites with fireplace and a double Jacuzzi, and a two-bedroom suite for a larger group. The cream of the crop in the main building is the Honeymoon Suite, sequestered off in a back corner of the first floor with a gorgeous view over the lake. All are decorated in a comfortable country manner, with patchwork quilts and antique or collectible furniture. For really large groups, the inn offers a separate cabin with three bedrooms, a living room with a large cathedral ceiling, a hot tub, and several scenic decks. The cabin doesn't include meals unless pre-arranged.

In addition to all the rooms, the inn includes a massive common area spread across the original cabin, a great room overlooking the lake and a dining room at the front of the inn overlooking the flowerbeds. There are several fireplaces and wood-burning stoves scattered throughout the rooms, with many comfortable chairs from which to enjoy them. This area is also well-stocked with more books, board games, and puzzles than one could enjoy over an entire summer. In one corner is an information nook with maps, flyers, brochures, and every other kind of local information you could want. There is also a television room with a VCR and a wide selection of tapes.

Breakfast will get you ready for any activity you choose. It starts with a buffet full of fresh fruits and homemade muffins and pastries, backed up by coffee, tea, and juices. Our breakfast spread also had a delicious baked egg and sausage casserole and a vegetable quiche. The menu choices range from various styles of eggs to waffles and pancakes. We found the buffet to be tasty and satisfying, allowing us to pick what appealed to us without wasting food. If you're lucky, Page or Jane will have made pumpkin muffins, our favorite, as part of the spread.

The pleasures of the inn extend beyond the buildings to include a sandy beach on the lake. In addition, the inn has canoes, boats, and kayaks for rent. Golf, horseback riding, and casinos are just a short drive away as well. Certainly the largest attraction outside the inn is the Nicolet National Forest at 661,000 acres. Shortly after its dedication in 1933 as a national forest, the Civilian Conservation Corps created many of the trails which are still in use today, including the Anvil Trail documented below. The forest spreads over an area 36 miles wide and 62 miles long with hundreds of miles of trails woven throughout.

With so much wilderness, you can expect to run into some of the natives. We saw numerous deer and, on one early morning ride, almost got run over by one crossing the trail. Perhaps the highlight of our stay was a black bear loping across one of the forest roads as we were driving to the trailhead. He stopped to look us over and we were happy to be in the car instead of the on the bikes. With many access points minutes from the inn, the Nicolet seems almost a part of the package.

Rides from Inn at Pinewood
While we've featured mountain biking here, there are scenic road rides in the area, looping around the wooded lakes, Eagle River, and other small towns. In addition to the many trails in Nicolet, most local communities have ski trails that are opened for mountain biking during the summer. The folks at Pinewood have plenty of brochures and other information on area biking opportunities.

Both rides for this chapter start from the same trailhead in the Nicolet National Forest. If you're feeling ambitious you can ride from the inn to the trailhead. The roads are paved (with no shoulders) until you actually get onto the forest roads, and they are not heavily traveled. That said, after riding these trails back-to-back, we were more than happy at the end of the ride to be able climb in the car and drive back to the inn. Trail maps for the rides below are available at the trailhead. For additional trail information, contact:

Nicolet National Forest Eagle River Ranger Station
P.O. Box 1809
4364 Wall Street
Eagle River, WI 54521
phone: (715) 479-2827
fax: (715) 479-1308

To reach the trailhead, follow these cues:

PtPt.	Cume	Turn	Street/Landmark
0.0	0.0		Exit parking lot from Inn at Pinewood onto **Silver Forest Lane**
0.4	0.4	L	**West Carpenter Lake Rd.**
0.3	0.7	L	**Highway 70**
6.7	7.4	R	**Fournier Rd., also Forest Road 2460** (gravel)
2.6	10.0	-	Anvil Trail entrance to right
0.1	10.1	R	**Trailhead Parking**

Terrain: To the untrained eye, signs that this area was shaped by glacial activity are few. However, the Nicolet North ride has one of the steepest ascents out of a ravine we've ever ridden. The good news is that the hills aren't overly long and the trails cut through beautiful wooded territory, so you may not mind the climbs.

Road Conditions: We rode these trails the day after a serious rainstorm but were delighted to find that, aside from one or two boggy areas and one small impromptu lake across the trail, the paths were in great shape. This is mostly singletrack riding with surfaces ranging from packed dirt to grass. There are roots and rocks in places as one would expect on this kind of ride. We also came back with some raspberry bush scratches, but since their presence probably explains why we saw the bear, we're not complaining.

Traffic: Despite riding these trails on a major holiday weekend, we saw nobody either on the trails or on the forest roads driving in.

Best Time to Ride: Fall in these woods is absolutely spectacular. If you come in mid-September you'll find MTV visuals without the associated noise level. If you like to ride early or late in the day, bring some warmer riding gear.

Nearest Bike Shop
Chain of Lake Cyclery
107 Railroad St.
Eagle River, WI 54521
(715) 479-3920

Anvil Lake (7.4 miles)

First laid out in the mid-1930s by the Civilian Conservation Corps, these trails found renewed popularity in the 1970s with the rise of interest in cross country skiing. During the non-snow months, these ski trails are excellent for mountain biking. While Nicolet North trails challenge the rider with elevation, roots, and rocks, the Anvil Trails are content to mostly throw hills at the rider. You can fine-tune the level of difficulty by choosing which trails to ride, with the West and East Trails providing the easiest way around. The Lake Loop and Ninemile are more difficult, with Devil's Run topping the charts.

Pt.-Pt.	Cume	Turn	Street/Landmark
0.0	0.0		From the Nicolet North ride board at the Forest Road 2460 parking lot; head back out to **FR 2460**
0.0	0.0	L	**FR 2460**
0.1	0.1	L	**Anvil Trail Access Path**
0.3	0.4	-	Looks like an intersection but isn't; keep right and down hill
0.1	0.5	-	Cross Ninemile Creek
0.0	0.5	L	**Ninemile Trail**
0.4	0.9	L	**East Trail**
0.5	1.4	L	**Military Trail,** there are tables and shelter here, plus two trails (West and Devil's Run) to the right
0.1	1.5	-	Return of Lake Loop Trail to the left
0.2	1.7	L	**Lake Loop Trail**
1.5	3.2	R	**Military Trail**
0.1	3.3	BL	**West Trail** (if you're feeling strong, take Devil's Run—they end up at about the same place. *Warning:* Devil's Run is an expert trail)
1.5	4.8	-	Trail to parking on Rt. 70
0.1	4.9	S	Intersection with Devil's Run, continue straight
0.4	5.3	SR	**Sharp right onto East Trail.** A gentle right would put you on Ninemile Trail, a more challenging route back
1.1	6.4	L	**Ninemile Trail**
0.5	6.9	R	**Butternut Trail**
0.1	7.0	-	Keep left through the false intersection
0.2	7.2	S	Ignore trail marker to right, continue straight to FR 2460
0.0	7.2	R	**FR 2460**
0.2	7.4	R	**Trail parking lot**
0.0	7.4	-	**Nicolet North ride board**

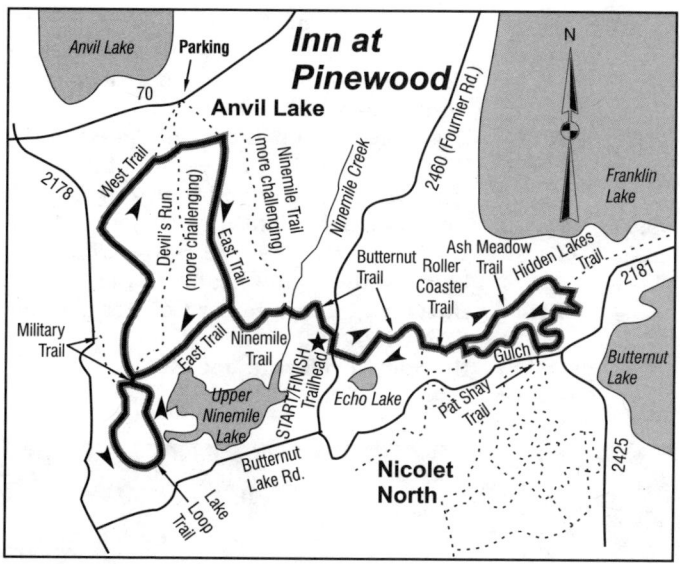

Nicolet North (4.3 miles)

Though this ride is just over half as long as Anvil, it took us about the same amount of time to ride. There are more and steeper hills. Every downhill and flat spot is laced with exposed roots and rocks. On the other hand, this ride through the Nicolet National Forest has some of the prettiest meadows and one forested glen that is as beautiful as any we've ever seen—we half expected to see fairies darting about. This ride is just a short sample of what Nicolet North has to offer with over 15 miles of trails, mostly intermediate or expert in skill level. At the end of a day that combined Anvil and Nicolet North, we were content to head home, though better lungs and legs than ours might spend the whole day exploring these trails.

Pt.-Pt.	Cume	Turn	Street/Landmark
0.0	0.0		From Nicolet North ride board at the Forest Road 2460 parking lot, head back out to FR 2460
0.0	0.0	**S**	Cross FR 2460
0.8	0.8	**BL**	**Roller Coaster Trail** (also heads to right)
0.2	1.0	**S**	Roller Coaster ends, **Ash Meadow** begins, Gulch is off to the right
0.5	1.5	-	False trail to the left, stay to right—it's well marked

Pt.-Pt.	Cume	Turn	Street/Landmark
0.4	1.9	R	**T with Hidden Lakes Trail** system, turn right
0.0	1.9	-	*Be careful*—trail goes down a steep ravine and right back up the other side
0.8	2.7	R	**Right at fork onto Gulch**; Pat Shay goes left. Watch out for deer here—one of us was almost run over by one crashing through the woods.
0.4	3.1	R	**Roller Coaster Trail**
0.1	3.2	L	**Roller Coaster;** Ash Meadow heads right. We're back on the trail we came out on
0.2	3.4	BR	**Butternut Trail;** Roller Coaster goes left
0.8	4.2	S	Cross FR 2460
0.1	4.3	-	**Nicolet North ride board**

Lumberman's Mansion Inn, Hayward, Wisconsin

Lumberman's Mansion Inn

Wendy Hinrichs Sanders
Jan Hinrichs Blaedel   Phone: (715) 634-3012
P.O. Box 885   Fax: (715) 634-5724
Hayward, WI 54843   Web: http://haywardlakes.com/mansion.htm
Rates: Budget – Moderate

E ven as it was being built, the Lumberman's Mansion Inn was getting rave reviews from the local paper. The July 8th, 1887 *North Wisconsin News* said the mansion would be "the finest house in town." The mansion is still a contender for that title over a hundred years later. Built by a local lumber baron to showcase his stock in trade, the inn features some beautifully restored woodwork including a broad oak staircase, maple floors polished to their original warm color, and pocket doors from local white pine. These pieces of craftsmanship are accompanied by many other fine touches, such as two decorative tile fireplaces, oak bookshelves in the library (with appropriate period literature), and antiques Jan and Wendy have collected for the house.

The rooms are a graceful blend of old and new. Several rooms have antique beds, but almost all also have whirlpool baths. We stayed in the Acorn and Oak room, which features an antique oak bed and large walnut armoire, accompanied by a view of the pond and park across the street. Generous in size, this room and the White Pine both provide ample space for spreading out. If you're feeling the need to compartmentalize, the mansion also offers two suites, the Birchwood and the Norway Pine. Both have a sitting room, separate sleeping room, and private bath with shower. The Birchwood features and Eastlake bed, while the Norway Pine has oak antiques and a view of the mansion's garden. The mansion's fifth room, the Maple Leaf, looks out over the porch and has a spoon-carved, bird's-eye maple bed along with a private bath.

Breakfast brings a complete helping of food and conversation. Jan and Wendy's breakfasts are tasty inventions using local goods and produce. Depending on the season, you might get something with a hint of cranberry or perhaps a tempting slice of apple pastry from the region's orchards. The breakfasts are complete works from the juice and coffee to start through the entrées that provide all the energy you'll need for a day of biking. Your hosts are also a wonderful resource for local activities if you don't fill up your dance card with bike rides on the numerous local trails.

The Chequamegon National Forest provides hundreds of miles of mountain bike trails, and the local country roads provide many more miles for touring. The Chequamegon Area Mountain Bike Association (CAMBA) maintains the trails and provides good maps to help get you into (and back out of) the woods. The area also hosts one of the largest mountain bike events in the Midwest, the Chequamegon Fat Tire Festival. With several other biking events throughout the summer season, the area is not just bike-friendly, but almost bike-obsessed.

Which is not to say that Hayward and environs don't provide plenty of other activities. There are a number of lakes in the region with the associated boating, fishing, and other water activities. Don't be too shocked if you happened to see a giant Godzilla-sized muskie off to the side of the road as you drive through town. It's just a display outside the Fishing Hall of Fame. In general, Hayward is a great destination for outdoor activities, with everything from a golf outing through horseback riding and hiking to a trip down a wild river. Organized events include the American Berkebeiner Ski Race, the Lumberjack World Championships and the Stone Lake Cranberry festival. On the more sedate side, the area also has some excellent antique shops.

If you've been on the bikes all day, a good soak in the whirlpool may be just the ticket for winding down. If you have a little energy left, you might walk across the street and contemplate Shues Pond. Either way you'll be happy to return again to the Lumberman's Mansion Inn.

Rides from Lumberman's Mansion Inn

The fact of the matter is that you could quit your job and move to Hayward, spend all your days riding, and probably still not ride all the trails and road routes that exist around here. The Chequamegon Area Mountain Bike Association maintains hundreds of miles of trails, ranging in difficulty from those appropriate for almost any beginner to some of the most challenging riding in the Midwest. Not all the beautiful riding in this area is on forested singletrack, though. There are miles and miles of well-maintained, little-traveled country roads as well. This area hosts a number of well-known biking events and is bike-friendly in a way that few rural areas are. Both rides in this chapter originate from the Berkebeiner OO Trailhead. To drive to the trailhead, follow these cues:

Pt.-Pt.	Cume	Turn	Street/Landmark
0.0	0.0		From the inn take **Kansas Ave.** towards town
0.2	0.2	**L**	**Rt. 63** (also **First St.**)
0.4	0.6	**S**	Intersection with 77; go straight
9.5	10.1	**R**	**Rt. OO**, across from Sawmill Saloon
3.4	13.5	**R**	**Birkebeiner OO Trailhead;** paid parking

Terrain: This area has its hills. The mountain bike ride on the Berkebeiner Trail is another of those rides that will give you new respect for the folks who can actually ski *up* these things. The road ride also has some ups and downs, but nothing that we felt was extreme (maybe they all seem easier in comparison to the trail hills).

Road Conditions: Both the trail and the roads are well maintained in this area. The trail is quite wide with a single track threaded down the center of the cleared area. The fire road at the end of the ride has some sandy sections, but is kept in good condition without many washboards or any swampy sections to contend with. The roads on the Tiger Cat Ride are in good shape, though most do not have shoulders to ride on.

Traffic: On the road we encountered very few cars. Drivers were courteous and we never felt like we had to compete for space on the road. We only saw one other rider the day we were out on the CAMBA trails.

Best Time to Ride: Like so many of these North Woods locations, it's hard to pick a bad time to ride between June and October. Earlier in the season you'll get more mild temperatures; later you'll get fall colors.

Nearest Bike Shop
New Moon Bike and Ski Shop
Highway 63 N
Hayward, WI 54843
(715) 634-8685

Though not a bike shop, you should also get in touch with the Chequamegon Area Mountain Bike Association (CAMBA) for trail maps and other information.

CAMBA
P.O. Box 141
Cable, WI 54821
(800) 533-7454
http://www.cable4fun.com/camba/

The Birkebeiner Trail (9.4 miles)

The American Birkebeiner is the premier American cross-country ski race. Consequently, its route is well maintained. In the summer, when there's no snow (usually), this makes for some wonderful mountain biking through the woods. This loop starts out on a portion of the Birky Trail and then branches back to the starting point on fire roads, snowmobile trails, and a short paved section.

Pt.-Pt.	Cume	Turn	Street/Landmark
0.0	0.0	S	Enter trail through passageway at the warming house
0.7	0.7	-	Unmarked trail left
0.5	1.2	-	Unmarked dirt track
1.7	2.9	-	Unmarked doubletrack
0.5	3.4	-	Unmarked doubletrack
0.2	3.6	-	Long ascent
0.7	4.3	**R**	**Dirt track**
0.3	4.6	**BL**	**Bear left**; lesser trails to right
0.1	4.7	**R**	**Phipps Fire Lane**
0.1	4.8	-	Stretch of sand
0.6	5.4	-	Unmarked doubletrack to right
0.1	5.5	**BR**	**As unmarked road comes in from left**
0.1	5.6	**BR**	Unmarked doubletrack goes straight
1.0	6.6	-	Unmarked road left
0.2	6.8	-	Unmarked road right
0.1	6.9	S	Unmarked intersection, continue straight
1.1	8.0	-	Unmarked path
0.6	8.6	**R**	**Rt. OO**
0.8	9.4	-	**Birkebeiner OO Trailhead**

Tiger Cat Ride (26.7 miles)

This ride takes its name from a local dam along the route. Though forests of the North Woods seem to take top billing around here, the lakes provide an enjoyable environment as well. This ride starts from the OO trail head ($5 parking fee on the honor system), runs down to and around a series of lakes, and then continues back up to the trailhead, all on paved roads.

0.0	0.0	R	**Rt. OO**
0.8	0.8	L	**OO turns left;** Pederson continues on straight
0.6	1.4	S	**Onto Clear Lake Rd.;** OO turns right, Telemark Rd. to the left
0.7	2.1	-	Paddock Rd.

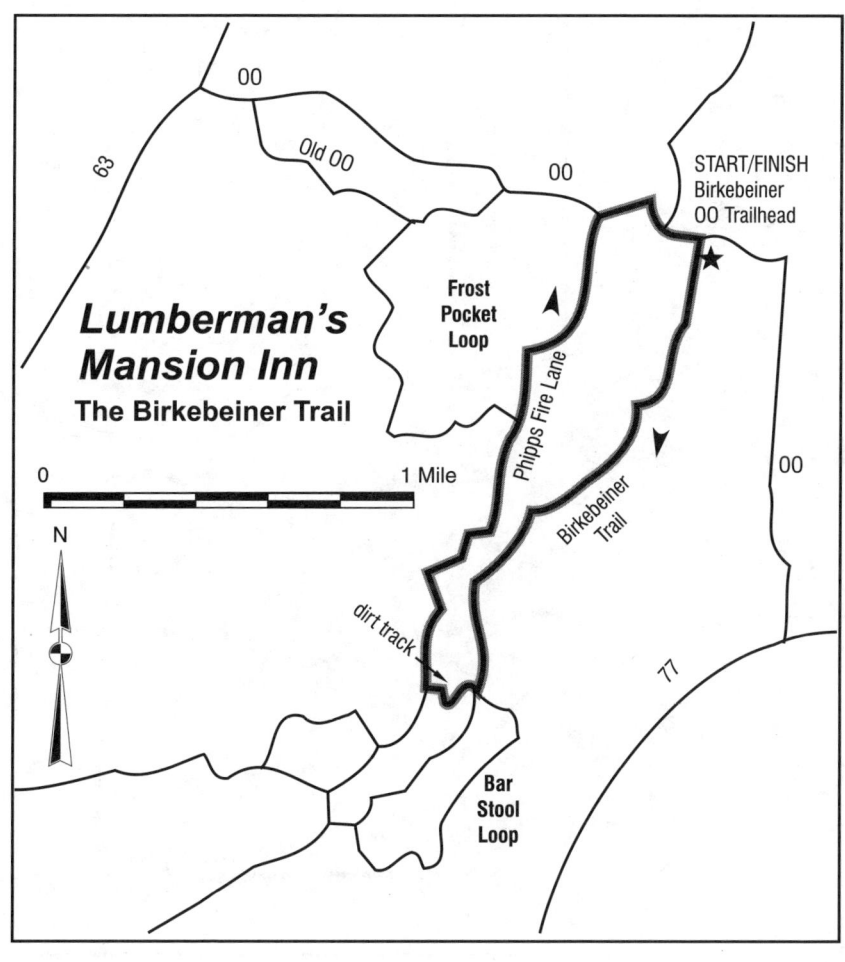

00

Old 00

63

00

START/FINISH
Birkebeiner
OO Trailhead

Frost
Pocket
Loop

Lumberman's
Mansion Inn

The Birkebeiner Trail

Phipps Fire Lane

00

0   1 Mile

Birkebeiner
Trail

N

dirt track

77

Bar
Stool
Loop

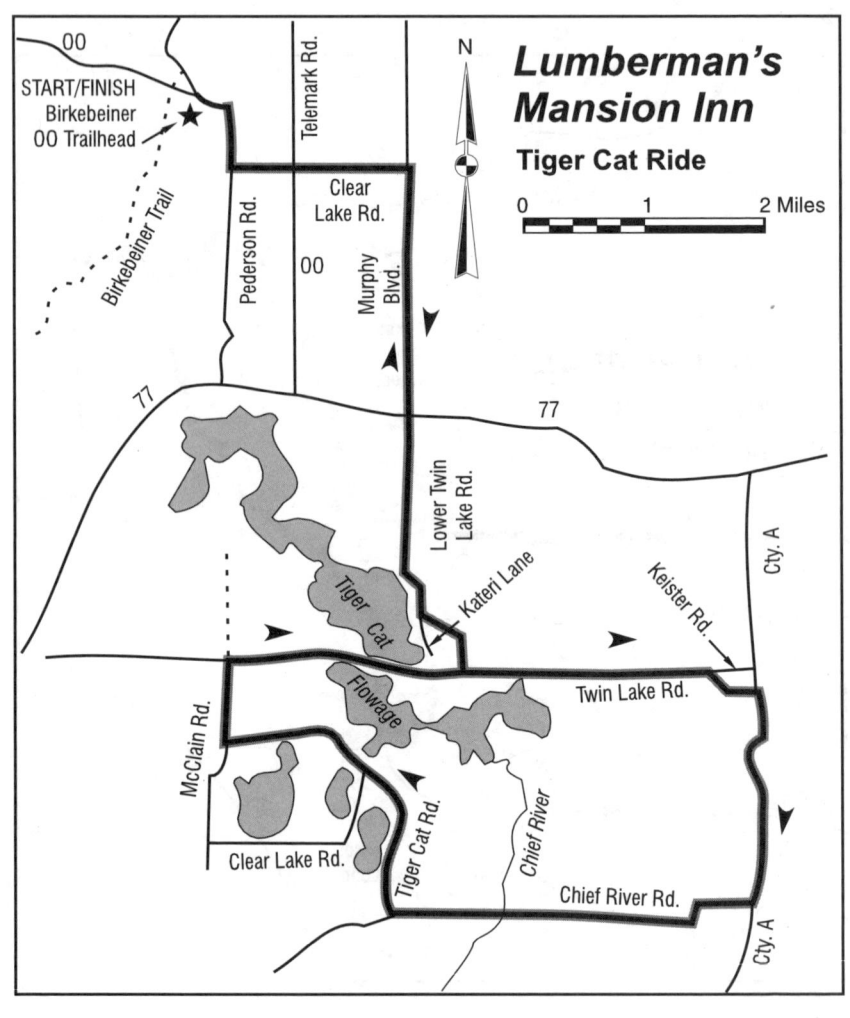

Lumberman's Mansion Inn

Tiger Cat Ride

0   1   2 Miles

N

00

START/FINISH
Birkebeiner
OO Trailhead

Birkebeiner Trail

Telemark Rd.

Pederson Rd.

Clear
Lake Rd.

00

Murphy Blvd.

77

77

Lower Twin
Lake Rd.

Cty. A

Tiger Cat

Kateri Lane

Keister Rd.

Flowage

McClain Rd.

Twin Lake Rd.

Clear Lake Rd.

Tiger Cat Rd.

Chief River

Chief River Rd.

Cty. A

Pt.-Pt.	Cume	Turn	Street/Landmark
0.3	2.4	R	**Murphy Blvd.**
0.0	2.4	-	Elaine Dr.
0.8	3.2	-	Boys Camp Rd. on left
0.6	3.8	-	Allan Rd. from left
0.6	4.4	S	Cross Rt. 77; across intersection name changes to **Lower Twin Lake Rd.**
1.1	5.5	-	Surface change—rougher pavement
0.2	5.7	-	Bluebird Ln.
0.4	6.1	BL	Kateri Ln. goes off straight/right, stay on **Lower Twin Lake Rd.**
0.7	6.8	L	**Twin Lake Rd.**
0.5	7.3	-	Grosbeak Ln.
1.6	8.9	BR	**Twin Lake Rd. curves right**; Keister Rd. goes straight
0.2	9.1	-	Voight Rd.
0.3	9.4	R	**County Rt. A**
1.0	10.4	-	Moose Lake Rd.
0.7	11.1	R	**Chief River Rd.**
0.8	11.9	-	Fromm Rd.
1.4	13.3	-	Shuler Rd.
1.1	14.4	R	**Tiger Cat Rd.**
0.3	14.7	-	Oriole Ln.
0.9	15.6	-	Tiger Cat Dam Rd.
0.1	15.7	BR	**Stay right on Tiger Cat;** Clear Lake Rd. is to left
0.4	16.1	-	Echo Point Ln.
0.3	16.4	-	Chickadee Ln.
0.3	16.7	-	Seagull Ln.
0.3	17.0	R	**McClaine Rd.**
0.8	17.8	R	**Twin Lake Rd.**
0.5	18.3	-	Farnesworth Rd.
0.3	18.6	-	Meadowlark Ln.
0.2	18.8	-	Mertig Rd.
0.4	19.2	-	Cross Tiger Cat flowage
0.3	19.5	-	Hummingbird Ln.
0.3	19.8	L	**Lower Twin Lake Rd.**
0.8	20.6	BR	**Stay on Lower Twin Lake Rd.;** Kateri Ln. to left
0.3	20.9	-	Bluebird Ln.
1.3	22.2	S	Across Highway 77 as road name changes to **Murphy Blvd.**
0.6	22.8	-	Allan Rd.
0.6	23.4	-	Boys Camp Rd.

Pt.-Pt.	Cume	Turn	Street/Landmark
0.8	24.2	-	Elaine Dr.
0.0	24.2	**L**	**Clear Lake Rd.**
0.5	24.7	-	Paddock Rd.
0.5	25.2	**S**	**Go straight onto Rt. OO** across intersection
0.6	25.8	**BR**	**Rt. OO to right;** Pederson to left
0.9	26.7	-	**Berkebeiner OO Trailhead**

The Old Rittenhouse Inn, Bayfield, Wisconsin

The Old Rittenhouse Inn

Jerry & Mary Phillips
P.O. Box 584
Bayfield, WI 54814
Rates: Moderate — Luxury

Information: (715) 779-5111
Reservations: (800) 779-2129
E-Mail: frontdsk@rittenhouseinn.com
Web: www.rittenhouseinn.com

We should probably admit a bias for The Old Rittenhouse Inn. It's hard to keep a clear head about the inn that provided a warm summer night with a full moon shining across Lake Superior as a backdrop to our wedding reception. The inn is well suited to play any number of storybook roles. Nestled on a hillside above Lake Superior, this 100-year-old Victorian mansion welcomes you across a generous wraparound front porch and promises security and comfort under every one of its many gables and dormers.

Most of the first floor is given over to dining rooms, a small front desk, and one of the guestrooms, which has a separate entrance from the porch. The three intimate dining rooms are each decorated in a different color. Normally such details as the plate rails, tiled fireplaces, stained-glass windows, and lake views—not to mention the polished woodwork and lace table cloths—might upstage the meal to be served. As we'll discuss a bit later, that's not a problem here.

The Old Rittenhouse Inn has 10 guestrooms spread across three floors. At the top of the mansion—and the price list—is a gorgeous third-floor suite, which was originally the mansion's ballroom. Dark pine paneling, a double whirlpool, a double-sided fireplace, and dormers looking out across the lake provide the perfect atmosphere for creating your own fairy tale.

High ceilings and tall windows give an almost open-air feeling to the other rooms, located on the first and second floors. Double, queen, and king beds are available, along with various combinations of fireplaces, whirlpools, and lake views. The rooms are decorated with period antiques, with one bed having a headboard that wouldn't fit under a modern 8-foot ceiling. All the rooms have plenty of space to spread out, though rooms in the seamlessly-crafted addition have more floor space than those in the original part of the inn. If all of these rooms are booked, the Rittenhouse has a number of other accommodations nearby at Le Chateau Boutin, the Grey Oak Guesthouse, and the Fountain Cottage.

If the building itself isn't enough to capture your delight, the attention to detail and effortless grace of the service will surely do the trick. The wait staff will remember you and what you had for breakfast from day to day. The front desk is always ready with advice about activities or assistance in ironing out the last detail for the day. An ever-present plate of all-too-tempting sweets on the second floor landing reminds the visitor of the staff's care.

Though not included with the room, the gourmet supper is a natural extension of the inn's hospitality. Jerry's gourmet menus are presented verbally by the wait staff, almost managing to satisfy your appetite before the first plate graces the table. There are usually four or five entrée choices surrounded by four other courses of pure culinary pleasures. By the end of the meal, your head, heart, and stomach will all be well fed.

The continental breakfast that is included with the room rate raises the bar for all future continental breakfasts, offering an extravagance of fruit, baked goods, and juice. If you dined at the inn the previous night, this breakfast may still carry you through to a late lunch. For a small additional fee, you can get the full breakfast, which starts out with everything in the continental breakfast before moving onto other lavish interpretations of traditional breakfast fare.

The Bayfield area was a camping site for the Ojibiway tribe long before the first western trappers arrived in the mid-1600s. Bayfield proper was established in the mid-1800s when locks at the other end of Lake Superior opened it up to navigation from the lower Great Lakes. Lumbering and commercial fishing have given way to cruises, kayaking, sailing, sport fishing, and a host of other recreational activities on the water and in the wooded hills around Bayfield. In the hills above town are a number of orchards which, depending on the time of year, have fresh berries or apples. The Apostle Islands lie just offshore and offer a variety of hiking trails, picnic sites, and lighthouses to explore. Madeline Island, the largest of the islands, is just a ferry ride away.

Though very small, Bayfield has a number of popular eating establishments. If you feel the need to eat good basic American cuisine in the company of every imaginable representation of pink flamingos, Maggie's is the place for you. It's a very popular hangout, so expect to put your name in and have some time to enjoy the company of your traveling companions. Gruenke's is another alternative; seafood is the signature offering. Over on Madeline Island, you can relax in Tom's Burned Down Bar, a deck and tent affair with a very casual attitude towards decorating.

Bayfield and the Old Rittenhouse Inn allow you to experience that rare combination of feeling away from it all while still being in a five-star setting. The town and the inn deliver on every element of a great vacation: privacy, relaxation, first-class but unobtrusive service, and surroundings that quietly make you feel as if you've always lived here—or, at least, would like to.

Rides from The Old Rittenhouse Inn

In addition to the rides documented below, you'll find shorter options on Madeline Island. There are also several options for mountain biking south of Bayfield.

Terrain: Bayfield sits on the edge of a rise of land above Lake Superior. There's literally nowhere to go but up out of town, unless you've equipped your bike with scuba gear. That makes the start tough, but coming home pretty easy. The Madeline Island ride, on the other hand, is gentler, with most of the ride being relatively flat. There are a few hills, but if you're riding a mountain bike, the gearing should be in your favor.

Road Conditions: On both rides, you'll find a combination of pavement and gravel/dirt. We recommend mountain bikes both for the gearing on the Danny DeVito ride and for the sand that you may encounter in some places.

Traffic: Traffic should not be an issue for most riders. The town is busiest in July and August, but even then, traffic drops off immediately when you get outside of town. On the island, speed limits are set at 40 mph max and traffic is generally minimal.

Best Time to Ride: We're partial to June. Tourist season has not yet cranked up to full volume so there are fewer crowds. With Lake Superior acting as a huge air conditioner, you won't encounter outrageous temperatures any time of the year. The fall color comes early this far north, so riding through the colors probably means a September booking.

Nearest Bike Shop: Rentals are available on Madeline Island, but for full service you'll need to head down to Ashland.

Bay City Cycles
412 W. Main St.
Ashland, WI 54806
(715) 682-2091

Danny DeVito Ride (9.2 miles)

This is the shortest road ride in the book, but don't for a second think it's the easiest. Like its namesake, it's short and full of attitude. Most of the attitude comes as a result of altitude—the first two miles of this ride are up ...and up ...and then up a little bit more. Admittedly, we're talking Wisconsin here, not the Alps, but this ride does start with an uphill. After one or two undulations, it relents and is happy to escort you home. We probably broke a few of the local speed limits on the way back down into town.

Pt.-Pt.	Cume	Turn	Street/Landmark
0.0	0.0		On Third St., headed uphill across from Rittenhouse
0.0	0.0	R	**Washington Ave.**
0.0	0.0	-	Broad St.
0.1	0.1	L	**Second St.**
0.1	0.2	-	Rice Ave.
0.1	0.3	-	Sweeny Ave.
0.1	0.4	-	Lynde Ave.
0.1	0.5	BL	Three-way intersection with Island Ave., 2nd, and Olson Rd. **Bear left uphill onto Olson Rd.**
1.2	1.7	-	Top of first climb
0.3	2.0	-	Surface changes to gravel
0.4	2.4	R	**Betzold Rd.,** back onto pavement
0.5	2.9	S	Betzold Rd. ends; stop and **continue straight onto County J.** (Turn left here to cut out worst dirt road and pick up below where Weidinger Rd. joins County J)
0.8	3.7	L	**Turner Road** (at bottom of downhill)
1.0	4.7	L	**Weidinger Rd.** (Dirt)
0.6	5.3	-	Driveway; continue uphill to right
0.3	5.6	-	*Caution:* patches of loose sand; use low gears
0.6	6.2	-	Surface changes to pavement
0.1	6.3	S	Weidinger Rd. ends; stop and **continue straight onto Country J**
0.4	6.7	-	Begin last payment in the hill climbing account
0.4	7.1	-	Begin living off the interest in the hill climbing account
0.7	7.8	L	T intersection; **turn left onto County I.** (County J goes right)
0.0	7.8	-	Unmarked dirt road
0.3	8.1	-	Betzold Rd. to the left
0.3	8.4	SR	Sharp right in the middle of an intense downhill.

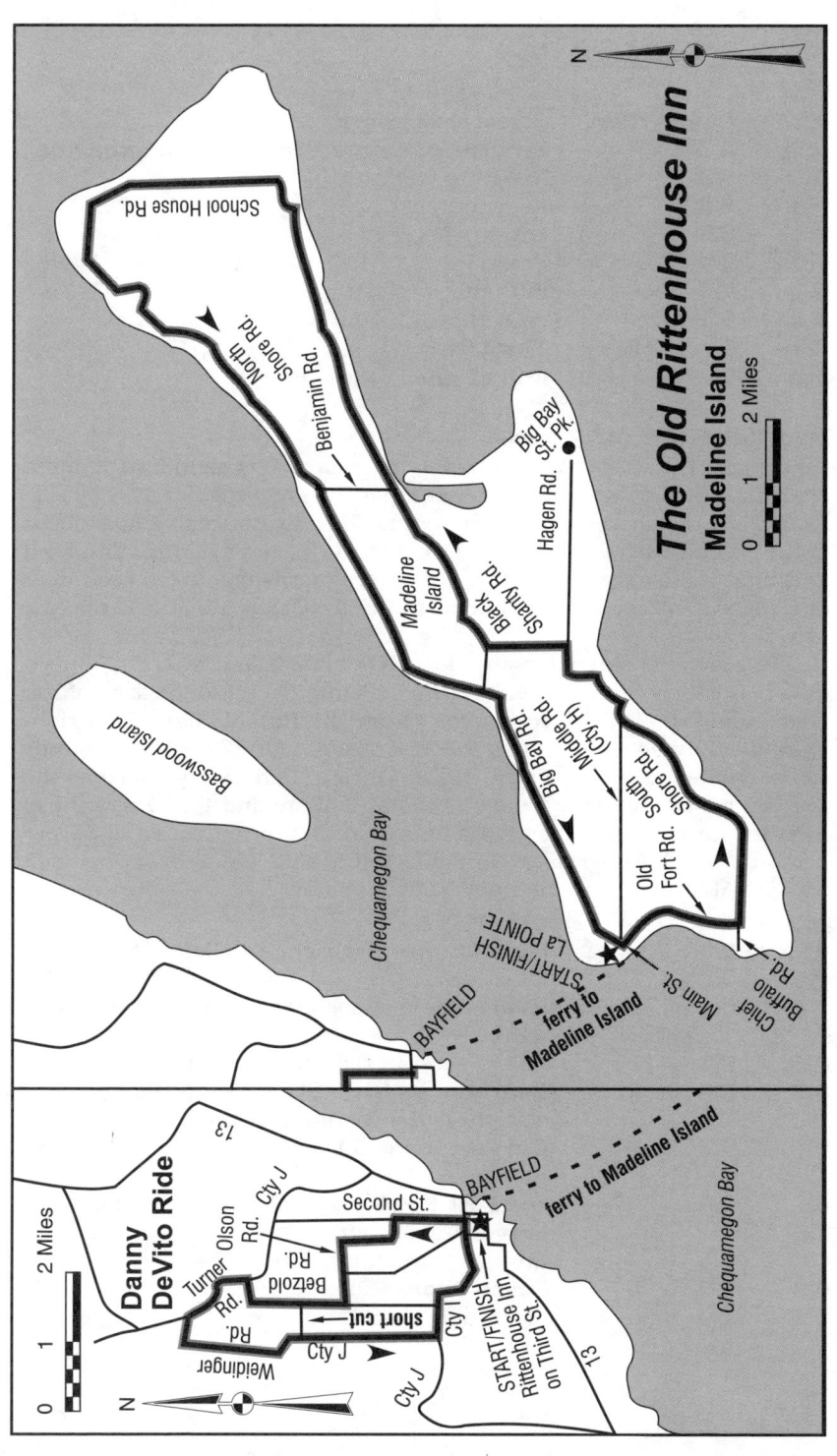

The Old Rittenhouse Inn
Madeline Island

Basswood Island

Chequamegon Bay

North Shore Rd.

School House Rd.

Benjamin Rd.

Madeline Island

Black Shanty Rd.

Big Bay St. Pk.

Hagen Rd.

Big Bay Rd.

Middle Rd. (Cty. H)

South Shore Rd.

Old Fort Rd.

Chief Buffalo Rd.

La Pointe

Main St.

START/FINISH

ferry to Madeline Island

BAYFIELD

0 1 2 Miles

Danny DeVito Ride

Weidinger Rd.

Turner Olson Rd.

Betzold Rd.

Cty J

13

Cty J

Cty I

Second St.

short cut

START/FINISH Rittenhouse Inn on Third St.

Cty J

13

BAYFIELD

ferry to Madeline Island

Chequamegon Bay

0 1 2 Miles

Pt.-Pt.	Cume	Turn	Street/Landmark
0.3	8.7	-	Tenth St. (County I becomes **Washington Ave.**)
0.1	8.8	-	Ninth St.
0.0	8.8	-	Eighth St.
0.1	8.9	-	Seventh St.
0.0	8.9	-	Sixth St.
0.1	9.0	-	Fifth St.
0.1	9.1	-	Fourth St.
0.0	9.1	**R**	**Third St.**
0.1	9.2	-	**End of ride** at Rittenhouse

Madeline Island (27.7 miles)

Starting in the island town of LaPointe, this ride is significantly more level than the DeVito ride. The opening miles are quite flat as they ride near or on the shores of Lake Superior. The only noticeable hills occur in the second half of the ride. You'll get beautiful views of this inland sea and may well see local wildlife. On several occasions we've seen deer and raccoons. This is a good opportunity to pack a lunch and make a lazy day of it.

To get to the starting point of the Madeline Island ride, you'll need to take the ferry from Bayfield over to LaPointe. To get to the ferry office, head uphill on Third Street across from the Rittenhouse. Turn right onto Washington Avenue, and follow it straight for two-tenths of a mile to the Madeline Island Ferry Office. During high tourist season, the ferry runs once an hour from 6:30am to 9:30am and then every thirty minutes until 6pm; it then runs hourly until 11pm. Cost is $3.50 per person plus $1.75 per bike. On the LaPointe side, the ferry access road T's with Main Street at the ride's starting point.

0.0	0.0	-	**Main St.**, heading right into LaPointe
0.0	0.0	-	LaSeur St.
0.1	0.1	-	Middle Rd. heads left (Lake Superior is to your right)
0.3	0.4	-	Public park on right with restrooms
0.2	0.6	**BL**	**Continue on Main St.;** what appears to be straight is the yacht club parking lot
0.1	0.7	**R**	**Old Fort Road** (3-way intersection where Main St. ends)
0.2	0.9	**BL**	**Old Fort Road meets Chief Buffalo and curves to the left**
0.6	1.5	-	Surface turns to gravel
0.2	1.7	**L**	**South Shore Rd.**
0.2	1.9	-	Mondamin Trail

Pt.-Pt.	Cume	Turn	Street/Landmark
0.4	2.3	-	Raymond Rd.
0.4	2.7	-	Unmarked road to left
0.1	2.8	-	Islewood Rd. to right
0.1	2.9	**BL**	**Only real option**
1.8	4.7	-	Unmarked road to left
0.1	4.8	**R**	**Middle Rd. (City H);** back on pavement
1.2	6.0	**L**	**Black Shanty Blvd.**
1.0	7.0	**R**	**Big Bay Rd.** (T intersection)
2.2	9.2	-	Big Bay Town Park
0.2	9.4	-	Benjamin Rd. to left
1.8	11.2	-	Unmarked road to left
0.9	12.1	-	Anderson Ln.
1.1	13.2	**L**	**Schoolhouse Rd.;** surface turns to dirt. At some unmarked point, this will become **North Shore Rd.**)
0.1	13.3	-	Chippewa Trail to right
1.2	14.5	-	Kron-Dahlin Ln. to right
1.1	15.6	-	Very sandy surface
5.0	20.6	-	Benjamin Rd. to left
3.5	24.1	**R**	**Big Bay Rd.**
3.3	27.4	-	Rice St. to left
0.1	27.5	-	Library St.
0.1	27.6	-	Whitefish St.
0.0	27.6	-	Nebraska Row
0.1	27.7	**L**	**Main St.**
0.0	27.7	-	Back at **entrance to ferry dock**

St. Croix River Inn, Osceola, Wisconsin

St. Croix River Inn

Bev Johnson   **Phone: (800) 645-8820**
305 River Street
Osceola, WI 54020   **Web: www.bbhost.com/stcroixriverinn**
Rates: Budget – Luxury

The St. Croix River Inn sits high on a bluff above the river from which it takes its name. Around the turn of the century, the St. Croix was a major transportation artery filled with riverboats moving goods and people in and out of the area. Osceola was a boat building hub, one of the last stops on the navigable river. The river is a more tranquil place now, with the upper St. Croix just a few miles north of Osceola having been named one of the first wild and scenic riverways in the United States. Though not quite the bustling hub of commerce it was during the heyday of river transportation, Osceola and surrounding areas continue to provide ample opportunities for recreation and relaxation.

From its perch high above the river, the St. Croix River Inn is a perfect home base. Built in the early 1900s for the local pharmacist, it stayed in the family until 1984 when it was converted into the luxurious bed and breakfast it is today. Approached from the street, the vaulted roofline of the Dutch Colonial structure and solid stone taken from a local quarry give the inn a cozy, almost cottage-like quality. Once you step through the front door, the inn seems to expand as if you had stepped through the looking glass. The inn's seven rooms, all named for riverboats built in Osceola, are spread across three floors. All the rooms have private baths with a Jacuzzi, most have river views, and a few have a fireplace as well.

The Jenny Hays, on the top floor of the inn, has one of the best views of the river. A floor-to-vaulted-ceiling Palladian window looks down from the top of the inn all the way to the river valley. A private deck and a cast iron fireplace make this a perfect cozy hideaway. The Osceola Suite is a huge room that rambles through separate dining, living, and sleeping areas. It has a fireplace, a TV/VCR, and a walkout patio. From the sleeping area you look out the windows over the river valley. Towards the street side of the suite is a wet bar and kitchenette. You could move in here and never leave the room for your entire stay—did somebody say "honeymoon"? The G.B. Knapp is another large suite with a separate dining area, a private four-season porch overlooking the river, and a Jacuzzi which sits beneath windows overlooking the river valley. The canopy bed and fireplace make the large space intimate and comfortable.

While the other rooms are not quite on the scale of the suites, they are all beautifully decorated and have individual touches that will delight you. The Linn J has a Jacuzzi beneath a skylight for those star-drenched soaks. The Nellie Kent, tucked away in a corner of the bottom floor, has a river view and will satisfy any nesting instinct you might have. The Minne Will is another suite and has a walkout patio at the edge of the bluffs.

Your first thought on waking up in one of these wonderful rooms probably won't be about leaving it. Bev Johnson, the innkeeper, does nothing to discourage guests from starting the morning slowly. Half an hour before breakfast you'll find coffee (or hot chocolate if you ask) and the morning paper outside your door. After that gentle warm-up, breakfast is delivered to your room, for a relaxed, leisurely morning repast. In several stays at this inn, we've not gotten the same thing twice. We've had fluffy omelets, stuffed puff pastries, and hearty scrambled egg, waffle, and sausage breakfasts—though not all at the same time! Of course, you'll get all the trappings one expects from a first class breakfast, such as fresh squeezed juice, fresh fruits, and home baked bread and sweet cakes.

The surrounding area offers a variety of activities beyond just trail riding and mountain biking. There's hiking, boating, and fishing along the river. Numerous golf courses are nearby. Stillwater, one of the region's best stops for antiquing, is a short drive away as well. Bev can provide lots of information depending on your interests.

When you stay at this enchanting and romantic inn, you'll feel about as far from the workaday world as a person can get. Whether lounging in a Jacuzzi overlooking the river or letting one of the fireplaces warm your soul as a blaze of changing leaves color a cool fall evening, it's hard to imagine that the Twin Cities are just over an hour away.

Rides from the St. Croix River Inn

This is hilly agricultural country and the roads tend to go up and down the hills instead of through cuts. We strongly recommend sticking to the off-road trails and park loops.

Terrain: Where you're not dealing with sandy river bottom, the countryside is deeply etched with valleys. Since the Gandy Dancer follows the river and is a rail trail, you won't have to confront the worst of the hills.

Road Conditions: The Gandy Dancer is composed of crushed limestone, providing a reasonably solid riding surface. The ride along the St. Croix is steeped in sand and gravel.

Traffic: Almost non-existent.

Best Time to Ride: We prefer this region in the very early summer, May and June, before the tourist season is in full swing. Fall is pretty, but this is also a hunter's paradise, so be aware of what the hunting seasons are and include that in your planning for when and where to ride.

Nearest Bike Shop: Also almost non-existent. You should come prepared to do your own minor bike maintenance.

Gandy Dancer Trail (11.9 miles)
The Gandy Dancer is a great recreational trail because it has small towns scattered evenly along its length every few miles. It starts with a climb out of the St. Croix River valley, but after that is fairly level. The trailhead is not far away from the inn, but we recommend driving because of the traffic and lack of consistent shoulders on Route 35. To drive to the trailhead, turn right out of the inn's parking lot onto Fourth Street. After one-tenth of a mile, turn left onto Cascade (Route 35) and follow it 7.6 miles to the Gandy Dancer Trailhead.

Pt.-Pt.	Cume	Turn	Street/Landmark
0.0	0.0	-	Access trail leaves back of parking lot and heads uphill
0.2	0.2	**S**	**Trail enters Old Highway 8**
0.1	0.3	-	Red Fox Trail
0.1	0.4	-	Industrial Parkway comes in from left; **diagonally across the intersection, the paved trail picks up again**
0.1	0.5	-	Underpass under Highway 8
0.2	0.7	**S**	Cross Pine Ave.
0.1	0.8	**S**	Cross Maple Dr.
0.3	1.1	**BR**	Trail comes in from left
0.3	1.4	**L**	Access trail T's with **Gandy Dancer**; surface changes to crushed limestone
0.9	2.3	**S**	Cross unnamed road
1.0	3.3	**S**	Cross unnamed road
1.4	4.7	**S**	Cross unnamed road (gravel)
0.3	5.0	**S**	Cross unnamed road
0.6	5.6	**S**	Cross Eighth St.
0.3	5.9	**S**	Cross Fourth St.
0.0	5.9	**TR**	Centuria
0.1	6.0	**S**	Cross Fourth St.
0.3	6.3	**S**	Cross Eighth St.
0.6	6.9	**S**	Cross unnamed street
0.3	7.2	**S**	Cross unnamed road (gravel)

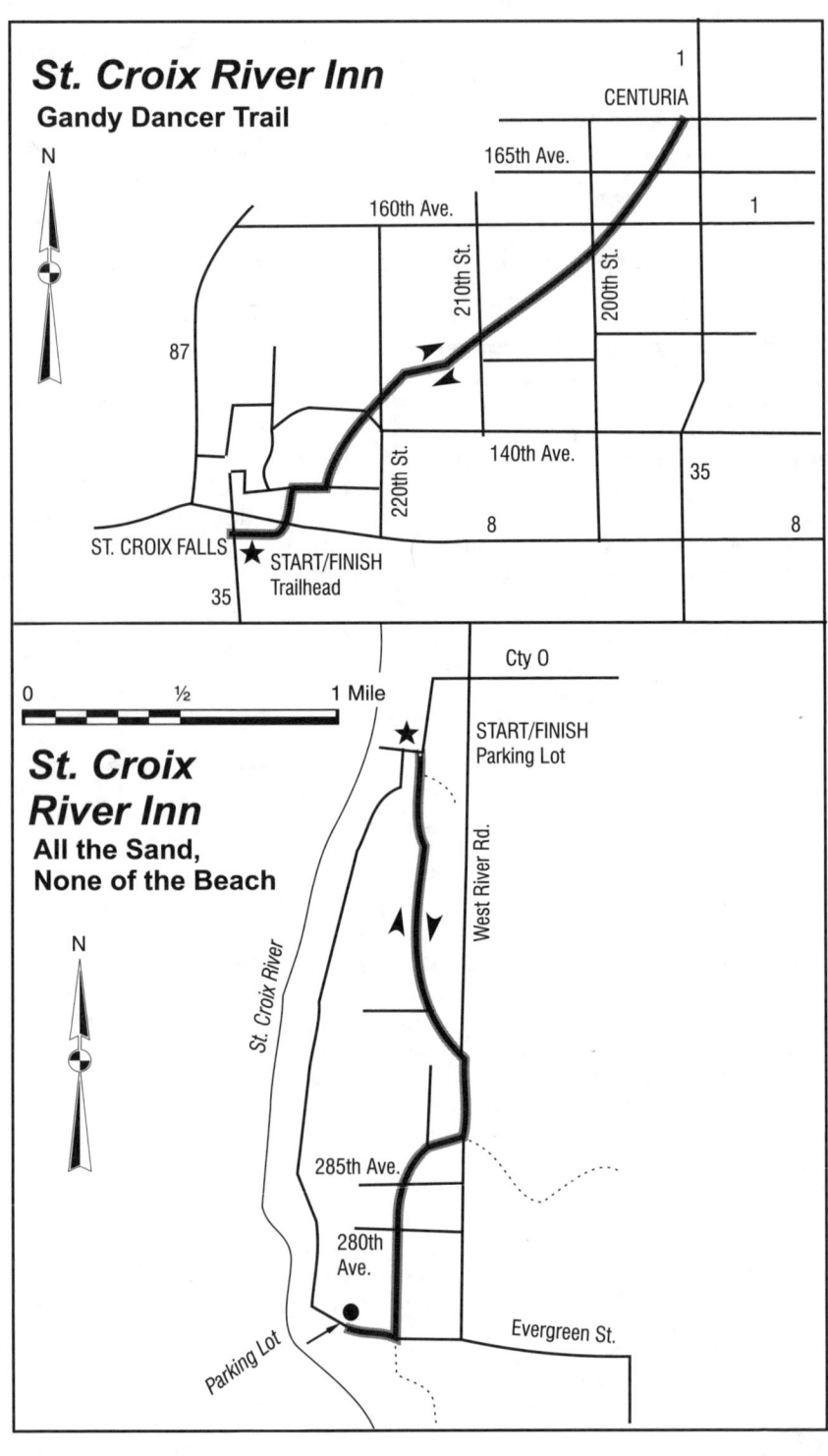

Pt.-Pt.	Cume	Turn	Street/Landmark
1.3	8.5	S	Cross unnamed road
1.1	9.6	S	Cross unnamed road
0.9	10.5	R	**Access trail** (paved surface)
0.2	10.7	BL	Another trail goes off right; **stay left**
0.3	11.0	S	Cross Maple Dr.
0.1	11.1	S	Cross Pine Ave.
0.3	11.4	-	Underpass
0.1	11.5	R	Paved path ends, cross Industrial Parkway and **head west on Old Highway 8**
0.1	11.6	-	Red Fox Trail
0.1	11.7	S	Road ends; **trail goes straight**
0.3	11.9	-	Back at **St. Croix Fall trailhead parking lot**

All the Sand, None of the Beach (14.2 miles)

Yes, this is a long drive to get to the riding in Governor Knowles State Park. But you do get to go through some beautiful wetlands on the way and the ride itself takes you well out into the pinewoods. This ride, as documented, is an out-and-back on part of a loop through the park. The other half of the loop is outrageously technical and downright impassable sometimes, so we advise bikers to stay on the documented ride unless you can obtain advance information regarding the condition of the second half of the loop. Driving directions to Governor Knowles State Park are as follows:

0.0	0.0	R	Out of inn parking onto **Fourth St.**
0.1	0.1	L	**Cascade (Highway 35)**
7.6	7.7	-	Gandy Dancer Trailhead
0.1	7.8	R	**Rt. 8**
0.4	8.2	R	**Highway 87**
20.8	29.0	L	**County O**
9.4	38.4	S	Intersection with West River Road, **go straight despite "Dead End" sign**
1.6	40.0	-	**Parking for the ride**

All the Sand, None of the Beach Cue Sheet

0.0	0.0	-	End of County O
0.3	0.3	R	**Hiking trail** into the woods
0.1	0.4	R	**Dirt road**
0.0	0.4	BR	Road turns left; **trail continues straight**
0.3	0.7	-	Trail to left; continue straight

Pt.-Pt.	Cume	Turn	Street/Landmark
0.8	1.5	-	Trail from right; continue straight
0.4	1.9	L	**Trail ends in T**
0.2	2.1	R	**West River Rd.** (gravel)
1.1	3.2	-	300th Ave.
0.6	3.8	-	Trail comes in from right, **continue on West River Rd.**
0.4	4.2	R	**Turn onto trail into woods**
0.1	4.3	-	Merge with riding and snowmobile trail
0.3	4.6	L	**T intersection, go left**
0.5	5.1	-	285th Ave. (dirt)
0.5	5.6	-	280th Ave. (dirt)
1.2	6.8	R	**Evergreen St.** (Trail continues on other side, but turn onto Evergreen)
0.3	7.1	TA	**Turn around**
0.3	7.4	L	**Evergreen St.** (trail continues on other side, but turn onto Evergreen)
1.2	8.6	-	280th Ave. (dirt)
0.5	9.1	-	285th Ave. (dirt)
0.5	9.6	R	Horse Trail straight; **turn right**
0.3	9.9	-	Merge with riding and snowmobile trail
0.1	10.0	L	**Onto West River Rd.**
1.0	11.0	-	300th Ave.
1.1	12.1	L	**Unmarked track**; watch closely
0.2	12.3	R	Trail continues straight as well, but **hang a right**
0.4	12.7	-	Trail from left; continue straight
0.8	13.5	-	Trail to right; continue straight
0.4	13.9	S	Trail joins dirt road coming in from right
0.0	13.9	L	**Onto County O**
0.3	14.2	-	**End of County O**

The Strawberry Lace Inn

Elsie & Jack Ballinger   Phone: (608) 269-7878
603 North Water Street
Sparta, WI 54656   Email: **strawberry@centuryinter.net**
Rates: Budget — Deluxe   Web: **www.spartan.org/sbl**

Don't be misled by the moderate rates of this authentically restored Italianate Victorian inn. The museum-quality antique furnishing, the resort-quality services and the overall care and attention to detail will delight and surprise even the most veteran bed and breakfast traveler. Jack and Elsie had a bit of a jumpstart over other new bed and breakfast owners. Jack taught industrial arts and Elsie taught home economics. If that weren't enough, they traveled extensively in Europe and applied their experiences as guests to their work as innkeepers. A little antique brokering rounds out the picture. The evident pleasure they take in both the inn itself and in the services they provide translates into ease and satisfaction for their guests.

If Jack and Elsie brought an interesting past to the table, the inn also stepped up to the plate. Built in 1875 as a residence for Major James Davidson, the house remained in private hands until Jack and Elsie bought the building with the intention of opening up a bed and breakfast. What followed was a year of deconstructing most of the house, then rebuilding it with modern amenities such as private baths in each room and air conditioning throughout. Despite the complete update, Jack and Elsie have preserved the look and feel of Victorian design and décor. Don't look for phones or televisions in your room. If you need a fix, there's a small television on the sitting porch, which Jack says is used mainly for The Weather Channel.

The first sight that greets you upon entering the inn is a lovely curved wood staircase that seems to float up from the first to the second floor. The living room, sitting room, and dining room all have brightly-polished wood floors and twelve-foot ceilings. Every room has at least one or two items to catch your eye. An enormous grandfather clock presides over the sitting room. A beautiful old (and in-tune) piano holds court in the parlor. The sitting porch has its original slate floor. And don't forget to look for the strawberries and lacework in every room of the house.

The most sumptuous room is the Servants Quarters. It's really a suite with a Jacuzzi, a fireplace, and a private wet bar. The room is built in the old servants' quarters at the back of the house and is a half-flight down from the second story. Its smaller windows, wood wainscoting, and subdued color scheme provides a delicious sense of privacy and isolation. Among repeat visitors, this is the most popular room.

The Major's Room, the Rose Room, and The Lilac Room share the second floor. While these rooms are more traditional Victorian bed and breakfast rooms, you'll appreciate the unique details in each room. The Rose Room has a king-sized bed tucked into a recessed archway. The Lilac Room uses three unique windows to show off an antique iron and brass bed. The Major's Room has a large yet cozy fourposter bed warmed by a fireplace.

If you enjoy the eccentric, the Tower Room is for you. Located at the top of the Italianate tower that caps the house, you'll have wonderful views out of windows in all four directions. You might not spend much time looking out the windows, though, as the room itself is a visual delight with light airy murals on all the walls. The queen-sized bed has a picket fence for a headboard and you can easily imagine yourself falling gently asleep in a peaceful country meadow. The steep climb up the stairways is worth the exhilarating open-air experience of the room.

If the building doesn't win you over, the service will. Characteristic of the whole experience is breakfast. It's a four-course extravaganza that will fuel even the most ambitious biker. The linen and china form an appropriate backdrop for the savory gourmet creations. Breakfast is a leisurely affair, with Jack and Elsie bragging that it takes over an hour to experience. They also keep track of what guests have for breakfast so you won't get a repeat even if you come back a year later.

The town of Sparta is proud to bill itself as "The Bicycle Capital of America." Visitors to town are greeted by a huge statue of an old high wheeler cyclist, and a number of bike shops and other bike-related services make this an ideal destination for readers _of Bed, Breakfast & Bike_. Speed's Bike Shop provides full-service repairs and rentals. Outspokin provides shuttle service along the trails. In addition, practically every diner and café pitches to the cycling crowd. Our favorite is A Slice of Chicago, serving up carbo-loaded pizzas. If you're interested in racing, you can sign up for the Monroe County Century Challenge, held the second week of August each year.

Sparta still feels a bit like the old resort town it was in the mid-1800s. Thanks to an abundance of artesian wells and "magnetic" mineral springs, Sparta was billed as "The Saratoga of the West." Even though the springs don't run anymore, the beautiful topography of Western Wisconsin's driftless area is still a strong attraction. Sparta also offers a variety of other activities including canoeing and fishing on the La Crosse River, an 18-hole golf course and numerous antique shops.

The Strawberry Lace Inn, Sparta, Wisconsin

Rides from The Strawberry Lace Inn

Sparta's most powerful claim to being "The Bicycle Capital of America" is the Elroy-Sparta bike trail, the very first rails-to-trails conversion in the United States. Through connections to the La Crosse River Trail, the Great River State Trail, the 400 Wisconsin State Trail, and the Omaha Trail, there are well over 100 miles of bicycle trails stretching from the Mississippi River through Sparta to the heart of the Wisconsin Dells region.

Terrain: Though the trails conform to the 3% grade common for railroad beds, as soon as you get off the trails and into the topography untouched by glaciers you'll find climbs much steeper than 3%, some of which go on longer than the build-up in a b-grade horror movie.

Road Conditions: The trails are crushed limestone, suitable for all but the skinniest tires. The roads included in these rides are two-lane country roads. By and large they are in pretty good shape, if very steep at points.

Traffic: Traffic on the trail is heavier on weekends. This is the oldest and one of the most popular trails for both walkers and riders. On the road portion of the ride, we saw almost no traffic at all. The route avoids main roads, which carry most of the local traffic.

Best Time to Ride: In late July and August you might want to ride early in the day to avoid the heat. The trail is shady in areas and the tunnels are cool even on the hottest summer days. In late September and early October, you'll be treated to an explosion of leafy color on the parts of the trail which are more wooded.

Nearest Bike Shop
Speed's Bike Shop
1126 John St.
Sparta, WI
(608) 269-2315

Outspokin Adventures
Shuttle Service
(608) 269-6087
(800) 463-2453

A Taste of Elroy-Sparta (33.8 miles)

On this physically challenging but extremely scenic ride you'll see delicate fauna, walk a ¾-mile-long tunnel and look out over expansive valleys from vantage points along the trail. Once off the trail and onto country roads, the ride leads into unrelentingly hilly terrain with many sweet cows and barking farm dogs cheering the rider along. If you prefer to just ride the trail and avoid the steep grades, Outspoken will shuttle you and your bikes from Sparta down to the Elroy trailhead.

Pt.-Pt.	Cume	Turn	Street/Landmark
0.0	0.0	R	**Turn right out of the inn's driveway**
0.4	0.4	-	Main St.
0.3	0.7	S	Cross U.S. 16
0.1	0.8	L	**Walrath St.**—look for the giant bicyclist!
0.3	1.1	-	*Caution:* rough railroad tracks
0.2	1.3	S	Railroad tracks followed by multi-road intersection
0.2	1.5	R	**Igloo Rd.**
0.5	2.0	-	La Crosse River Trail to right
0.5	2.5	L	**Elroy-Sparta Trail parking lot** (just past overpass)
0.3	2.8	R	**Elroy-Sparta Trail**
1.3	4.1	S	Cross Impala Rd.; ride around trail gate
6.7	10.8	-	Beginning of Tunnel #3; dismount, break out the flashlight!
1.2	12.0	-	Rest area—water and bathrooms
2.8	14.8	R	Norwalk trailhead; **turn onto road**
<0.1	14.8	L	**Rt. 71**
0.3	15.1	S	Rt. 71 curves left; **go straight on County U**
0.2	15.3	R	**Follow County U to right**; start of long steep climb
3.2	18.5	R	**County XX**
6.5	25.0	R	**Kansas Rd.**
2.6	27.6	R	**Jansing Ave.**
0.9	28.5	L	**Jamboree Rd.**
1.6	30.1	L	**Ideal Rd.**
2.2	32.3	S	**South Water**
0.2	32.5	-	La Crosse River Trail and railroad tracks
0.5	33.0	-	Walrath Street and the giant bicyclist
0.1	33.1	S	Cross U.S. 16
0.7	33.8		**Strawberry Lace Inn**

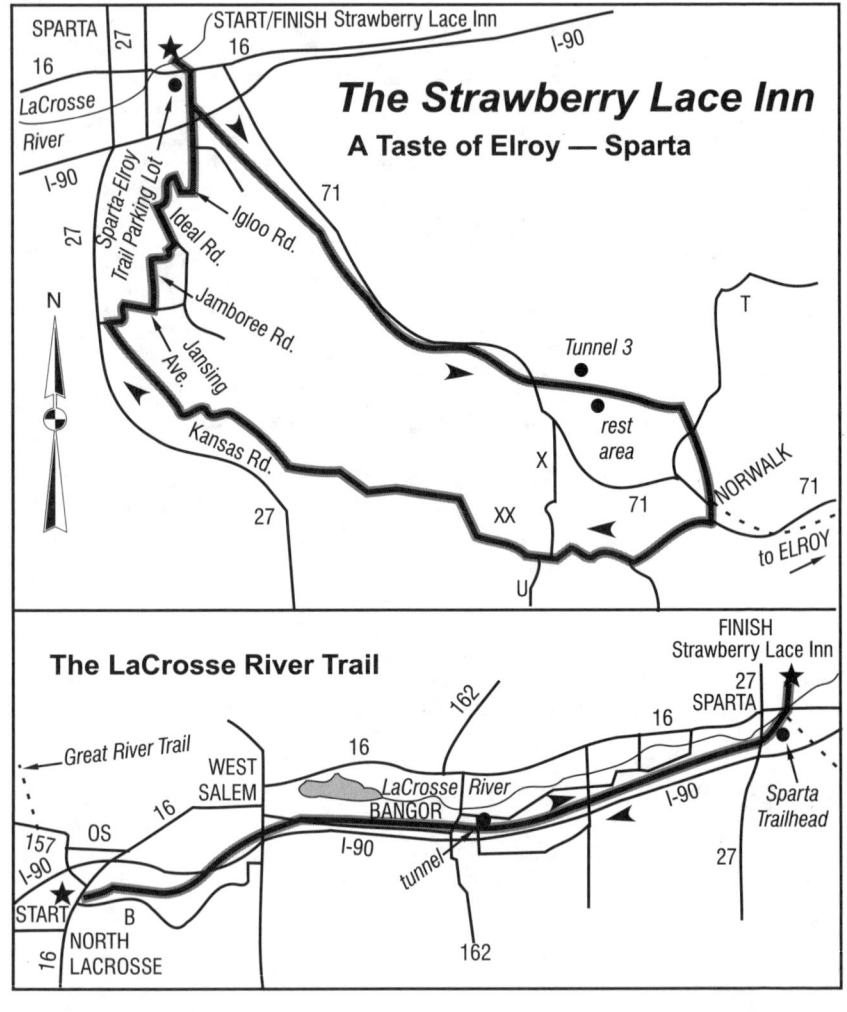

SPARTA
16
LaCrosse
River
I-90
27

27

START/FINISH Strawberry Lace Inn
16
I-90

The Strawberry Lace Inn
A Taste of Elroy — Sparta

Sparta-Elroy
Trail Parking Lot
Igloo Rd.
Ideal Rd.
Jamboree Rd.
Jansing Ave.
Kansas Rd.
71
27

N

Tunnel 3
rest
area
X
XX
71
U
71
T
NORWALK
to ELROY

The LaCrosse River Trail

FINISH
Strawberry Lace Inn
27
SPARTA
16

Great River Trail
162
16

157
I-90
START
16
NORTH
LACROSSE
B
OS
16
WEST
SALEM
LaCrosse River
BANGOR
I-90
tunnel
162

I-90
27
Sparta
Trailhead

The La Crosse River Trail (22.7 miles)

The La Crosse River trail starts just east of the Mississippi River and La Crosse, Wisconsin. We had a delightfully chatty drive down to the trailhead in La Crosse courtesy of Tom from Outspokin, who provides shuttle services all over the region. We paid $30 to be delivered to the trailhead with our tandem, then rode the bike back to the inn.

After unloading your bikes from the van, you'll find the first parts of this trail go through some beautiful marshes where you'll see a wide selection of birds and wildlife. After a long initial climb away from the Mississippi River Valley you have a relaxing ride through western Wisconsin farmland.

Pt.-Pt.	Cume	Turn	Street/Landmark
0.0	0.0		Trailhead at La Crosse (also the Great River Trailhead)
0.3	0.3	-	Go around gate
3.5	3.8	-	Interstate 90 underpass
1.5	5.3	-	Cutoff to left to Veteran's Memorial Park and campground
1.4	6.7	-	Go around gate
0.1	6.8	S	Cross unmarked road; beginning of West Salem
0.2	7.0	S	Cross South Leonard
0.1	7.1	S	Cross South Mill
1.8	8.9	-	Unmarked road
0.3	9.2	-	Driveway
0.3	9.5	-	Driveway
1.7	11.2	-	Highway 162
0.4	11.6	-	Village Park (Bangor)
0.2	11.8	-	Short tunnel
0.1	11.9	-	14th Ave. South
0.3	12.2	-	Unmarked road
0.8	13.0	-	Unmarked road
2.5	15.5	-	Unmarked road (Rockland, WI)
2.4	17.9	-	Iceberg Rd.
1.3	19.2	-	Hammer Rd.
2.2	21.4	L	**South Water St.** (Sparta Trailhead is just across the street)
0.5	21.9	-	Walrath St. and the giant cyclist
0.1	22.0	S	Cross U.S. 16
0.7	22.7	-	Strawberry Lace Inn

Victorian Treasure, Lodi, Wisconsin

Victorian Treasure

Kimberly & Todd Seidl
115 Prairie Street
Lodi, WI 53555
Rates: Budget – Deluxe

Phone: (608) 592-5199
Reservations: (800) 859-5199
Fax: (608) 592-7147
E-mail: innkeeper@victoriantreasure.com
Web: www.victoriantreasure.com

When Kimberly and Todd named their inn the Victorian Treasure, they set a high standard for their inn. Luckily for their guests, the Seidl's more than met the challenge. You'll have no problem thinking of this inn and the sweet little town that surrounds it as treasures and want to return here again and again.

The inn is really two stately Queen Anne houses, beautifully restored and remodeled, sitting on a slight rise above Prairie Street in Lodi, Wisconsin. The Bissell Mansion was built in 1897 and the Palmer House, right next door, was built in 1893. Just a block off of Lodi's quiet main street, these two buildings seem to have settled comfortably into their small-town surroundings.

The Bissell Mansion holds the public spaces of the inn starting, with the accommodating wrap-around porch. Inside, a sitting room, a parlor, and a dining room provide ample space and comfort for the casual encounter and conversation that are a hallmark of good bed and breakfasts. Three guestrooms, all with private baths, occupy the second floor. Queen Anne's Lace showcases a fourposter bed with a crocheted lace canopy. Several beautiful windows bathe the room with warm light, and its bath includes a two-person whirlpool. The Wild Ginger has its own second-floor porch and an antique clawfoot tub in which to soak. The bed has an ornately carved antique ash headboard, while the rest of the room seems arranged to suggest relaxation and contemplation. The Victorian Rose Suite invites you into two rooms of luxury and retreat. The sitting room includes a stereo/CD, a microwave, a bar refrigerator, and a coffee maker, but no TV, finding the right mix of modern comfort without post-modern confusion. A cozy alcove houses a two-person whirlpool and the sleeping area centers around a Victorian Eastlake half-canopy bed.

Though Palmer House is all Queen Anne on the outside, the floor plan inside has been updated. The entire house is given over to just four rooms, two on the first floor and two on the second floor. Todd and Kimberly have laid out the space and decorated it so skillfully that one forgets that this is not how all Victorian Houses look inside. Intricate wallpapers, burnished woodwork, antique furniture accents, beautiful fireplaces and mantel pieces all conspire to give these rooms a real sense of a Victorian interior.

The Angelica Suite on the first floor is comprised of three graceful rooms, with original brass light fixtures, stained glass, and a private front porch. The parlor has a dining table and sofa. From the parlor, a set of thick pocket doors sets off the bedroom with a high bed (bed steps are provided) in front of a fireplace with an antique oak mantelpiece. The huge two-person whirlpool is off the bedroom through another set of pocket doors.

The Dahlia Suite is not quite as spacious as Angelica, but its love seat sitting area, the cherry-mantled fireplace, and the demi-canopy bed seem to be just the right size for a cozy and intimate retreat. Upstairs, the Lilac Suite has an iron open-canopy bed draped in sheer fabrics. The ashwood fireplace casts warmth on both the bed and the two-person whirlpool. Set in the vaulted ceiling is a stunning stained-glass window.

The Magnolia Suite spreads across two full rooms. The sitting room includes a two-person whirlpool across from the fireplace, along with a stereo and wet bar. The bedroom is given over to an Eastlake walnut bedroom complete with canopy.

If the perfect restorations, decorations, and amenities set high expectations for breakfast, you won't be disappointed. Though Todd has a great deal of training in the culinary arts, this kind of fare comes only from a chef who loves what he does. He applies his knowledge and passion to create delicate crumbly fruit pastries, floating airy quiches, and a host of other pleasing dishes which fill the table, attract the eye, and delight your palette. While everything has a light touch that emphasizes taste and texture, you leave the breakfast table completely satisfied, wondering if Todd ever thought of opening up a restaurant.

While we all know that inns take on the character of the innkeepers, that fact has never been demonstrated more clearly than at the Victorian Treasure. Kimberly and Todd met in college when both were pursuing hotel and restaurant management. After several years working in first class establishments, it is our good fortune that they decided to create one of their own. Their focus on the mechanics and details of guest comfort imbues the inn with a quality of experience rarely found.

Lodi seems the perfect town to host an inn like the Victorian Treasure. Nestled in the Wisconsin River Valley, the town recently celebrated its sesquicentennial and holds the longest-running agricultural fair in the state. The original Main Street is still active, with many 100-year-old buildings housing bustling businesses. High on the list of pleasant small-town diversions is Susie the Duck, who raised a clutch of ducklings in the stream that runs through downtown forty years ago. The town adopted Susie, and her descendents—a long line of Susies—still populate the little stream. Ducklings can be seen in late spring, and there is a feeding station where Main Street crosses the stream. Other attractions include nearby hiking, skiing, eagle watching, or perhaps a day on Lake Wisconsin. Todd and Kimberly can help you lay out a day's or a week's worth of activity.

Rides from Victorian Treasure
These are some of the prettiest road rides we've included in this book. Wandering through the Wisconsin River Valley and surrounding bluffs, you'll be treated to some amazing vistas, charming farms, and sparkling waterscapes. Come prepared to climb, especially on the Devil's Lake Loop.

Terrain: On the Ice Age Trail loop the hills are more benign, as most of the ride is confined to the river valley itself. The Devil's Lake Loop has some notable long uphills and one section that should probably be a spiral staircase—we don't know how cars would navigate it.

Road Conditions: These roads are all in good shape, with no surprises for the cyclist. Most of the roads don't have shoulders, but we've laid out routes that shouldn't require them, anyway.

Traffic: There's very little traffic to deal with in the Ice Age Trail ride. On the roads surrounding Devil's Lake, you'll encounter more cars, so some caution is advised. Speed limits help control the situation, especially in the park itself. With a few very short exceptions, this route stays off the most heavily-traveled roads.

Best Time to Ride: By mid-summer, this ride is a lush festival of green and blue between trees, sky, and water. The temperature can get a little over-the-top in late July or August, but it rarely stays there for long. Early summer will provide some balmy days while September and October hold crisp promises.

Nearest Bike Shop: There is no local bike shop, but our favorite Madison, Wisconsin, bike shop is less than an hour away to the south.

Budget Bicycle
1230 Regent Street
Madison, WI 53706
(608) 251-8413

The Ice Age Trail Ride (21.7 miles)
This ride isn't really on a trail, but the roads it traverses do pass by the Ice Age Trail, which traces the furthest extent of the glaciers in Wisconsin. Almost all of this ride is on quiet rural roads with the exception of one short section on Route 60 right at the end. This is by far the more mellow of these two rides and almost seems like an extended ride in a pretty park.

Pt.-Pt.	Cume	Turn	Street/Landmark
0.0	0.0	**R**	Out of the driveway of the Victorian Treasure onto **Prairie St.**
0.1	0.1	**L**	**Lodi St.**
0.0	0.1	**R**	**Water St.**
0.1	0.2	-	Mill St.
0.1	0.3	-	Pleasant St.
0.1	0.4	-	Canning St.
0.2	0.6	-	Nestiles Rd.
0.1	0.7	**L**	**Riddle St.** (Mysteriously becomes **Lodi-Springfield Rd.**)
1.7	2.4	-	Lodi Marsh Wildlife Area
1.0	3.4	-	Lee Rd.
1.8	5.2	**BR**	Black Hill Rd. from left
0.6	5.8	**BL**	Latham Rd. from right
0.5	6.3	**R**	**County V**
0.8	7.1	-	Buethin Rd.
0.1	7.2	-	Bitney Rd.
0.7	7.9	**BR**	Brereton from left
0.5	8.4	**R**	**Lueth Rd.**
1.4	9.8	**S**	Onto **County Y**; Loper Rd. goes left, County Y goes right
0.6	10.4	-	Mussen Rd.
0.3	10.7	**S**	**Hornung Rd.** continues straight; County Y turns left
1.4	12.1	**R**	**Fish Lake Rd.**
0.7	12.8	-	Lake access
0.4	13.2	**BR**	**Schoepp Rd.**
1.0	14.2	**R**	**Mussen Rd.**
0.7	14.9	**L**	**Crystal Lake Rd.**
0.5	15.4	-	Emerald Tr.
2.2	17.6	**S**	**County Y** comes in from right and joins **Crystal Lake Rd.**
2.7	20.3	**S**	County Y merges with Rt. 60 from left; stop and **continue straight onto Rt. 60**

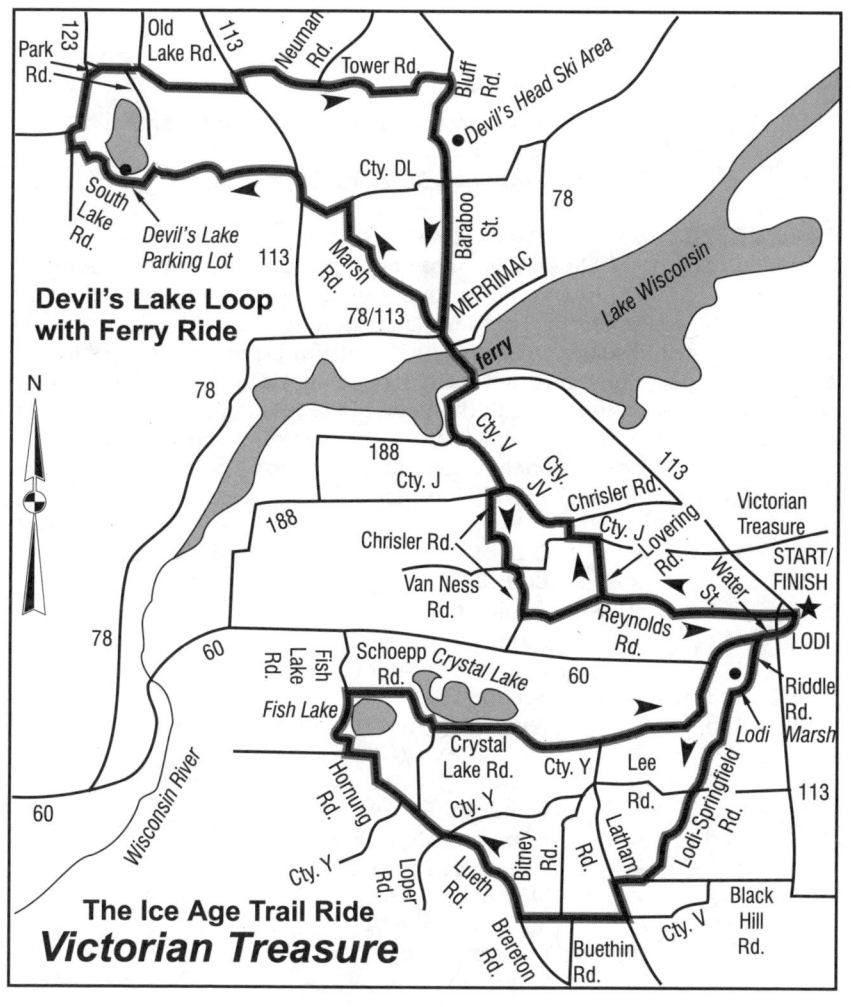

Park Rd.

123

Old Lake Rd.

113

Neuman Rd.

Tower Rd.

Bluff Rd.

Devil's Head Ski Area

South Lake Rd.

Devil's Lake Parking Lot

Cty. DL

Baraboo St.

78

Devil's Lake Loop with Ferry Ride

113

Marsh Rd.

78/113

MERRIMAC

Ferry

Lake Wisconsin

N

78

188

Cty. V

Cty. JV

Chrisler Rd.

113

Victorian Treasure

Cty. J

Cty. J

Lovering Rd.

START/ FINISH

188

Chrisler Rd.

Van Ness Rd.

Reynolds Rd.

Water St.

LODI

78

60

Fish Lake Rd.

Schoepp Rd.

Crystal Lake

60

Riddle Rd.

Lodi

Fish Lake

Crystal Lake Rd.

Cty. Y

Lee Rd.

Lodi-Springfield Rd.

Marsh

113

60

Wisconsin River

Hornung Rd.

Cty. Y

Cty. Y

Loper Rd.

Lueth Rd.

Bitney Rd.

Latham Rd.

Cty. V

Black Hill Rd.

The Ice Age Trail Ride
Victorian Treasure

Brereton Rd.

Buethin Rd.

Pt.-Pt.	Cume	Turn	Street/Landmark
0.2	20.5	-	McCulley Rd.
0.4	20.9	**BR**	As Lodi St. goes straight
0.1	21.0	-	Riddle St. **(Rt. 60 becomes Water St.)**
0.2	21.2	-	Nestiles Rd.
0.1	21.3	-	Canning St.
0.1	21.4	-	Pleasant St.
0.1	21.5	-	Mill St.
0.1	21.6	**L**	**Lodi St.** (turning across flow of traffic)
0.0	21.6	**R**	**Prairie St.**
0.1	21.7	-	**Victorian Treasure**

Devil's Lake Loop with Ferry Ride

Highway 113 crosses Lake Wisconsin on a ferryboat operated as long as the lake is ice-free, but you'll probably want to confine your riding to more temperate seasons. This ferry ride is just one of the many highlights of this ride, along with views of beautiful Devil's Lake, nestled in the high bluffs. When getting on the ferry, especially on the Merrimack side, you can walk your bike to the head of the line, but you'll get loaded on last. There are metal grids on the ferry, so you'll want to walk your bike aboard. There are concessions and restrooms on both sides of the lake, so this makes a nice mid-ride rest stop.

0.0	0.0	**R**	**Out of Victorian Treasure driveway**
0.1	0.1	**R**	**Lodi St.**
0.0	0.1	**R**	**Sauk St.**
0.0	0.1	-	Railroad tracks
0.1	0.2	-	Grand Ave. to left
0.1	0.3	-	Second St.
0.0	0.3	-	Wisconsin Ave./Washington Ave.
0.1	0.4	-	Merton Ave./Church Ave.
0.0	0.4	-	Strangeway Ave.
0.1	0.5	-	Meadowview Ave.
0.0	0.5	-	Bobwhite Court
0.1	0.6	-	Pheasant Court
0.1	0.7	-	Meadowview Ave.
0.2	0.9	-	McCulley Ave.
1.9	2.8	**R**	**Luvering Rd.**
1.0	3.8	**L**	**County J**
0.5	4.3	**BR**	Van Ness comes in from left
0.2	4.5	**BL**	Chrisler from right
1.1	5.6	**R**	**County JV**
0.3	5.9	**S**	County JV becomes **County V** (which also turns right)

Pt.-Pt.	Cume	Turn	Street/Landmark
0.8	6.7	**BL**	Gortner Rd. comes in from right
0.1	6.8	**R**	**Rt. 188**
0.7	7.5	-	Pleasant View Park Rd.
0.2	7.7	-	Pleasant View Park Rd.
0.4	8.1	**L**	Rt. 188 ends, **Rt. 113** begins. This is the entrance to the ferry
0.3	8.4	**L**	**Rt. 78/113**
0.1	8.5	**R**	**Baraboo Rd.**
0.2	8.7	-	Church St.
0.1	8.8	**L**	**Cemetery St.** (becomes **Marsh Rd.**)
2.6	11.4	**L**	**County DL**
0.8	12.2	**R**	**Rt. 113**
0.3	12.5	**L**	**South Lake Rd.**
1.9	14.4	-	Camping
0.6	15.0	-	Railroad tracks
0.3	15.3	-	South Shore parking lot
1.1	16.4	-	Beginning of steep winding climb
0.5	16.9	-	Climb tops out
0.1	17.0	**BR**	**South Lake Rd.** makes 90-degree turn
0.2	17.2	-	Unnamed Rd
1.1	18.3	**R**	**Park Rd.**
0.2	18.5	**R**	**Rt. 123/DL**
0.1	18.6	**BL**	**Follow Rt. 123 to the left**; Park Rd. goes straight
0.4	19.0	-	Railroad tracks
0.1	19.1	**BR**	Old Lake Rd. from left; **stay on 123**
1.8	20.9	**L**	**Rt. 113**
0.0	20.9	**R**	Tower Rd.
0.4	21.3	-	Neuman Rd.
2.0	23.3	-	Unmarked road
1.1	24.4	**R**	**Bluff Rd.** (becomes **Baraboo St.**)
1.4	25.8	-	Devil's Head Ski Area; mountain biking available
0.4	26.2	-	County DL
1.1	27.3	-	Reusch Rd.
0.5	27.8	-	Dan-Mar Court
0.7	28.5	-	Cemetery St.
0.1	28.6	-	Church St.
0.2	28.8	**L**	**Rt. 78/113** or **Main St.**
0.1	28.9	**R**	**Rt. 113** and **ferry**
0.2	29.1	**R**	**Rt. 188**
0.5	29.6	-	Pleasant View Park Rd.

Pt.-Pt.	Cume	Turn	Street/Landmark
0.2	29.8	-	Pleasant View Park Rd.
0.6	30.4	**L**	**County V**
0.1	30.5	**BR**	As Wartner Rd. goes straight
0.9	31.4	**S**	**Onto County JV**; County V goes left
0.1	31.5	**R**	**JV forks**
0.1	31.6	**R**	**County J**
0.4	32.0	**S**	Go **straight on Chrisler Rd**. as County J curves right
1.2	33.2	**L**	**Van Ness Rd.**
0.1	33.3	**R**	**Chrisler Rd.**
0.8	34.1	**L**	**Reynolds Rd.** (becomes **Sauk Rd.**)
1.3	35.4	-	Lovering Rd.
1.5	36.9	-	Rough pavement
0.4	37.3	-	McCulley Ave.
0.2	37.5	-	Meadowview Ave.
0.1	37.6	-	Pheasant Court
0.1	37.7	-	Bobwhite Court
0.0	37.7	-	Meadowview Ave.
0.1	37.8	-	Strangeway Ave.
0.0	37.8	-	Merton Ave./Church Ave.
0.1	37.9	-	Wisconsin Ave./Washington Ave.
0.0	37.9	-	Second St.
0.1	38.0	-	Grand Ave. to left
0.1	38.1	-	Railroad tracks
0.0	38.1	**L**	**Lodi St.**
0.1	38.2	**L**	**Prairie St.**
0.1	38.3	-	**Victorian Treasure** driveway

Selected Recipes

1. Arbor House Carmel Corn

The Arbor House in Madison, Wisconsin, puts big baskets of this out as an evening snack and sometimes has it available as a biking or cross-country skiing snack.

16 cups popped popcorn
1 cup pecan halves
1 cup almonds
1 cup walnut halves
2 cups firmly packed brown sugar
1 cup butter
½ cup dark corn syrup
½ teaspoon salt
½ teaspoon baking soda

Preheat oven to 250 degrees. Put popcorn and nuts in a large roasting pan. Keep warm in oven. Place brown sugar, butter, syrup, and salt in a large saucepan. Bring to boil, stirring constantly. Stop stirring and cook to 250 degrees on candy thermometer (about 5 minutes). Stir in soda. Drizzle over popcorn, toss to coat. Bake at 250 degrees for 10 minutes, 20 minutes for crisper corn. Yields 20 cups.

2. Lemon Poppyseed Muffins

Blacksmith Inn
Bailey's Harbor, WI

1 (8 ounce) package cream cheese
½ cup softened butter
1¼ cup sugar
2 eggs
2¼ cups flour
1 tablespoon baking powder
½ teaspoon salt
¾ cup milk
1 tablespoon grated lemon rind
1 tablespoon Poppyseeds

Glaze

1½ teaspoon lemon rind
1 tablespoon fresh lemon juice
½ cup powdered sugar

Beat cream cheese and butter together until smooth. Beat in sugar. Beat eggs in one at a time. Combine flour, baking powder and salt; add to creamed mixture alternately with milk. Add lemon rind and poppyseeds. Grease 10 large muffin cups. Fill 2/3 full. Bake 20 minutes at 350 degrees. Spoon glaze over cooled muffins.

3. Baked Egg and Cheese Casserole

The Fargo Mansion Inn
Lake Mills, Wisconsin

2 cups shredded cheese
1 dozen eggs
2 cups shredded fresh broccoli
1 small can of mushrooms, stems and pieces
½ cup diced green pepper
½ cup milk
6 tablespoons butter

Preheat oven to 375 degrees. Grease a 9" x 13" glass pan. Sprinkle 1 cup shredded cheese over bottom of pan. Break eggs evenly over cheese. Break yolks. Spread broccoli, mushrooms, and green pepper evenly over eggs. Sprinkle second cup of shredded cheese over vegetables. Drizzle milk over top. Place butter evenly over top. Bake 30-40 minutes or until firm. Cool 5 minutes. Cut into 6 equal portions. Garnish with parsley, sliced bananas, and orange. May be prepared the night before and refrigerated.

4. Cheddar Egg Bake

Green Tree Inn
Elsah, Illinois

12 eggs
2 cups half-and-half
2 cups milk
Cheddar cheese
Dry breadcrumbs
Optional: broccoli and/or onions

Layer dry breadcrumbs on the bottom of pan. Beat eggs, half-and-half, and milk for 5 minutes. Add salt and pepper to taste. Add optional broccoli and/or onions to eggs if desired. Pour eggs on top of breadcrumb layer. Bake at 350 degrees until eggs have risen and set. Sprinkle with cheddar cheese.

5. Dry Cherry Buttermilk Scones

Hill Street Bed and Breakfast
Spring Green, Wisconsin

1 large egg
3 tablespoons brown sugar
1 teaspoon vanilla
2½ cups cake flour
1 tablespoon baking powder
½ teaspoon baking soda
½ teaspoon salt
¾ stick butter, cold
1 cup dried cherries or apricots (chopped)
½ cup half-and-half
¼ cup granulated sugar
4 teaspoon dry buttermilk blend, little water

In a bowl whisk together buttermilk, brown sugar, and vanilla. In another bowl stir together flour, baking powder, and salt. Add butter in small pieces until evenly mixed. Add cherries to buttermilk mixture, mix lightly (add a little water if mixture is dry). Spread on parchment-lined cookie sheet in a 10-inch circle. Brush top with buttermilk and sprinkle with sugar. Bake at 375 degrees for 20 minutes. Cut into 12 pieces.

6. Cream Cheese Crescent Rolls

House of Nahum
Harrisburg, Illinois

1 crescent roll package
1 (8 ounce) package cream cheese
1 egg yolk
1 teaspoon vanilla
1/3 cup sugar
Margarine

Warm cream cheese 30 seconds in microwave to soften. Mix sugar, egg yolk, vanilla into cream cheese. Pat out half of crescent rolls in lightly buttered 8" x 8" square pan. Spread mixture over dough. Sprinkle cinnamon on top. Pat out remaining crescent and evenly put over mixture. Sprinkle sugar and cinnamon on top. Bake at 350 degrees for 20 minutes. Spread margarine over top and bake 10-15 minutes longer. Cool and cut.

7. Pumpkin Muffins
Inn at Pinewood
Eagle River, Wisconsin

1 ¾ cup flour
½ cup sugar
1 teaspoon baking powder
½ teaspoon baking soda
½ teaspoon salt
½ teaspoon cinnamon
½ teaspoon nutmeg
½ teaspoon allspice
1 ¼ cup packed pumpkin (not pie filling)
½ cup buttermilk or plain yogurt
1 large egg lightly beaten
vanilla
3 tablespoons melted butter
¾ cup chopped nuts

Heat oven to 375 degrees. Combine dry ingredients. Combine pumpkin, egg, butter, and buttermilk. Add dry ingredients to wet ingredients, don't over mix. Pour into muffin pan. Sprinkle tops with brown sugar and cinnamon. Bake for 20 – 30 minutes.

8. "Inncredible" Eggs

Inn at Pinewood
Eagle River, Wisconsin

8 slices bread
2/3 cup cheddar cheese
1½ cup ham, sausage, or veggies (or any combination of the three)
8 eggs
4 cups milk
4 teaspoons mustard

Crumble bread into small pieces into a 9" x 13" pan. Mix bread with cheese. Beat eggs and milk, add mustard. Add ham, sausage, and veggies mixture. Spice to taste. Pour over breadcrumb and cheese layer. Let stand for 15 minutes. Bake 1 hour at 350 degrees, or 40 minutes at 400 degrees.

9. Pumpkin Butter

Inn at Pinewood
Eagle River, Wisconsin

16 ounces packed pumpkin (not pie filling)
½ cup apple cider juice
½ cup sugar
½ teaspoon nutmeg
½ teaspoon cinnamon
¼ teaspoon cloves

Combine all ingredients in a pan and bring to a boil. Lower heat to simmer and cook for 15 minutes. Yields 1¾ cup.

10. Coffee Cake
Inn at Rocky Creek
Rochester, Minnesota

1 cup white sugar
½ cup brown sugar
2/3 cup shortening
1 cup buttermilk
2 eggs
2 cups flour
1 teaspoon soda
1 teaspoon brown sugar
1 teaspoon cinnamon

Topping
¼ to ½ cup chopped nuts
¼ cup brown sugar
1 teaspoon cinnamon
1 teaspoon nutmeg

Using a mixer, cream sugar, shortening, and eggs; mix well. Add flour, baking soda, and cinnamon alternately with buttermilk. Pour into a 9" x 13" pan. To make topping, combine chopped nuts, brown sugar, cinnamon, and nutmeg together in a bowl. Mix to create a crumb-like consistency. Sprinkle over batter. Bake at 350 degrees for 30-40 minutes. Serve warm. The batter can be mixed the night before and refrigerated and baked in the morning.

11. Chocolate Chip Scones
JailHouse Inn Bed and Breakfast
Preston, Minnesota

2 cups all-purpose flour, sifted before measuring
4 cups flour for working
1 tablespoon baking powder
½ teaspoon salt
¼ cup sugar, plus 2-3 tablespoons
¾ cup semi-sweet chocolate chips
1¼ cups heavy cream
3 tablespoons unsalted butter, melted

Position a rack in the middle of the oven and preheat the oven to 425 degrees. Select a heavy-duty baking sheet but do not grease.

Sift together the sifted flour, baking powder, salt, and the ¼ cup of sugar into a bowl. Toss together with a fork to mix thoroughly. Mix in the chocolate chips. Pour in the cream and mix with the fork until the mixture holds together. The dough will be sticky.

Transfer the dough to a lightly-floured work surface and sprinkle lightly with flour. Knead the dough 10 times, pushing it away from you with the heel of your hand, folding it back over itself and giving it a quarter turn each time. Pat into a 9-inch disk. Brush with the melted butter and then sprinkle with the 2-3 tablespoons sugar. Cut dough into 10 pie-shaped wedges and transfer each to the baking sheet, leaving about a 1-inch space between the wedges.

Bake until the tops are golden brown, about 15-17 minutes. Serve warm or at room temperature.

12. Smoothie
Landers House
Utica, Illinois

8 frozen strawberries
1 frozen banana
8 ounces vanilla yogurt (1 container)
1 cup orange juice
1 tablespoon peanut butter (optional)

Combine all ingredients in the blender and blend. Serve in wine glasses and garnish with a fresh strawberry. Yields two servings.

13. Blueberry Blintz Soufflé
Landers House
Utica, Illinois

4 thawed blueberry blintzes
3 eggs
8 ounces of sour cream
¼ cup sugar
1 teaspoon vanilla extract

Preheat oven to 350 degrees. Grease two individual soufflé dishes and place two blintzes in each. Beat all the rest of the ingredients together and pour over blintzes just to cover. Drizzle some butter over each and bake for one hour. Serve immediately and garnish with fresh blueberries. Yields two servings.

14. Salsa Cheesecake

The Old Rittenhouse Inn
Bayfield, Wisconsin

2 tablespoons melted butter
½ cup very fine breadcrumbs
¾ pound cream cheese
¼ pound Roquefort cheese
1 cup sour cream
2 tablespoons flour
1 cup grated Parmesan cheese
½ cup fresh salsa
4 large eggs

Garnish:
Leaves of fresh kale
Fresh cilantro
Minced cilantro
Minced parsley

Preheat the oven to 350 degrees. Brush sides and bottom of a 9-inch springform pan with the melted butter and carefully coat with ¼ cup breadcrumbs. Tap out excess.

In the bowl of an electric mixer, combine the cream cheese and Roquefort cheese. Add sour cream, flour, Parmesan, and salsa, beating well between additions. Scrape bowl, turn motor to high, and add eggs one at a time. Scrape bowl and beat well to make certain all is blended properly. Pour batter into prepared pan. Sprinkle with remaining breadcrumbs.

Carefully wrap bottom of pan in foil and set in a larger baking dish filled with hot water. Or place pan in oven over another filled with hot water. (Cake will be a bit higher if baked in a water bath.) Bake 1¼ hours. Cool in oven, with door ajar, one hour.

Place one or two leaves of fresh kale on each serving plate. Top with a slice of cheesecake. Then garnish plate with cilantro and sprinkle with minced cilantro and parsley. Serve warm or at room temperature.

15. Chocolate Lover's Muffins

"We love the richness of this muffin, especially with bittersweet choco-late," says Innkeeper Jerry Phillips of the Old Rittenhouse Inn in Bayfield, Wisconsin. "With cocoa powder, chocolate liqueur, and chocolate pieces, they're a triple chocolate treat!"

2 eggs
1½ cup vegetable oil
1½ cup chocolate liqueur
2/3 to 1 cup buttermilk
1½ cups flour
1 cup sugar
½ cup cocoa
2½ tablespoons baking powder
1 cup semisweet chocolate chips or bittersweet pieces (about one 4-ounce bittersweet bar) chopped in the food processor or grated

Preheat oven to 350 degrees. Grease or line 12 to 13 muffin cups. In a medium-sized bowl, whisk together eggs, oil, liqueur, and buttermilk. In a large bowl, mix flour, sugar, cocoa, baking powder, and chips or pieces. Pour the milk mixture into the flour mixture and mix well. If mixture is very thick, add a little more buttermilk (but batter will be thicker than cake batter, for instance). Divide batter between 12 or 13 muffin cups. Bake for about 20 minutes or until a toothpick inserted in the center comes out clean. Remove from oven and cool muffins in pans for 5 minutes. Remove from pans and serve immediately.

16. Quick Cherry Coffee Cake

The Park Street Inn
Nevis, Minnesota

1 box (9 ounces) yellow cake mix
1 egg
¼ cup water
½ cup canned cherry pie filling
1 tablespoon sugar
½ teaspoon cinnamon

Mix cake, egg and water according to cake mix directions and pour into greased round cake pan. Spoon dollops of cherries over the top, then sprinkle with sugar and cinnamon. Bake at 350 degrees about 35 minutes or until toothpick comes out clean.

17. Wild Rice and Ham Quiche
The Park Street Inn
Nevis, Minnesota

1 cup cooked cubed ham
1 cup wild rice, cooked and cooled
1 cup (4 ounces) shredded cheddar cheese
1¾ cup milk
1 cup buttermilk biscuit mix
4 eggs

In a greased 10" pie plate, layer ham, rice, and cheese. In a bowl, combine milk, baking mix and eggs; beat until smooth. Pour over cheese. Bake at 400 degrees for 30 – 35 minutes or until a knife inserted near center comes out clean. Let stand 5 minutes before cutting. Serves 6 - 8.

18. Pincushion Baked Apple Pancakes
Pincushion Mountain Bed and Breakfast
Grand Marias, Minnesota

1½ cups pancake mix
1 cup whole milk
3 eggs
2 tablespoons sugar
Dash of vanilla
3 Red Delicious apples
1 cup finely chopped walnuts
2 teaspoons nutmeg
2 teaspoons cinnamon
3 tablespoons brown sugar

Preheat oven to 450 degrees. Mix pancake mix, milk, eggs, sugar and vanilla. In another bowl mix walnuts, nutmeg, cinnamon and brown sugar. Melt ½ stick butter in a 7" ovenproof skillet. Cut unpeeled apples in half and remove core. Slice apples thickly and put in the skillet and sauté until soft but not mushy (usually 10 minutes on low).

Sprinkle nut mixture evenly over the top of sautéed apples. Pour pancake batter over the top of apples in the skillet. Add a little nut mixture over the top. Cover and bake in oven for 20 minutes. Take pancake out of the oven and cut into wedges. Serve warm with syrup; yields 2-3 servings.

19. Rockwell's Spaghetti Sauce

Rockwell's Victorian Bed and Breakfast
Toulon, Illinois

1 pound ground beef (or more if desired)
1 pound canned tomatoes
2 six-ounce cans tomato paste
2 medium onions, sliced thin
1 clove garlic, chopped fine
2 cubes beef bouillon
3 cups water
1 teaspoon salt
¼ teaspoon pepper
1 teaspoon sugar
1 teaspoon oregano
1 teaspoon basil

Brown ground beef, add onions and garlic. When the onions are clear, add beef bouillon, tomatoes, tomato paste, water, salt, pepper, sugar, oregano and basil. Bring to a boil, and then turn heat down to simmer for one hour or longer. Do not cover.

20. Fresh Spinach and Portabella Mushroom Crepes

Victorian Treasure
Lodi, Wisconsin

Crepes:
3 eggs
2 tablespoons flour
Pinch salt
¼ cup milk

Combine and stir all ingredients well. Coat small sauté pan with a little butter and turn heat to medium. Pour in just enough batter to coat pan bottom. When crepe batter is set, turn over, brown lightly. Repeat for 8 crepes.

Sauce:
3 tablespoons butter
2 tablespoons flour
1½ cups milk
½ cup fresh grated pepper jack cheese
2 tablespoons sun dried tomatoes, diced.

Melt butter in a saucepan on low heat, add flour and cook for 5 minutes. Add milk, stir to combine. Cook on low heat for 10 minutes. Add cheese, stir until incorporated. The sun dried tomato is used as a garnish over the sauce.

Filling:
2 ounces butter
4 ounces red onion, julienne
4 ounces Portabella mushrooms, diced
8 pieces artichoke hearts, quartered
4 ounces fresh spinach
1 ounce fresh (or 1 teaspoon dry) basil
8 ounces cream cheese, softened

Melt butter on medium heat in a saucepan. Sauté red onion, mushrooms, and artichoke hearts until lightly brown. Add spinach and basil, lightly cook until wilted. Place in a bowl with softened cream cheese, lightly combine. Divide evenly among eight crepes by placing in center of crepe and folding over the ends. Keep crepes in warm oven, or reheat in microwave before serving. Place 2 crepes in center of plate, ladle sauce down the center, garnish with diced sun dried tomatoes.

21. Spiced Zucchini Nut Muffins
Victorian Treasure
Lodi, Wisconsin

1½ cups flour
1 cup sugar
1 teaspoon cinnamon
½ teaspoon nutmeg
¼ teaspoon ground cloves
½ teaspoon baking soda
½ teaspoon baking powder
½ teaspoon salt
2 eggs, beaten
2 teaspoons vanilla
1 cup zucchini, unpeeled, grated
½ cup walnuts, chopped

Preheat oven to 350 degrees. In a large bowl, mix dry ingredients. Make a well in center of dry ingredients, add eggs, vanilla, zucchini, oil, and nuts. Mix well with spoon. Fill greased muffin cups to top. Bake 15-20 minutes. Yields 12 muffins.

22. Black Forest Cherry Cake

Wander Inn Bed and Breakfast
Watertown, Minnesota

2 round 9" chocolate cakes (chocolate cake of your choice, preferably a moist recipe)
4 teaspoons rum or rum extract
Cherry pie filling
1 teaspoon powdered sugar
1 pint heavy whipping cream, whipped
1 small chocolate bar

Sprinkle one layer of chocolate cake with two tablespoons of rum or rum extract. Reserve 6-8 cherries from pie filling and set aside. Spread remaining pie filling onto cake layer. Combine whipped cream and powdered sugar and mix on high until firm, spread approximately 1/3 of cream onto pie filling. Cover with second cake layer. Sprinkle remaining rum or extract on second layer. Spread remaining cream onto top and sides. Take saved cherries and arrange on outside rim of cake, sprinkle top of cake with grated chocolate. Keep chilled until ready to serve.